PRAISE FOR *THE SPIRIT OF VILLAROSA*

This wonderful book shows the love and admiration of a son for his father without concealing the occasional tensions in their relationship. The father, Horace Ashton, must have had the most interesting, action-packed lives of anyone on ~~~~ in his day. This story brings to life the places he vis~~~~ customs of the people he met, especially those of H~~~~ also tells Marc "Butch" Ashton's incredible sto~~~~ es enormous insight into Haiti during the more th~~~~ y he lived there. As a significant player in the Haitian p~~~~ tor for so many years, his contribution was particularly valu~~~~ . This is a must-read for Haiti enthusiasts.

Robert C. Felder, Vice-Consul of the United States Embassy in Haiti (1966); Deputy Chief of Mission at the United States Embassy in Haiti (1990s); Ambassador of the United States of America to Benin, (1998–2000)

What a captivating, heart-rending father-son story in the unique setting of Haiti! Father Horace Ashton, an adventure-seeking, renowned photographer inspires his son Butch to become a successful entrepreneur in agri-business and tourism as both settle into the rich and mysterious culture of Haiti, including still vibrant Vodou ceremonies. As longstanding Haitian values deteriorate through the years, Butch is kidnapped by vicious killers seeking ransom. Memories of the courageous exploits of his father sustain him and help him plan his escape. What an uplifting family story and intimate introduction to the physical beauty and deepening challenges in contemporary Haiti!

Ernest Preeg, Ph.D., Ambassador of the United States of America to Haiti (1981–1983); author of *The Haitian Dilemma*; Chairman, Haiti Democracy Project

Most Americans view Haiti as a mysterious place—exotic, dangerous for outsiders, American visitors, or ex-pats living there. Horace and Marc Ashton made their home there and discovered a country largely unknown to Westerners. Each contributed to the Haitian economy and culture for decades, despite trying times of brutal dictatorship, political unrest, violence, widespread destruction, and natural disasters. As economic conditions worsened and kidnapping for ransom became a terrorist tactic worldwide, Marc underwent a harrowing experience. As a Latin Americanist and Graham Green *aficionado*, I find this novelistic story better than one Greene—author of the Haitian-based *The Comedians*—could have fictionalized. This true story is a great read.

Paul C. Clark, Ph.D., Latin American Scholar; Lieutenant Colonel, United States Army (Retired)

As a medical student working in Haiti in 1957, I had the pleasure of meeting the Ashton family at the Hotel Splendid, where I stayed that summer. Because the Ashtons had let the American ambassador use Villarosa, they took a cottage at the hotel. How vividly I recall the string of baby parrots sitting on a rail in the kitchen screaming to be fed and the interior of the cottage enriched with furnishings brought down from their home above the city! Horace and his lovely wife introduced me to the wonders of their world, while their son Butch and I ran all over the city, despite the curfew that would someday ring in Papa Doc.

Reading this staggering account of Horace and Marc Ashton awakened in me just how much my own life had been influenced by knowing them at a time when Haiti was in full bloom. Every day now, I am reminded of their love for orchids, parrots, old plantation buildings, landscaping and creation of courtyard gardens, painting of historic buildings on Grand Isle, and even the selection of a wife from England with a Peschier Port-au-Prince ancestor. And to think now that I would dare to dance to the music of this man and his family so beautifully presented in this book. I am indebted to Butch for this masterpiece.

Glynne C. Couvillion, M.D.

$\mathcal{T}$HE SPIRIT OF VILLAROSA

The SPIRIT OF VILLAROSA

A Father's Extraordinary Adventures; A Son's Challenge

As told by Horace Dade Ashton &
Marc Ashton with Libby J. Atwater

Two Harbors Press, Minneapolis

www.thespiritofvillarosa.com

Two Harbors Press
322 First Avenue N, 5th floor
Minneapolis, MN 55401
612.455.2293
www.TwoHarborsPress.com

ISBN-13: 978-1-63413-847-5
LCCN: 2015920588

Distributed by Itasca Books

Cover Photograph: The side view of Villarosa, depicted in this painting by Horace Ashton when he was in his late eighties, belongs to the private collection of Marc Ashton.

The photograph of Horace Ashton on a girder photographing New York City was obtained from the Nelson-Atkins Museum in Kansas City, Missouri, and the authors have the museum's permission to print it in this book.

Cover Design by James Arneson
Typeset by MK Ross

Printed in the United States of America

For Dad

"The child is father of the man . . ."

—William Wordsworth

CONTENTS

DISCLAIMER

Much of the material in this book came from stories that Horace Dade Ashton tape recorded at the age of eighty-six and had transcribed, in addition to articles written by and about him during his lifetime. Facts have been researched and verified where possible, but we ask the reader's tolerance if a few dates appear out of sync or even slightly skewed.

At the time of the recordings Mr. Ashton said, "Fortunately I have been blessed with a very vivid memory, which has served me well, even up to the time of this writing at the age of eighty-six."

If there is anything that professionals who help others tell their stories have learned, it is that over time we all seem to acquire a selective memory. Horace Ashton had a life more adventuresome than most, a mind more curious and intelligent than many, and a spiritual vision and faith more richly investigated than nearly all the masters and sages of ages past. If he makes an occasional error in recollection, let us be sympathetic to the sheer volume of material and number of experiences this learned, self-taught man digested during his days on earth.

ACKNOWLEDGMENTS

The stories left behind by my father, Horace Dade Ashton, form the basis of this work. They might not have been published had I not been kidnapped and promised my father that I would tell his story if I survived. I thank him for having the foresight to record his amazing escapades for future generations.

Most of all I would like to thank my family for their love, support, and encouragement when I needed it. I wholeheartedly thank my loving wife, Myriam; my beautiful daughters, Daska and Militsa; and my grandniece Kerry Ashton, who spent countless hours on the text.

Many others contributed to this work and deserve my gratitude:

My very dear friend for nearly sixty years, Dr. Glynne Couvillion, who knew my father in his later years and whose constant encouragement was of utmost importance to me.

My "big" brother, Burdette, who passed away unexpectedly on August 17, 2014 and did not get to see the finished product. He was most supportive of my effort and spent numerous hours laminating the scrapbook from which I was able to copy some of the random articles and photos included in this book. His untimely death greatly saddens me.

My wingman, Carlos, who has "got my six" and given me the freedom to maneuver.

I am and always will be indebted to my good friend Bob[*] for all his help and support immediately after the kidnapping.

---

[*]   Last name omitted for obvious reasons.

Bob spent a great deal of time with my father discussing religion, and he has continually encouraged me to tell this story. Sadly, his wife, Pat, passed away on February 17, 2015. Bob told me that my father appeared to him as he sat by Pat's bedside during her final hours.

Most of all, my driving force, my seven wonderful grandchildren, Juan Carlos, Miya Rafaella, Natalia Lucia, Lara Sofia, and especially Naime, Anya, and Marc Anthony, who are of age to appreciate and better understand, have been my primary inspiration toward fulfilling my commitment to tell the story. I hope they will be motivated and inspired by their great-grandfather's extraordinary life and one day will share this work with their respective grandchildren.

My thanks to my cousins and many friends who have constantly encouraged me to publish the story, too many to name, but you know who you are.

My coauthor Libby J. Atwater waited thirteen years to bring my father's and my stories to life and created this final manuscript with me. Her persistence has inspired me.

Editor Margaret Ganton helped shape this work in its early stages, and it has grown from her input.

If "it takes a village to raise a child," it takes a collaboration of dedicated individuals to write a book.

I am sincerely grateful for all the love, support, and help I received.

Marc Ashton
December 31, 2015

From the Explorers Club Archives

ASHTON, Horace D.—Born King George County, Virginia, July 29, 1883, educated Baltimore, Maryland. Went to Russo-Japanese War as correspondent for *Collier's Weekly*, later traveled in South America and Orient for illustrations for leading magazines and newspapers. Was for several years official photographer for President Roosevelt, accompanying him to Panama. Managed first transcontinental passenger-carrying automobile tour, winter 1911–1912. Engaged for several years in the production of scientific motion pictures. Member, American Academy of Sciences; Member, New York Microscopical Society; Fellow, Royal Geographic Society, London; Fellow, American Geographical Society. Has conducted original explorations in South America and North Africa, including the Sahara. Made a special study of Haiti, visiting the interior and living with the natives. Lecturing on Morocco, Haiti, the Sahara, and allied subjects. Magazine contributor.

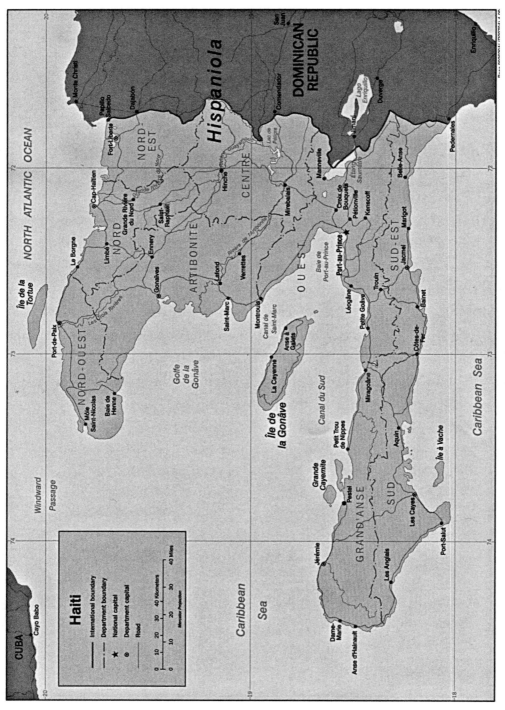

Map of Haiti

CHAPTER 1

Villarosa

**The entrance to Villarosa, our family home since 1953,
featured an ornate gate. (see page 342)**

Marc "Butch" Ashton
Port-au-Prince, Haiti
April 5, 2001

Roosters crow incessantly, and the pleasant aroma of strong coffee
cooking over the charcoal fires of my shantytown neighbors teases

the warm, moist breeze. I walk out among the bright splashes of crimson and tangerine bougainvillea growing in ceramic pots on my second-story terrace, looking over the city as I do every morning to assess the conditions in the streets below and, thus, my chances of getting to and from work.

Surveying the city, I spot barricades of burning tires in the streets. The thick, black, acrid smoke punctuated by slashes of orange flame is an all-too-common sign of trouble in Port-au-Prince these days.

I look down upon the mile-long road built in 1953, when my father purchased and rebuilt Villarosa, our family home since I was fourteen years old. In the early days, our tranquil view was magnificent as we meandered up this lonely road. Perched atop a foothill that has a spectacular view of Port-au-Prince and its bay and surrounded by dense forest, our paradisiacal home had been well outside the borders of Port-au-Prince. Until the mid-eighties, the rose-colored villa was a private tropical oasis where three generations of the Ashton family lived.

In the new millennium, Myriam and I live here alone, but our children and grandchildren come here often. Today they will all be here for lunch as the family gathers for the baptism tomorrow of our first grandson.

Villarosa stands amid nature in 1953.

Population growth encroached upon Villarosa's pristine surroundings.

Our view is no longer tranquil. Since the mid-eighties, the slums of Port-au-Prince have spread up the hill to encircle Villarosa like a salivating predator. Stripped of trees and rife with ever-increasing signs of poverty, this area has unofficially come to be called *Les Bidonvilles de Villarosa[1]*, and the squatters in this shantytown have become my neighbors. Only the legend of my father's extraordinary mystical powers prevents them from invading and stealing our trees to make charcoal. Several years ago, a visit by UNICEF ambassador and well-known actress Julia Roberts, officially placed the slums of Villarosa on the map.

The signs of increasing poverty and desperation are everywhere. For the past several years our electric power lines have bare wires thrown over them. Squatters "borrowed" our electricity to light up their meager dwellings, known as *ti-kays*, one-room homes that lack enough space for the families to all sleep inside at one time. As a result, my neighbors sleep in shifts throughout the day and night.

Villarosa's water supply, which our family provided in the mid-fifties by building a pipeline from the spring two miles up the mountain, carries water to our reservoir. Lately it must be patrolled weekly to disconnect those who tap into our water line for their own needs, leaving our family without enough water.

Our lives today differ greatly from when my parents first brought me to Haiti as an infant in 1940 after my father, Horace Dade Ashton, became the United States Cultural Attaché to the American Embassy in Haiti. We lived in a developing country and benefited from my father's status. My parents had servants, and I had a nanny because they were so active in the social and cultural scene in Port-au-Prince during the last five-plus years of World War II. From my nanny I learned to speak Creole, a language

---

1   *Les Bidonvilles de Villarosa* translates to "The Slums of Villarosa," a large shanty-town that squatters built around our property in the early seventies. The area was named for our family home, which had become a landmark, to designate it from other shantytowns.

spoken by all Haitians.[2]

When the political situation in Haiti changed dramatically in the early sixties after Dr. Francois Duvalier, known as Papa Doc, declared himself "President for Life," the United States government placed an embargo on Haiti. All American investors were forced to cease operations, and President Kennedy ordered the United States Navy to evacuate all American citizens in 1963. His goal was to oust dictator Papa Doc.

While I had returned to Haiti, I knew it was best to send my younger brother, Todd, who was only sixteen, stateside to stay with my older brother, Burdette, in Indianapolis. Most Americans had already left Haiti due to the political situation. Although it was difficult to have both brothers so far away, I knew it was the best decision.

After Todd graduated from high school in Indianapolis, he joined the United States Coast Guard. Ironically, he saw active duty in the Mekong Delta during the Vietnam War, a conflict I was fortunately spared.

Only a handful of Americans stayed in Haiti during this difficult period. My father had known Dr. Francois Duvalier when Dr. Duvalier was the Haitian representative to the U.S.-funded program to eradicate a yaws epidemic. He and Papa Doc shared mutual respect, and my father did not feel in danger, nor was he prepared to abandon his home and life in this island nation.

* * *

By 1975 the population of Port-au-Prince had increased more than tenfold since 1953, when my father bought the property. To protect our home, I built an eight-foot-high concrete block wall

---

2   Based largely on eighteenth-century French with some influences from Portuguese, Aramaic, Spanish, Taíno, and West African languages, Haitian Creole emerged from contact between French settlers and African slaves during the Atlantic slave trade in the French colony of Saint-Domingue (now the Republic of Haiti). Today Haitians are the largest Creole-speaking community in the world.

almost entirely around our eight-acre property, except where it sits on the edge of a steep cliff. It and the twenty-four-hour armed guard I keep stationed at the dark green wrought-iron gate with another patrolling the property fend off would-be invaders.

Despite these precautions, Myriam and I know we are no longer safe. We have even taken defensive driving and shooting classes with our grown daughters so we will all be prepared to defend ourselves if the need arises. I carry a pistol with me whenever I leave home, but this morning I leave my pistol behind. If I get caught up in a street demonstration, I feel my chances of survival are better if I am unarmed.

As I do every day, I drive carefully around the chickens, goats, and crowds of people milling around the makeshift businesses that thrive along Canapé Vert Road. Huts called *cailles-pailles*, composed of boxes, straw, scraps of tin, and debris, held together with mud and cement, cling precariously to the hillside. Junked cars and trash litter the roadside, adding to the general squalor visible through the haze of charcoal smoke from cooking fires. Vendors selling fruits and vegetables, charcoal, or fixing tires haggle over prices in loud Creole. The people and animals occupy the road. I drive slowly and honk the horn to urge them out of my way.

Working until early afternoon, I apply my defensive driving skills after leaving our Toyota dealership to head home for lunch with Myriam, our daughters, and our grandchildren. Because of the crowded conditions, I run late.

April 5, 2001
1:55 p.m.

Myriam's voice cuts through the static on my two-way radio, and I sense concern. "Ash One, Ash One. Where are you?" she asks frantically.

I press the talk button and turn onto the hill as I begin bouncing my four-wheel-drive Land Cruiser along our rutted Canapé Vert Road. "Be home in five minutes, Myriam."

Our children and grandchildren await, and I look forward to seeing them.

Suddenly a vehicle emerges from behind a group of junked cars and cuts me off. It skids to a stop only inches in front of me, raising a cloud of dust.

"*Tonnerre!*"[3] I exclaim.

My heart pounds as terror seizes me. This is an all-too-familiar nightmare. But I had planned and trained for it. Acting on reflex, I throw the Land Cruiser into reverse. At the same time, I glance in my rearview mirror.

Too late! A car with two men inside pulls up behind me and stops. I am trapped between the two vehicles.

Men pile out and run toward me.

I reach for the radio to alert Myriam.

One man standing at the front bumper aims an Uzi machine gun at me through the windshield. Two others stand at either side of my car, pointing handguns at my head. I notice a fourth gunman at the rear, sighting him through the back window.

I drop the radio and place my hands on the steering wheel, gripping it tightly.

Too late again.

---

3   Creole word for "damn it."

Chapter 2

Surrounded

Butch
April 5, 2001
1:56 p.m.

It is said that when a person is faced with imminent death, his whole life flashes before him, and he relives it in a split second. As I wait for the bullets to tear through my body, this is partly true. But it isn't just my own life that tumbles in fast-forward mode across the screen of my mind. I also think of my dad.

My father was Horace Dade Ashton—renowned photographer, lecturer, filmmaker, explorer, scientist, student of religion, diplomat, and artist. In my moment of peril, I see his life flashing before me, inextricably entwined with mine as it had been for most of our lives.

In this world there are leaders and there are followers. My father was a born leader. He exuded confidence and always gave the impression that he knew what he was talking about. Horace Ashton commanded respect just by being who he was. As a boy, I observed how my father influenced others, how he persuaded them to think his way or do things his way, and how he entertained the ever-present audience parading through our house with tales of his adventurous life.

Among several of his great achievements as Cultural Attaché was the founding of Union School, a small correspondence-course school for the children of American expats living in Haiti. Union School quickly became the most important American school in Haiti, and it holds that rank today. I received my primary education from kindergarten through eighth grade there and made many friends and great memories during that period.

As I look back on my childhood and teens, I realize that life's circumstances compelled me to be creative and not hesitate to "think outside the box." My parents' influence taught me that all things are possible.

After my father retired from his position as Cultural Attaché, my mother, Gordana Ashton—consummate hostess and "the doyenne of the diplomatic corps," as I affectionately described her—turned our Haitian home into a unique kind of bed-and-breakfast, where an odd collection of paying guests would often stay for two or three months at a time. News of our tropical guesthouse rapidly spread by word of mouth in America and Europe: "You've got to go to Haiti to meet Horace Ashton and listen to his fascinating stories!"

People loved my father and would sit and listen to him for hours. Congressmen, generals, celebrities, and other important people came to visit him. Known for his wit and intelligence, Horace Ashton was described as an attractive raconteur, who never failed to hold the attention of his audience, and a captivating storyteller.

To be honest, I'd privately doubted the truth of his stories. How could one man have done all that he claimed? But I had too much respect for Dad to openly question him. It was obvious he loved to tell the tales as much as our visitors loved to listen to them.

Nonetheless, when my father was eighty-six, I urged him to record his stories on tape before he forgot them. He liked the idea of the stories living on after he was gone, although I hadn't a clue what I was going to do with them.

After my father's death in 1976 at the age of ninety-three,

my aunt Martha, his elder sister who was then ninety-five years old, sent me two scrapbooks she had kept. I had not known they existed, and the scrapbooks were filled with articles documenting Dad's extraordinary life.

A few months later, I sat alone on his favorite cane chair in his empty studio, my feet on his red Turkish rug and one of the scrapbooks in my lap. As the pleasant fragrance of the ylang-ylang tree he'd planted long ago drifted through his open window, I heard the unmistakable sound of a large snake slithering through the dense vegetation below. I slowly turned the pages of the legacy he'd left me. A lump grew in my throat, and tears clouded my vision as I realized that all his remarkable stories were true.

* * *

Now, so many years later, my life threatened by a Haitian tragedy he had thankfully never known, I can clearly picture my father sitting in that same cane chair, his beloved dog Bouki asleep at his feet on the Turkish rug. Clean-shaven, impeccably groomed, and wearing his trademark colorful bow tie—maroon today—he pauses to relight his ever-present pipe. Perhaps he is gathering his thoughts, perhaps adding suspense while his audience waits in anticipation.

This time, I am the audience.

My father looks up, and his gray eyes shine with amusement as his lips curl in a half-smile. I hear his comforting, distinct, pleasantly modulated voice. It is the kind of voice that has traveled and borrowed inflections from all over the world.

CHAPTER 3

Birth of a Spirit

Horace Dade Ashton
July 29, 1883

Thanks to my guardian angel I lived a charmed life. I survived plane crashes that took the lives of others, malaria in the desert, poisonous snakes, Vodou ceremonies, and most dangerous of all, two divorces. I was led to an oasis when I was about to die of thirst and mysteriously guided out of the dark depths of underground caves when I lost my way. This angel introduced me to life's mysteries, brought me opportunities, and watched over me whenever I was in peril—even at the hour of my birth in an open sailboat in the middle of the Potomac.

Of course I don't remember my birth, but as a child I heard my mother tell this story many times. In 1883, my parents lived near my father's family in King George County, Virginia, where his father was a prominent physician and surgeon. Feeling uncomfortable in anticipation of my birth, my mother wanted to see her mother. She persuaded my father, John Burdette Ashton, to take her to visit her parents in Charles County, Maryland, where her father was an Episcopal minister.

They stayed a few days at my mother's childhood home until, unexpectedly early, her labor began. She wanted her doctor in Virginia to deliver her child, so she and my father decided to return home as quickly as possible. The only transportation available was an open sailboat, and the Potomac River was twelve miles wide at that point.

A stiff breeze filled the sails as my parents began their voyage. Halfway across the river the wind suddenly died. There they sat, becalmed in the middle of the Potomac while my mother's labor pains grew more and more pronounced.

With no medical help available, my father had to take charge. Although he was not a physician as his father and brothers were, he was a farmer who'd assisted with animal births. Trusting his instincts, he helped my mother deliver me right there in the boat. The date was July 29, 1883.

I have always credited my enduring love for the sea and my sense of calm to the circumstances of my birth. No matter what happened, I have always held the belief that everything would turn out all right, and it always has, even though my life has been full of adventures and surprises.

My parents named me Horace Dade Ashton, after my paternal grandfather. Although I did not train as a doctor, I must have inherited some of his medical skills, for I have also delivered several babies, performed surgeries, and acted as a healer on many occasions.

* * *

The Ashtons came from a historic Virginia property, and historic antecedents were later described by *Farm & Country magazine*[4] as follows:

Oldest Family Farm: Waterloo Continues Producing

When Horace Vernon Ashton[5] looks out across the Potomac River from Waterloo Farm, his view is about the same as that seen by generations of his ancestors. Waterloo, in King George County, is con-

---

4   Kathleen Hoffman, "Oldest Family Farm: Waterloo Continues Producing" in *Farm & Country* magazine, 3 May 1986. *Farm & Country* magazine was a publication of the Virginia Land Bureau and has ceased publication.

5   Horace Vernon Ashton was the son of Horace's sister Martha, who married a cousin with the same last name.

sidered the oldest family farm in the state. It was developed from a grant given by Richard Townsend in 1653. . . . Ashton, descended from George Washington's family, has spent a lifetime feeling the dual pull of the land and the river—and while earlier Ashtons and their predecessors undoubtedly felt their own affection for the farm, the strength of its current hold on the 63-year-old Ashton does justice to its age and deep tradition. . . .

I grew up on Waterloo Farm in Virginia, with my two sisters, Martha, who was two years older than I, and Eliza, who was two years younger. Like me, my father had a great love for nature, and I was told he'd caught specimens of all snakes native to the Atlantic Coast region of the United States for the Smithsonian Institution in Washington D.C. (perhaps a prelude to my own adventures with snakes). Sadly, my father, John Ashton, died at the young age of thirty-one, when I was only three. My mother was left to raise three small children and tend a farm on her own.

Life on the farm was happy, and I kept busy by helping my mother and sisters run our family home. In those days we had no telephone or telegraph, no electricity or motors. Our transportation was limited to horseback or vehicles drawn by horses or oxen. When we traveled on the river, we took side-wheel steamboats over long distances, and for shorter distances we used sailboats. I remember fondly the whale-oil lamps we burned in the rural Virginia and Maryland of my youth, their soft glow casting monsters' shadows on my bedroom wall.

I was a curious child who liked to explore and try new things. Being the only son, I was given the freedom to follow my instincts and challenge my intellect. As I grew older, I remained fascinated by technology and the way things worked. In my lifetime I witnessed an array of exciting technological developments: the evolution of flight—from ballooning, through the Wright brothers' first flight, and ultimately the jet airplane; radio; telephone; printing presses; the great harvesting machines; photography and motion pictures; elevators and skyscrapers; sewing machines; automobiles and internal combustion engines; steamships to cruise ships; scuba diving; the building of the Panama Canal; television; atomic reactors; landing on the moon; and the dawning of the computer age.

When I was thirteen, my mother sent me to study at St. Paul's Episcopal School in Baltimore. However, my real adventures began at the age of fourteen, when I spent my summer vacation working as a cabin boy on a brigantine, sailing from Baltimore to Costa Rica and back. The ship delivered coal to the small Central American country and returned with a load of coconuts, a tropical delicacy in the United States.

I soon discovered that life experience offers far more instruction than any classroom. The open ocean, endless sky, and travel to distant lands appealed to me and stimulated my wanderlust, as it was my first adventure abroad. The captain of the ship was a family friend who had taken me under his wing after my father's death. This friend taught me how to sail, a skill that became a lifelong passion. My trip to Costa Rica was the first of many sea voyages I would take.

* * *

A few months later, in the fall of 1898, I was fifteen and back at boarding school in Baltimore. On the heels of my exciting seagoing summer adventure, the confines of the classroom made me feel cooped up. The triviality of school life held little interest for me. Fortunately, my tenure at St. Paul's would be short—lived because of an incident that occurred one evening during study hour.

My schoolmates and I were in the library working on our assignments when one of the boys found something amusing in his textbook and began laughing aloud. The headmaster, a swarthy, bearded man with a stiff right elbow, was a strict disciplinarian. He strode to the study table and stood, arms folded across his chest, glaring at the youth.

"Mr. Mitchell, please stand," he commanded.

When Mitchell complied, the headmaster raised his arm and struck the small boy with such force that the child fell down and hit his head, leaving him stunned. Witnessing the severity of the headmaster's rage caused me to react without considering the consequences. I leapt from my chair, grabbed the heavy wooden ruler I'd handcrafted for geometry class, and crashed it down on the swarthy man's head.

He crumpled to the floor—knocked out cold.

In that moment I realized I'd no longer be welcome at St. Paul's. I ran to my room, packed my few belongings—a comb, brush, and toothbrush—and left school for good.

Planning to return to my family in Washington, D.C., I walked to the railroad depot, where I convinced the kindly ticket agent to lend me the fare (which I returned to him a few months later). As the train clicked along the tracks, and I watched Baltimore flash by the window, I felt both terribly ashamed and guiltily thrilled to be free.

When I arrived in Washington, I went to my cousin's home. I did not want my mother to know about my expulsion from St. Paul's. My cousin took me in and kept my secret to avoid upsetting my mother, who was gravely ill. I visited her in the hospital where she died a few months later, never having learned of my disgrace.

Having decided my school days were over for good, I immediately started looking for work. Two days later I joined the throngs on Pennsylvania Avenue, shouting, "Peace programs! Peace programs! Celebrate the United States's victory in the Spanish–American War!"

As I hawked the Peace Jubilee programs I dreamed of becoming an adventurer and going off to war. Like many young men, I romanticized the excitement of battle. While I stood in the middle of the nation's capital, I imagined the battleship *Maine* being blown apart in Havana harbor; Theodore Roosevelt leading the Rough Riders up San Juan Hill; and Señorita Cisneros being rescued from prison by an American correspondent who wore my face. My sea voyage had opened my eyes to the world, and I would never be content to sit on the sidelines. I yearned to know all there was and be in the thick of the action.

Selling peace programs was only a temporary position, and my next job proved more confining than any classroom. Through my cousin's contacts I was hired as an auditor for the Southern Railroad, where I was one of about seventy-five men. We all sat in one large room, tracking the earnings of each train. As you can imagine, the work was deadly repetitious and tedious. However, I devised a novel way to relieve the monotony.

All seventy-five auditors were required to refer to a single tariff book that we shared by circulating it around the room. When I wanted to look at the book, I would shoot a rubber band to attract the attention of the person holding it. This method worked quite well and made my job a bit more bearable, until one day my aim got the better of me. After I shot the rubber band through the air, a nearby colleague jumped up and screamed, holding his eye. I was fired on the spot.

Shortly after losing my job as the slingshot auditor, I developed typhoid fever. I was confined to Alexandria Hospital, where my sister Martha was a nurse. At the beginning of the twentieth century, there were no antibiotics, and if one was fortunate enough to survive this dreadful disease, the recovery period took months. I was glad to have Martha involved in my care until she resorted to typical sibling tricks. Typhoid fever severely affects the intestinal tract, and many foods, such as fresh fruits and vegetables, are prohibited. As I convalesced, my sister teased me by passing through my room carrying trays of ripe red tomatoes and tangy cucumber pickles— foods I loved but was unable to eat.

After two months in the hospital, I was finally strong enough to sit in a chair beside my bed. I detested being idle, and I'd seriously had enough by that time. No matter what the doctors said, I figured that since I was able to get out of bed, I was well enough to leave the hospital. I rang for an attendant and offered him a bribe in exchange for my clothes. He gladly accepted the money. Dressing quickly, I waited until the corridor was quiet and then sneaked out of the hospital, clinging to the railings for support.

Somehow I made my way to the Washington trolley, purchased a newspaper, and returned to my room at the boarding house where I'd lived before being hospitalized. I went to bed to rest, but despite my illness, rest did not come easily, for I was still unemployed. While in bed, I read the job listings in the newspaper.

One ad sounded particularly interesting: "Wanted— an experienced snapshot and view–photographer. Apply Clinedinst, 1207 F Street, Washington, D.C."

The next morning, I took the streetcar downtown to apply for the job. I found the address but was still so weak that I had to pull myself up the long stairway to the studio by the handrail. Breathing heavily, I paused to gather strength before knocking on the door. When I asked to see Mr. Clinedinst about the job, the receptionist led me straight into his private office for an interview.

"Well, young man, what experience have you had as a photographer?" Clinedinst asked, eyeing me suspiciously over the rims of his small round spectacles.

I'd only taken a few pictures in my life, using a friend's camera, but I was very keen on the idea of being a photographer. I handed him several small snapshots I'd made with a borrowed Kodak box camera—one of the early "you push the button; we do the rest" models.

He glanced at my samples but gave no comment. Naturally, I had no way of knowing then that Mr. Clinedinst was just as desperate to hire someone as I was to find employment. His last photographer had quit without notice only days before.

Clinedinst handed me a strange new–model Kodak. "Take this out on the street, snap six pictures of prominent people, ask their names, and come back."

I left the office and hurried across the street to a camera store. "My friend just loaned me this camera," I told the store owner. "Could you please show me how it works?"

The man gave me a brief introduction to the instrument that would become my lifelong companion. Full of youthful enthusiasm, I sauntered down the street to a large department store where prominent people might shop. I stood outside and waited.

A few minutes later, an ornate horse–drawn carriage pulled up in front of the store. When the door opened, a huge cloud of smoke burst forth from the interior, followed by two ladies wearing fur–trimmed capes and elegant hats graced with velvet and plumes.

I cranked the handle on the camera and snapped my first picture.

Startled, the well–dressed ladies raised their hands to hide their faces. "Don't," they begged. "Oh, please don't print that picture of us!"

At the beginning of the twentieth century, ladies did not smoke cigarettes in public, and my smoky picture would cause quite a scandal if it were published.

"I'm so sorry. I didn't mean to frighten you," I assured them. "Of course I won't use that picture if you'll allow me one more photograph."

Smiling with relief, the two agreed and climbed back into their carriage. At my signal, they stepped out again. I snapped the picture and then asked, "Ladies, will you tell me your names, please?"

"Why, of course! This is Countess Cassini, and I'm Alice Roosevelt."

CHAPTER 4

Capturing Moments in Time, 1900–1902

Horace

I couldn't believe my luck photographing Alice Roosevelt and Countess Cassini. Hoping to capture the images of other well-known Washingtonians, I remained in front of the department store. In about an hour, I had used up the roll of film. I returned to Clinedinst's studio, where I waited nervously while my pictures were developed. When all of them showed important people arriving at the department store, I breathed freely.

The next day was the opening session of Congress. I filled my pockets with rolls of film and made my way to Capitol Hill early to catch the senators and congressmen as they arrived. Whenever an important-looking, well-dressed man approached the Capitol from the streetcar stop, I'd say, "Beg your pardon, sir, are you a member of Congress?" If he answered yes, I'd measure off three of the four-foot squares on the concrete sidewalk. Then I'd aim my camera, signaling the man to come forward. Afterward I'd ask his name and thank him. That morning, I shot five rolls of film before noon, taking action photographs of sixty members of Congress.

The following morning I placed all my pictures proudly on Mr. Clinedinst's desk for review. He examined them one by one, his eyes narrowing behind his spectacles while I stood in front of his desk, shifting my weight back and forth.

Suddenly, his stern face broke into a wide grin. "Fine work, young man. Fine work indeed." He stood and extended a beefy hand to shake mine firmly. "Looks like I've got myself a new photographer. And you've got yourself a job, Mr. Ashton."

The art editor of *Collier's Weekly*, the largest and most popular publication of its kind at the time, bought all of my pictures from Capitol Hill for a double-page spread, paying well for first publication rights. Hundreds of copies were sent out on a syndicate basis to papers all over the United States because Clinedinst used his father's invention—the half-tone process that reproduced photographs for print publication. (Prior to this, all illustrations had been made from engravings or woodcuts.)

Some might attribute the way I practically fell into my first job as a photographer to blind luck. Others might say it was a combination of my own ingenuity and undiscovered talent. Still others might say it was my belief in divine intervention, or belief in myself, or just because I was in the right place at the right time.

I assure you, this was no coincidence. It was just the first of many unique and interesting opportunities—all connected like a domino train, as you will see—that were placed in my path by my guardian angel throughout my entire life.

I will, however reluctantly, admit that an element of good fortune played a role in launching my photography career so successfully. Early on I was fortunate to photograph many people of prominence, and my pictures were printed in a number of publications. With my camera I captured the president and his family; diplomats and their families; senators, congressmen, and their families; cabinet members; visiting dignitaries; and military and naval chiefs.

My subjects varied but not my skill with a camera, which always led to more interesting assignments. I became well-known as a photographer for a number of reasons: I was determined and believed I could do anything to which I set my mind; I was one of the few professional photographers in Washington, D.C. at the time; the people I photographed were prominent, gracious, and accommodating; and my employer's invention and use of half-tones could disseminate my work to numerous publications at once. I also had an eye for composition and a talent for capturing a complete story in a single shot. Within a short period of time, individuals and groups began to request my services.

* * *

In 1902, Mount Pelée erupted violently on the Caribbean island of Martinique, and an emergency team headed by Professor Louis Aggasiz of the University of Pennsylvania was dispatched to the island nation to see what help they could render. They asked me to accompany them as the official photographer. I was always keen for a new adventure, especially if it involved a sea voyage.

Very little description of the disaster had reached us prior to our departure, so we were not prepared for the horror that greeted us on our arrival four days later.

Our ship anchored three miles out in Martinique's harbor and was soon inundated by volcanic ash. Falling like black snow upon the deck, it piled to a depth of about one inch per day, for several days. The air was thick with a haze that stung my eyes and made my throat sore.

Immediately after we anchored, I was allowed to go ashore with the first detachment of sailors to survey the ruins and photograph them. We found hundreds of bodies of men, women, children, dogs, cats, donkeys, and chickens decaying in the streets. Under the fierce tropical sun, despite the screen from the ash cloud, the decaying corpses gave off an odor that was almost unbearable. Several times, I had to drop my camera quickly in order to heave my stomach contents at the side of the road.

After trekking through the devastated wasteland

that had once been the capital city of St. Pierre, we felt hopeless. Not a soul survived.

Later that day, we heard shouts from the area where the island's prison had stood. Our despair briefly turned to joy when we discovered the sole survivor of this cataclysmic event: a prisoner who'd been locked in an underground cell.

Groups of sailors were dispatched to all parts of the city to bury the dead and to search for other survivors. Sadly, there were no other survivors. The island resembled Pompeii after the first great eruption of Mount Vesuvius. A broad stream of molten lava and rock had poured down the mountainside, destroying everything in its path. Not a house in St. Pierre was left standing. The entire city was a sad and odoriferous shambles.

We remained in Martinique for one week. I was so distraught by what I had seen and photographed that I hardly ate a mouthful the entire time.

As we left the island and headed home, we finally emerged from the still—falling ashes and sailed beyond the smell of the dead. The relief of the open sea and bright sunlight felt to me like a stay of execution must feel to a death—row inmate. Only nineteen years old, I had seen enough death and destruction to last a lifetime.

* * *

I was relieved to return to Washington, D.C. and photograph the living. I continued to enjoy my work immensely, but, as always, I hated to be idle. One day, after I had caught up with all my assignments, I began to inspect some odd pictures left lying about.

Two photos caught my eye. One was a picture of a young horseman jumping hurdles and the other depicted President Theodore Roosevelt. The young horseman's head was in exactly the same position as President Roosevelt's head as he bowed to a crowd from his carriage. It struck me that it might be amusing to paste the president's head on the flying horseman. I did so and showed it to my boss.

"Where'd you get that?" he asked.

Well, I hardly ever told a lie, so I explained what I'd done. Mr. Clinedinst was more interested than ever. He took some sandpaper and India ink, and we smoothed the composite picture down, and then photographed it. Looking at it with a naked eye, nobody would guess it was a fake.

We then submitted the picture to a magazine editor who was so completely taken in that he offered $500 for it. Theodore Roosevelt jumping hurdles was newsworthy. Knowing we had to come clean, we told the editor the truth and admitted the photo was a fake. "Why don't you get the real one?" he suggested.

Always ready for a new challenge, I marched up to the White House and persisted until I finally got in to see the president. I showed him the photograph, and Theodore Roosevelt stared at the image in astonishment. After I explained what I had done, the president agreed to go to Chevy Chase and do some hurdle jumping.

Collier's Weekly paid $5,000 for first publication rights to the real picture and used it as a double-page spread. The president loved the picture and had it blown up by the Eastman Kodak Company to the largest ever made at that time (eight by ten feet) and hung it in the East Room of the White House.

I'd made an important new friend in the process and obviously a lasting impression on the president. Some years later, I would be appointed official White House photographer and accompany President Roosevelt all over America and other parts of the world. But before that, as a result of my sale of the hurdle photo, I would get a life-changing call from the editor at *Collier's Weekly* in New York.

Chapter 5

Taken

Butch
April 5, 2001
1:57 p.m.

I sit alone in my locked car, surrounded by four men with guns pointed at me. Panic churns in my gut, and my mouth is dry with a metallic taste—the taste of fear. Time begins to crawl.

I swallow hard and then suck in a deep breath in an attempt to control my terror, knowing that my only chance to stay alive is to remain calm enough to assess the situation. Fortunately, my pistol is not in the car. I feel thankful that I'd made that unknowingly wise decision this morning, because if these thugs see me armed, they'll shoot me without a second thought.

Violence is a big part of life in Port-au-Prince today, the place I had once bragged about as being the "safest city in the world." Politics aside, Haiti had been a safe place to live under the rule of Jean Claude Duvalier, the son who succeeded Dr. Francois Duvalier as President for Life and became known as Baby Doc. Under his rule there were fewer slum-dwellers and not as much abject poverty.

I understand the misconceptions most of the world had of Haiti during this difficult period because I lived through it. Few people realize that prior to Papa Doc's election as president—with the open support of the United States—Haiti was controlled by a handful of wealthy families. The majority of Haitians were poor farmers. Papa Doc's primary accomplishment was to generate a social revolution that created a middle class. Even though his tactics were ruthless and too many innocent victims were killed, he employed methods that were far less destructive and controversial than those of the Castro regime in Cuba.

Papa Doc's presidency concurred with major social and political upheaval in Central and South America. Communism spread at a disturbing pace during this time. Cuba exerted its influence on Haiti and its next-door neighbor, the Dominican Republic. The "theology of liberation" fanned the fire. Amid this upheaval, both Papa Doc and Baby Doc Duvalier sided with the United States.

Upon Papa Doc's demise, Baby Doc was thrust into power at only nineteen years old. Despite being completely unprepared, Baby Doc swiftly improved the regime's image. He replaced his father's "Old Guard" with a younger, broader entourage of advisors and cabinet members, most of whom were well prepared and well educated abroad. By these actions, Baby Doc greatly improved Haiti's relationship with the United States and gained American support for increased investment in the private and public sectors.

Soon after Baby Doc took office, a group of business people formed a new Haitian-American Chamber of Commerce (HAMCHAM), of which I was a founding member. We formed this group to encourage and facilitate private investment, and our combined efforts generated several hundred thousand labor-intensive jobs.

During Baby Doc's sixteen-year reign, more schools, medical clinics, and infrastructure improvements, such as seaports, airports, and highways, were built than in any other time in Haiti's history. He headed Haiti in the right direction. The economy grew rapidly and human rights improvements granted freedom of speech and the press, which allowed open opposition.

Baby Doc was very popular, and had he heeded the advice of many to renounce his title of President for Life and held elections, he would have handily won fair and honest elections.

However, after he married in 1980, he chose instead to listen to the entourage that came with his marriage. They insisted he retain the title President for Life, a stance that proved unacceptable to the international community that sought democratic reform. Baby Doc's choice proved to be the beginning of his end.

When Pope John Paul II visited Haiti in 1983, he assailed the inequality and hunger that pervaded the nation and proclaimed, "Things must change here." His words supported the growing internal opposition to Baby Doc's rule while his international support waned.

Having lived in Haiti most of my life, I felt that the country's best years were from 1972 through 1984, when the government focused on improving living conditions and creating opportunities for all through free enterprise. Haiti had no kidnapping, no "necklacing,"[6] and very little crime during that period. As long as people did not actively try to overthrow the government, they had nothing to fear. While Papa Doc ruled with an iron hand, Baby Doc had the good sense to wear a velvet glove on it.

After Baby Doc was forced out of office in 1986, the country and its citizens slid downhill. Inequalities grew more pronounced, and hunger became a widespread problem that remains today. Many Haitians who had been living in the United States returned home and brought with them the violence and weaponry they had learned about and obtained in America. Some, who had been released from American prisons and deported, brought the kind of trouble Haiti had never seen before.

Since the Haitian Army disbanded in 1995,[7] a force originally

---

6   Necklacing is a torturous practice in which people are forced to swallow gasoline, doused with it, lit on fire, and burned alive.

7   After years of military interference in politics with dozens of military coups, Haiti disbanded its military in 1995.

formed and trained by the United States in the 1920s, the country is at the mercy of roaming gangs of thugs, known as *zinglendos*, mostly financed and empowered by the ruling politicos. The naiveté of the Haiti I'd once known—the land my father had loved, the beloved island paradise where I'd grown up, married, and raised my own family—seems forever lost. "*Honneur,* respect"—honor and respect—the words Haitians used to greet one another and the backbone of our culture—have all but disappeared. Haiti's tragedy has never been clearer to me than at this moment—in my own car on my private road with four men aiming firearms at my head.

* * *

One of the thugs pounds repeatedly on my car window with the butt of his gun while the others keep their weapons trained on me. Reluctantly, I press the button and unlock the doors with a click. It is either that or the rapid crack of firearms, the shatter of windshield glass . . . and my immediate death.

The gangster who pounded on my window now shoves me roughly into the passenger seat. I hear the doors slam as four Haitian men in their mid-twenties, still holding guns on me, jump into my car—one in the driver's seat and three in the back. A strong odor of perspiration assaults my nostrils, and the air inside the car grows close.

The rational side of my brain reasons that they obviously want something more than merely to shoot me or I would not still be alive with my heart hammering in my chest. But whatever these men want, they will probably still shoot me. Car shootings have become a daily occurrence in Port-au-Prince and often happen for no reason at all.

My training has reinforced the cardinal rule to never, never go anywhere in a car with your captors, but I have no choice. Glancing frantically out the window, I see the vendors along the roadside scattering rapidly, their eyes cast down, unseeing. I know most of these people. I provide cement to rebuild their houses whenever the mudslides wash them away. I give many of them work to help them earn money. I let them use our water and electricity, albeit begrudgingly. The older ones knew and respected my father.

Run to Myriam and tell her what's happening, my thoughts scream at them as I try to make eye contact. I silently plead with my neighbors for help, but they pretend not to notice my abduction. They turn away as if my coffin is already closed.

I am trapped in the passenger seat, perspiring heavily. My mind racing, I numbly watch the digital car clock flip from 1:59 to 2:00 p.m. I fight off the insane urge to laugh hysterically as my mind plays the opening of tonight's newscast.

"Two United States citizens have been shot and killed in Port-au-Prince in the past two weeks. Today, a third—American businessman Marc 'Butch' Ashton—was abducted in front of his home at Villarosa and . . ."

My thoughts churn with wild imaginings of murder, torture, kidnapping, and God knows what else is about to happen to me.

Had my father, the great explorer, ever felt this pounding fear, this utter sense of helplessness?

Dad had faced death many times and in many ways in his lifetime. I find it hard to believe he was never scared, but I know he was fearless. Risking his life was part of the thrill for him. He put absolute trust in his guardian angel and held on to his belief that everything would turn out for the good.

I don't have a guardian angel as he claimed to. I don't even want to have one—I think the whole idea is nonsense. And I am not fearless.

In my terror, my mind wanders to safer times. Again I see my father leaning forward in his chair in storytelling pose, an alert expression on his face. I breathe in the familiar aroma of pipe tobacco and listen to the comfort of his clear voice telling me about the Wright brothers and their flying machines—telling me I am not going to die today.

CHAPTER 6

First Flights, 1903

Horace

While I had immersed myself in photographing prominent Washingtonians, two brothers named Orville and Wilbur Wright, bicycle makers from Dayton, Ohio, were engaged in endeavors that would change the way people traveled. They were working on a flying machine.

Flight had always fascinated me. I followed the progress of early experiments intently and took an interest in the flights of dirigibles and balloons. I knew that attempts to build flying machines had been going on for years with little success. No one had been able to create a machine that was heavier than air and could fly. Popular scientists of the day claimed it was impossible. The press scoffed at the idea, reporting that inventors would get airplanes into the sky as soon as the law of gravity was repealed. The Wright brothers' work was met with derision.

Few people are aware that in 1896, even before the Wright brothers built anything that could fly, Professor Langley, director of the Smithsonian Institution, had built a steam—powered model airplane. Seven years later, months before the Wright brothers' famous attempt at Kitty Hawk in 1903, Professor Langley had a larger airplane he'd designed and built, called Aerodrome, ready for a test flight. It had four parallel wings, two in front and two behind, attached to a long fuselage.

Langley and his colleagues constructed a large houseboat equipped with a long rail and catapult on its roof to launch their invention. They anchored the houseboat in the middle of the Potomac River for privacy. Unfortunately, this location didn't afford the hoped-for privacy, and the houseboat was surrounded for days by a number of open rowboats, manned by newspaper reporters and photographers. I was among them, a twenty-year-old photographer in a rowboat in the middle of the Potomac, coincidentally near the scene of my birth. My anticipation mounted as I waited for what might be the first flight by a flying machine.

Despite the invasion of the press and their weeks-long criticism of his efforts, Professor Langley and his assistant, Professor Manly, decided to wait no longer. The two men sat astride the fuselage, signaled someone on the houseboat, and the flying machine took off on its first voyage.

Balancing unsteadily, I stood in the rowboat, camera ready. As the plane's tail left the houseboat, I snapped a photograph of the plane with its nose five feet above the water. Then it dove, throwing Manly into the river and making a terrific splash. I sat down hard on the wooden rowboat seat, clutching my camera to my chest.

The plane had flown for fifty feet, but it was not enough to crush the resultant newspaper reports and scathing criticism of Langley's efforts.

Soon after this momentous event, I was a guest at the home of Alexander Graham Bell, inventor of the telephone, attending one of his informal Thursday afternoon gatherings. During the discussions over the professor's failure, I heard the great astronomer Simon Newcomb, head of the United States Naval Observatory, explain very logically that no heavier-than-air machine would ever fly.

Shortly after the failure of Professor Langley's plane and my visit to Dr. Bell's home, news that the Wright brothers were about to attempt their first flight spread to the press. Because of earlier ridicule, we weren't welcome. However, I eagerly made my way to the isolated, windswept sand dunes off the Atlantic Coast near Kitty Hawk, North Carolina.

The date was December 17, 1903, a day history would remember. I hid in the sea-grape bushes in the early morning chill, staking a position alongside Jimmy Hare of *Collier's Weekly*. Jimmy and I each hoped to photograph the Wright brothers' first flight.

As we waited, we observed the brothers' unique invention. The Wright Flyer featured two sets of parallel cloth wings attached to a fuselage, held together by wire and struts, and a small gasoline motor. For takeoff, the brothers rigged the plane up to a tall tripod that had a couple of railroad car wheels attached to the top. The tripod was located at one end of a long, wooden monorail. After the brothers started the plane's motor, the wheels attached to the tripod were dropped, launching the plane into the air.

Breathlessly, we watched and turned the handles on our cameras while the plane soared to a dizzying altitude of what I estimated to be about sixty feet and then settled down to a gentle landing, reportedly having traveled 120 feet in twelve seconds.[8]

Orville Wright, who piloted the 650-pound machine, was later quoted as saying, "This flight lasted only twelve seconds, but it was nevertheless the first in the history of the world in which a machine carrying a man had raised itself by its own power into the air in full flight, had sailed forward without a reduction in speed, and had finally landed at a point as high as that from which it began."

While this first flight is the one history remembers, Wilbur Wright actually achieved better results on their fourth and final flight of the day: 852 feet in fifty-nine seconds.

---

8   The first three photos seen upon entering the Wright Brothers' exhibit at the Smithsonian Air and Space Museum in Washington, D.C., were taken by Horace Dade Ashton.

Unfortunately, I was not the only photographer who captured the now—famous photographs of the Wright brothers' first flight, but it was a thrilling sight to witness. I would continue to follow the Wright brothers' progress with great interest and would photograph some of their future flights.

Being present at that world—changing event further fueled my own passion for flying machines. Little did I realize then what role airplanes were to play in my future and how many perils they would present.

CHAPTER 7

Asia Beckons, 1903–1904

Horace

Not long after I witnessed the Wright brothers' pivotal event in the history of transportation, I received a telegraph from the editor of *Collier's Weekly* asking me to meet him in New York to discuss future employment. Naturally, I was curious and headed to New York City immediately.

When I arrived, the editor said, "Mr. Ashton, I am impressed by your work, and I'd like to offer you a job. You know the Russians and the Japanese are currently fighting over the Korean Peninsula, right? It's only a matter of time before war breaks out. How would you like to be a war correspondent for *Collier's*?"

"Yes, I would. I will!" I replied while trying to maintain some semblance of professionalism and coolly shaking my new editor's hand, despite wanting to jump up on his desk and hug the man.

Only two years earlier, as I'd sold peace programs in the streets of the nation's capital, the excitement of foreign lands and the pitch of battle had entranced me. I could not believe my good fortune. At the ripe old age of twenty, I was about to cover the Russo–Japanese War.

I returned to Washington immediately, eager to pack my bags. I then traveled by train to San Francisco. From there I boarded a steamship to Yokohama. In 1903 steamships burned coal, and this one carried 252 passengers and traveled at a speed of fifteen knots. En route to Japan we stopped in Honolulu for several days, and I saw enough of that beautiful mid—Pacific paradise to fall in love with it.

One day at Waikiki Beach I joined other steamship passengers on an outrigger to watch the spectacular performance of the local surf riders on the mountain-high waves. A huge breaker capsized our boat, and we were all thrown into the sea. Being a fair swimmer, I grabbed a terrified young lady struggling near me and pulled her to shore. Ivy, who was on her way to Japan to join her husband, was understandably grateful, and we were friends for the balance of the voyage.

Aboard ship, I met a remarkable Chinese gentleman, Yuan Shikai, who became my companion for a daily promenade around the deck. He impressed me immensely with his memory. We would chat, and he could tell me the exact dates and the names of all commanders in every important battle of the American War for Independence and the War Between the States. He spoke perfect English and told me he had taken postgraduate courses at Harvard and Oxford universities.

Yuan Shikai was then the Chinese commissioner to the St. Louis Exposition, and he was returning home to his country when I met him on the ship. (He would later become the president of China.) Every day, he astonished me with his intellect. From him I learned about the Chinese mentality, the history of China, the life of its people, and Oriental etiquette, which would serve me well in future travels.

When I left the ship at Yokohama, he told me to be sure to call on him if I ever came to China or if I was ever in need of more information about his country and people.

Yuan Shikai awakened my curiosity about China and other lands I never dreamed I'd visit. His words inspired me to travel and live among different cultures.

Further inspiration came from Will Levington Comfort, a correspondent for William Randolph Hearst's newspaper, *Manila America*, whom I befriended during the war. Since neither of us were drinking men, Will and I spent very little time with the other seventy–five war correspondents in the hotel bar. Through our long conversations we discovered we had many interests in common. One evening, while discussing interesting people we had met while doing our jobs, I told Will all about Yuan Shikai.

He listened raptly and then said, "Horace, you would really like this gentleman I met on the ship that brought me to Tokyo from Manila. He's an abbot of an ancient Buddhist monastery on a small island off the coast of China, south of Shanghai. He invited me to spend a few months in his monastery to study esoteric Buddhism after the war is over."

Growing more and more amazed as Will told me incredible stories about the abbot, I yearned to learn firsthand about this 3,000–year–old religion. Full of clarity, I was certain that I had to go to the monastery in China and meet the abbot. I begged Will to ask the abbot if I could accompany him to the monastery. He promised he would.

I was interested in studying different religions because I believed religion defined a culture most accurately. For the rest of my life, I would follow the inspiration ignited by these two men, using photography as my passport.

* * *

In Japan, however, I soon discovered that my job for *Collier's Weekly* would not open doors for me in this closed and secretive society. Since the country was preparing for war with the Russians, my access to several sites was limited—but limited in such a clever way that it took me a while to catch on.

When our ship entered the harbor of Yokohama, several nice–looking young men boarded our vessel with the pilot and immigration and customs officers. One of them approached me and said, "Sir, please allow me to be your guide for your stay in Japan."

I laughed and replied, "Thank you, but I have no need for a guide."

He didn't leave. When we arrived ashore, he insisted on helping me with customs, got me a rickshaw, and then followed me to the hotel in a second rickshaw.

The next morning I found a large map of Japan in my letterbox. The Welcome Society of Japan supposedly gave this to all visitors. Several red circles were drawn on the map around areas that I later learned were "non-photographic" zones. I would discover what this meant as I traveled around the country.

Before I finished my breakfast, my self-appointed guide appeared, persistently offering his services. He had learned that I was a war correspondent. "Sir, the war minister appointed a contractor to go to the front with each group of journalists and provide all necessary meals and comforts in the field. I would like to be your personal valet, secretary, and interpreter."

"This is nonsense. I have no need of such services," I assured him. Thankfully, he departed, and I was on my own—or so I thought.

I soon got to work taking photographs of recruiting and war preparations in and around Yokohama. Then I headed to Nagasaki, where the Japanese Navy was stationed. While traveling south on a train crowded with Japanese soldiers, I discovered my would-be guide sitting directly behind me. Appearing to be as surprised as I, he explained he was going to visit his uncle in Kyoto. "What a coincidence," I replied, not believing this for a minute.

The next day, my journey continued by boat through Japan's Inland Sea. I checked my map and figured we would pass the opening to the harbor where the bulk of the Japanese fleet was stationed. Hoping to take a picture of the Japanese battle cruisers, I went to my cabin, locked the door, and then quietly set up my camera. I opened the porthole and watched for the harbor opening. Just as I raised my camera, ready to shoot, a great canvas tarpaulin fluttered down, covering my porthole. I returned to the deck and found my young friend sitting in a deck chair and smiling.

When I arrived in Nagasaki, I joined the other journalists at the hotel and informed the United States diplomatic corps of my whereabouts. Although Nagasaki was supposedly a "non–photographic" zone, I hoped to get pictures of naval operations there. I had concealed my camera in a trunk while traveling, and now as I walked the streets of the city, I hung my camera over my shoulder, holster–style, and wore a raincoat over it.

* * *

Between the ever–diligent Japanese intelligence and my friend Ivy, whom I'd rescued from drowning in Hawaii, I never had a dull moment in Nagasaki.

On February 22, 1904, a large United States cargo transport arrived in the harbor to take Americans who were serving in the Philippines back to the United States for their home leave. Because it was the anniversary of George Washington's birth, an American national holiday, I received an invitation from the United States consul to attend the Washington's Birthday Celebration that night on the ship. He offered to place his private launch, manned by two sailors, at my disposal.

As coincidence would have it, Ivy was staying at my hotel, but her husband, also a war correspondent, had already gone to Korea. I asked her to accompany me to the celebration, and since she had also received an invitation, she agreed to let me escort her.

The invitation stated that the celebration was a formal affair, so I dressed in white tie and tails and awaited her in the lobby. Ivy arrived wearing a dark green, low–cut evening gown covered with sequins that sparkled like a million stars. Her beauty staggered me.

I took her arm, and we left the hotel, walking a short distance along the seawall to the consul general's launch. We climbed aboard and rode out to the ship. The launch rocked slowly, the stars shone above, and the sequins on Ivy's gown glittered in the moonlight. She smelled heavenly, like flowers in Hawaii. At twenty years old, I was more than a little smitten.

The ship was packed with people, and shortly after we arrived I lost sight of Ivy among all the handsome officers in full−dress uniforms. I found myself surrounded by a group that was seriously drinking to the Stars and Stripes. After the fifth toast to the flag, I was seized by a strong sense of responsibility and decided it was my duty to save Ivy once more. It took a long time to find her in the crowd, but I finally located her standing with a group of people around a punch bowl, looking a little worse for wear. As Ivy's legion of admirers glared at me, I gently guided her to the companionway and asked the boatswain to summon our launch.

We descended the ship's ladder and stood on the tiny platform below. By this time, the bay had developed quite a swell, and the ship rolled a little while the launch bobbed up and down in the water like a seesaw. Waiting, I measured the rhythm and jumped on the launch's deck at the appropriate moment, landing safely. As the launch bobbed again, I reached for Ivy's hand, intending to help her jump aboard at the right time. Before she could, this beautiful young lady in her stunning emerald evening dress lost her footing and plopped into the water between the launch and the ladder. With the help of the sailors, I pulled her aboard. She was drenched from head to foot, so I rushed her inside the cabin and wrapped her in a blanket as the launch headed toward shore.

When we neared shore, we learned that the tide had fallen dramatically. Even the roof of the launch's cabin was at least eight feet below the top of the seawall from which we'd departed. The exposed seawall was covered in a thick layer of green slime.

Our prospects for landing looked hopeless, but for propriety's sake I needed to bring Ivy back to the hotel. She couldn't stay out all night with me. I asked two men on the seawall above to haul me ashore, which they did. In the process my shirtfront scraped off its share of the wall's green slime. I urged Ivy to stand on the roof of the cabin so that the sailors could steady her while the rest of us pulled her up the wall. Fortunately, she made it, despite collecting the balance of the slime on her once–beautiful dress.

I longed to reach out and wipe the smudge of green slime marring her porcelain cheek, but instead I gave her my silk handkerchief and basked in her weak smile of gratitude. It was nearly midnight, and we hesitated to return to the hotel in our bedraggled condition. But what choice did we have? After some discussion, Ivy and I decided it was the only reasonable thing to do and continued toward the hotel.

Just as we mounted the front steps, the lights miraculously went out. The lobby was nearly empty except for the night clerk and a couple of bellhops, who averted their eyes. We returned to our respective rooms, tired and dirty, but safe and alone. At this point in the story, someone invariably says, "Sure you did," with a wink and a smile. I'm telling you, this is my story and I'm sticking to it.

* * *

One morning at the hotel in Nagasaki, I was awakened by strange noises so I rushed to my waterfront window and looked out. I saw several Japanese transports with the zigzag insignia on their funnels at anchor in the bay directly in front of the hotel. Hearing loud voices in the corridor outside, I knew there was no way I could sneak my camera out undetected and get a shot of those ships. However, I knew the floor above me was empty, so I ran downstairs to the lobby and got the manager to move me (and my trusty camera, still hidden in the trunk) up to another room.

I opened the jalousie door of my new room and peered up and down the open waterfront corridor, all the way to the bamboo curtains that screened each end. Not a soul in sight. I crept back into my room, opened my trunk, and prepared my camera. Crawling on my hands and knees to avoid detection from the outside, I raised my camera, ready to shoot.

Suddenly I felt a heavy hand on my shoulder. A young policeman with a Sam Browne belt, sword, and pistol said politely, "Honorable sir, please return honorable camera to trunk." By this time, I had acquired a healthy respect for Japanese intelligence and didn't even ask him how he knew where my camera had been hidden. I was just thankful he didn't try to confiscate it.

* * *

My final encounter with Japanese intelligence could have cost me my life. Shortly after I left Nagasaki, I managed to join the Pilgrimage Society's excursion to visit Buddhist shrines in different parts of the country. At the society's headquarters, I was outfitted properly with tight blue denim pants, straw sandals, a blue smock—like shirt with the society's insignia on the back, and an inverted straw basket that I wore as a hat to hide my face.

When we entered a village, a small boy ran alongside me, peered up into my face, and then began yelling in Japanese and pointing at me. The police arrived in a few minutes and took me into custody.

I was frightened and unable to speak Japanese, and none of the local residents spoke English, so I was locked up as a Russian spy. When the police searched me and could not find my passport, they were convinced I was a spy and sent me to a prison in Nagasaki, where I was kept incommunicado for three days in a cold cell with no blanket. My shoes had been removed, along with my small rucksack containing all my belongings for the trip.

"I want to see the American consul," I demanded repeatedly. Each time I made this request, I received no reply.

On the fourth morning, a young police captain who spoke English arrived to interrogate me.

"Sir, please contact Mr. Lloyd Griscom, the United States minister in Tokyo," I pleaded. "I am a correspondent for *Collier's Weekly*, and Mr. Griscom can verify this information."

The police captain nodded and quickly left my cell. Thanks to his quick action, I was released in a few hours.

As excited as I was to be a war correspondent, I never did get to the front in the first war I covered. The naval battles were limited when the Japanese Navy sank the Russian cruisers in the harbor of Seoul, Korea. I tried to join the army war correspondents, but Richard Harding Davis of Boer and Spanish–American Wars fame was already covering that area. Discouraged by my short–lived but not uneventful career as a war correspondent, I headed back home. On the way, another escapade in the guise of a job opportunity found me.

* * *

Returning from Japan on a small Northern Pacific steamer, we stopped in Vancouver, British Columbia. There I learned that the contractors constructing an important extension to Seattle's water supply had advertised for a man to go down inside the thirty–inch pipe that was to bring water about a thousand feet down from a new reservoir in the mountains. I telegraphed and applied for the job. The answer came immediately because there weren't so many lunatics at large.

A week later, I reported for the job and was told I would receive $500, if and when I completed the inspection and elimination of any rough spots on the joints inside the entire length of pipe. After checking to make sure the upper water valves were closed, they outfitted me with heavy duck overalls, a strong rope around my chest, and a miner's lantern on my forehead. As I made ready to enter the pipe, the expressions on the faces of the men standing around me were not reassuring.

I was slowly lowered inside the pipe, signaling to stop along the way as I tapped off the irregularities with a hammer. During the entire descent and ascent, I felt no sense of danger and actually found the experience interesting. I emerged from the manhole three hours later—with only a few skinned knuckles and slightly bruised knees, hips, and shoulders—to find a group of newspapermen and photographers expecting to photograph a corpse being hauled out. Undaunted, they found an angle for their story.

The next day my picture appeared in the local paper under this headline: "War correspondent helps Seattle win the war against water shortage."

* * *

My biggest assignment of the Russo—Japanese War occurred in 1905 when I returned again to United States soil, this time from a spiritual adventure in the Orient.

I photographed the event that brought an end to the world's most advanced naval conflict to date—the signing of the peace treaty at Portsmouth, New Hampshire. It was President Roosevelt's intervention and his persistence that led to the cessation of hostilities between the two empires. As I mentioned, I'd made a lasting impression on the president earlier. I was fortunate to witness and photograph Count Okuma and Count Witte signing the treaty, which had been arbitrated by Roosevelt aboard his yacht, the *Mayflower*.

CHAPTER 8

Ransom

Butch
April 5, 2001
2:02 p.m.

The thug in the driver's seat, who appears to be a low- to middle-class Haitian with little actual experience as a driver, turns my car around with difficulty. I wince as he races the engine and grinds the gears. He then speeds off down the hill as roosters, donkeys, and people flee in all directions.

I mentally force myself to calm down, to stop imagining horror, and to focus on a strategy to save my life. To assess what I am up against, I risk turning—slowly and deliberately—to face my captors in the backseat. They are still pointing guns at my head. The leader, a fairly well-dressed young man sitting to my left behind the driver, looks almost amused.

"Mr. Ashton, you have nothing to worry about," he says in heavily accented English. "We are both businessmen. You sell cars to make a living. I sell lives. Whether or not you approve of my business is of no consequence to me. You remain calm, and you will be okay."

I take a deep breath and let it out. Now I know what is going on. *I'm being held for ransom. To collect it they need to keep me alive . . . at least for now!*

"Messieurs," I begin and then direct my plea to the leader,

since he's the one doing the talking. "My life is worth everything I have, and you can have it all. I'm a sick man with a heart condition. I need medicine to survive. Just let me go home safely to my family."

"What do you have?" he demands.

"My car; take my car."

He laughs mirthlessly. "*Blanc*,[9] we already have your car. How much money do you have?"

"All I can lay my hands on at this time is $20,000, maybe $30,000," I offer.

"No, *blanc*." He spits out the word like an epithet. "We have decided your life is worth $1.5 million. One-point-five-million U.S. dollars! You understand?"

How did they come up with that outrageous amount? Why would they think I have that particular sum of money available to me?

"It's really very simple. You pay that amount or you die." To reinforce his words the leader stabs his gun against the side of my head.

Good heavens! They must think I've sold Villarosa. It just so happens that Myriam and I have been in quiet negotiations with the Haitian government over the past several weeks for the sale of our property as a residence for the prime minister, and $1.5 million was very close to the figure under discussion.

The prime minister visited Villarosa several times, always accompanied by his security agents. He had decided to purchase the property with the full approval of the president of the Republic. Members of his security force and others must have heard bits and pieces of these negotiations and identified me as "wealthy"—an easy hit. They knew my daily routines and used them to their advantage, taking me when I was unarmed and unwary.

With all the poverty and misery in Haiti and the complete

---

9   White man.

collapse of any form of law and order, kidnapping was the new method of making easy money.

But who would have told these lowlifes that? How could they possibly know? Who are these guys, and who is behind them?

"Unfortunately for me, you're wasting your time," I say, struggling to sound more confident than I feel. "I don't have a million-and-a-half dollars, nor do I know where to get that kind of money. Your demands are impossible. Please be reasonable."

The one who'd first menaced me through the front windshield with the Uzi is difficult to ignore because he sits directly behind me with the machine gun barrel pushed against the back of my head. His eyes and manner seem to indicate he has a sadistic nature. He is, no doubt, an experienced criminal, most probably high on crack—an uneducated thug from one of the slum gangs that currently roams the country.

I shift my gaze back to the leader and try to reason. "Look, killing me gets you nothing, and I very much want to live. Please, messieurs, ask for an amount I can provide."

He doesn't say anything. I only hope he is considering my request and rethinking his ransom demand.

"Your only other choice is to shoot me now," I add, still facing the Uzi as sweat drips off my forehead and into my eyes. "But then you'll have nothing but my murder to deal with."

* * *

As my hijacked car speeds down the hill and I await my fate at the hands of four Haitian gunmen, I try to make sense of my situation. The philosophical question about the worth of one's life is not expected to be answered with an exact dollar figure, but it appears the cost of Villarosa—my "inheritance" from my father—is the price of my life.

How ironic that I've been kidnapped because these *zinglendos* think I've sold my home and have one-and-a-half million dollars.

From the very beginning and for the nearly fifty years I have lived there, I've had a love/hate relationship with Villarosa but a true love affair with Haiti. Now Villarosa and my beloved adopted county might literally kill me.

My father loved Villarosa unconditionally from the moment he saw it. In 1953 he bought the historic hilltop villa for the woman who finally captured his nomadic heart—my mother, Gordana Dimovic. Having come from a wealthy, titled Yugoslavian family, she gave up many of the finer things in life for the love of a creative adventurer and settled for a simpler life in Haiti. My father knew she'd always wanted a grand home, and he felt she deserved to have a mansion fit for a queen.

The eight-acre property featured a breathtaking 360-degree view that extended as far as the eye could see—mountains, forest, the city of Port-au-Prince, all the way out to the glittering turquoise sea—but the existing house did not take advantage of the view back then. It was drab and in poor repair. Villarosa, chosen as one word by my parents and named for the rose color they painted it, needed a complete renovation.

Undaunted and unconcerned about cost or the extent of the work, my father tore the old house apart, spending as much money to remodel Villarosa and make the view its main attraction as he had to purchase the entire property. Working steadily for over a year, he turned the villa into a palatial paradise with modern systems and a new road, sprawling layers of gardened terraces, tall pillars and curved portals, ornate wrought-iron gates, beautiful stonework and tile, a large swimming pool, and bright, tropical flowers with lush foliage hanging and draping every surface. He hired and supervised teams of manual laborers to carry sand and mix concrete, but he did the woodwork and planted most of the trees and flowers himself, particularly the palms and orchids.

My father and I were very different. For Dad, no matter what the cost or what impact it might have on our future, building a dream house for his wife and children was a labor of love. For me, at the age of thirteen, it was just the opposite. I felt resentment and disappointment toward my father, and I despised Villarosa because I thought throwing good money at a mansion in need of so much repair was a ridiculously rash move.

Nonetheless, as Dad rebuilt the villa, I helped him with many of the projects and worked by his side in his woodworking shop without complaint. My teenage mind was elsewhere then. As a result, I didn't learn as much from him as I might have, nor did I pay attention to the tales of adventure he shared with me as we worked.

Now, as I face death at the hands of thugs who think I've sold my father's beloved Villarosa and offer to trade my life for the price of it, I long for another chance to hear Dad tell those tales again. I realize now that I had much to learn from him.

I cling to the armrest with one hand, and with the other I wipe the sweat dripping down my face. For a second, I allow myself to close my eyes and smell the sawdust in my father's woodworking shop. For a second, I am safe. I am a young boy working at my father's side to rebuild a grand home for his family. . . .

His pipe, long since gone out, dangles from his mouth, and a confident look of contentment spreads across my father's sun-browned face as he cuts a piece of trim to the perfect angle. He begins to tell me again about the most inspiring journey in his entire life.

This time I listen to every word.

CHAPTER 9

Spiritual Explorations, 1904–1905

Horace

In the years following the Russo—Japanese War, I first began to expand my religious education by studying other major world religions: Buddhism, Hinduism, Judaism, Islam, and Vodou. I always found the study of religion fascinating, and throughout my lifelong spiritual journey, I would explore many different paths, travel to interesting places, and meet unusual people.

Immediately after I returned to the United States from Japan, I received a letter from my journalist friend Will Livingston Comfort, who had sparked my interest in Buddhism with his stories of the abbot. Comfort invited me to join him in Shanghai a month later and accompany him to the monastery. Thrilled at the opportunity to meet the abbot, I packed quickly, and then boarded a ship back to the Orient.

From Shanghai, Will and I traveled together by train and then on horseback to the Chinese monastery, where we were warmly received. We were introduced to the rules and restrictions of monastic life and soon became members of a heterogeneous group of young monks.

We slept in small individual cells, only four hours a night, on a thin grass mat on a stone floor with no covering except our saffron robes. Our days were spent taking instruction in Buddhism, meditating, and working for and helping the poor and the aged in the small fishing village.

At nightfall, we placed a small basket over our heads to conceal our faces and then passed through the village tapping our chopsticks on our wooden begging bowls. The grateful people whom we had helped during the day filled our bowls with rice and fish, our only meal for the entire day. After we collected our repast, we'd seek a quiet place to sit and eat in silence and proper thankfulness.

My studies with the abbot presented me with impressive experiences that expanded my thinking. While listening to his lectures every day, I noticed that he always looked straight into my eyes and spoke in perfect English. For several days, I changed places in the semicircle of about thirty monks. The abbot still found my eyes and spoke in perfect English. Will and I were the only English-speakers in this group of many nationalities.

One day I asked a monk from French Indochina, who spoke French and Chinese, what language the abbot spoke. He replied that the abbot was speaking a southern Chinese dialect. I repeated my question to a Japanese monk. He stated that the abbot was speaking perfect Japanese. Others confirmed that the monk was speaking their language. Was this group of thirty individuals undergoing mass hypnosis, or was the abbot actually "speaking in tongues"? I must believe the latter.

During my stay at the monastery I had my first out-of-body experience. One afternoon, while seated in the prescribed Buddha posture—with my legs crossed and my hands resting gently on my knees—I leaned back against a great pine tree and meditated. Suddenly I heard the voice of the abbot at my shoulder. I did not move or turn my head.

He said softly, "Close your eyes now, and I shall give you a demonstration of what you have learned about the astral body as separate from the physical body. When you are sufficiently developed and when there is a real need to do so, you can travel with the astral body to any place in the physical world. Do you understand?"

"I do," I replied from within my meditative calm.

"Open your eyes," the voice said.

I obeyed and found myself about forty feet off the ground, looking down into the backyard of my sister Martha's house in Virginia. I could plainly see her calling and feeding a large flock of chickens. It was early morning in Virginia, and there were four small children outside. When I'd left Virginia a year earlier, there had been only three. I could hear all the sounds of the barnyard and the voice of my sister and the children distinctly. This made me very happy.

Then I heard the abbot's voice.

"Close your eyes," he said.

I did. When the voice instructed me to open them again, I found myself seated, as before, under the pine tree, looking across the soft, glittering waves reflecting the late afternoon sun on the China Sea.

I looked around. No one was near.

* * *

I was so enthused by what I learned during the almost eleven months I spent in the Buddhist monastery that I felt a need to broaden my religious horizons. I traveled alone by train and by ship for several weeks, and sometimes on horseback, to India and Tibet to study more about Buddhism and learn the Hindu philosophy.

After my ship docked in Calcutta and I had checked into my hotel, I decided to take a stroll in a nearby park. While in the park I sat on an empty bench to observe the strange life passing before me. Rickshaws pulled by scrawny, barefoot youths darted here and there, avoiding the occasional sacred cow wandering its own neighborhood. Young children with dark, luminous eyes laughed and chased each other, apparently unaware their tattered clothes were but rags.

Suddenly an elderly man with a long gray beard appeared beside me on the bench. I had not even seen him approach. Clad in gray jodhpurs made of homespun cotton and covered by a long coat of the same material, he wore a mauve turban. His dark eyes were clear and deep, and he smiled warmly. "We've been waiting for you," he said.

That was odd, as I had not told anyone of my intention to study in India or announced my arrival in Calcutta. "Thank you, kind sir," I replied. "Perhaps you can help me. I would like to contact, if possible, one or two of the great masters of Buddhism who live here."

"Ah, I see," he answered, as if he knew something important that I did not. "Please join me in the morning. Be prepared to walk great distances."

The next morning, the man appeared in front of my hotel, and I began the next leg on my journey of spiritual discovery. Along dusty roads we walked through the Indian countryside, passing many small, poor villages. The air surrounding these villages was often hazy from the wood fires the women used for cooking.

Two days later, as we approached a small village, I spotted a crowd assembled in the village square near what I assumed was a market. As we drew nearer, I saw that the villagers were all seated in the Buddha position, facing a small shelter. Inside the shelter an old bearded man sat with his eyes closed. Just as we reached the edge of the crowd, the man opened his eyes and beckoned us to step forward.

We did so and saluted him in the customary manner, with bowed head, hands in prayer position, and *namaste*[10] in our hearts. "I pay homage to the Blessed One, the Worthy One, the Truly Enlightened One," I repeated three times, to prepare my mind in the Buddhist way.

The old man spoke perfect English. "Welcome," he said in a voice that sounded like a deeply resonant song. "You may stay with us as long as you like. In time, I will call for you, and then you may ask me any questions you have. I will instruct you."

---

10   Hindu word meaning "the divine in me recognizes the divine in you."

I remained in this village for one week before my teacher sent us on several days' march to another teacher. My reception was equally cordial, and I remained a week with this instructor. From this second village, my guide and I made our way up to the foot of the Himalayas by easy stages, walking through Kashmir, encountering several other spiritual teachers on the way.

In Kashmir my guide left me, and I faced the hardest part of my journey alone. I soon joined a caravan of yaks. We climbed for days through ice—clad passes, across perilous—looking swinging bridges that spanned great gorges until we finally arrived at a large monastery on the border of Tibet. I was welcomed and again allowed to remain as long as I chose.

Despite the primitive living conditions, rarefied mountain air, and unfamiliar food, I considered this experience the highlight of my life. Remarkably, it was during my stay in this ancient and very remote Buddhist monastery in Tibet that I had my first close encounter with Jesus.

CHAPTER 10

Seeking the Divine, 1905–1906

Horace

At the Tibetan monastery I was assigned a sleeping cell that I soon learned was the very one in which Jesus had lived for several years. Little or nothing has been published regarding the teen years of Jesus. Yet, after reading the documentation in this monastery's archives, I became convinced that Jesus had indeed spent time here. Nearly 2,000 years earlier, he had traveled to Tibet as a teenager with his uncle, an Essene monk. Jesus had slept on this same cold stone floor where now, so many centuries later, I lay my head.

According to the story recorded on the monastery's clay tiles, Joseph had found Jesus in the temple talking with the Pharisees and was so vexed by this that he wanted to put Jesus to work in his cabinet—making shop with his two brothers. Mary had gently suggested that since their son was so highly developed spiritually, they should encourage him to develop his gift further by sending him to Joseph's brother, a monk who dwelled in a monastery by the Dead Sea. A few months after Jesus had joined his uncle, a group was organized to make a pilgrimage on foot across Arabia and Afghanistan to a monastery in Tibet. The young Jesus was allowed to join them.

Long after the others had departed, Jesus remained in the monastery, where his cellmate was a young Tibetan monk. Several years later, when Jesus was ready to leave, his cellmate accompanied him to Egypt. The young monk then went on ahead of Jesus to Greece and Palestine to prepare the way for the new Messiah.

When the New Testament was written and compiled two hundred years after Jesus's Crucifixion, there were more than seventy gospels from which to choose. (This is generally agreed upon by Tibetans and Christians.) As they were sorted and read, this part of the life of Jesus was suppressed. Everything that Jesus taught about reincarnation was also thrown out, as it was considered too controversial.

You might doubt this story because Tibet is a long way from Palestine. I know I did until the monastery's librarian showed me the ancient clay tiles on which the cuneiform records of the monastery were written. They recorded Jesus's stay in the monastery before he went forth to Egypt, where he was initiated and only then received the title of the "Christ." These particular cuneiform tiles were later copied, and impressions were made and then presented to the British Museum by Sir Aurel Stein, president of the Royal Geographical Society.

This story may be controversial to some, but to me this explanation accounted for the obvious lack of information in the New Testament as to the activity and whereabouts of Jesus between the ages of twelve and twenty-five. I felt deeply honored to have been assigned his cell in the monastery, and from that point on, I made it my mission to live his teachings.

* * *

I eventually left the monastery in Tibet, and after returning to the states to take on some photographic assignments and replenish my bank account, I traveled to Persia (now Iran). There I investigated the teachings of Zoroaster, a prophet who began his ministry in 660 B.C., about 1,000 years before the prophet Mohammed. According to Persian tradition, Zoroaster was revered as a prophet of the "true religion," and his teachings were written in a book called the *Zend Avesta*. Zoroaster believed in one God, a supreme being who created the world and represented good. This God was opposed by an evil spirit. The followers of Zoroastrianism believe that humans have the freedom to choose between good and evil.

From Persia, I journeyed to Palestine to study the Talmud in its homeland. From Palestine, I went to North Africa and took instruction in the Koran for several months. During this period, I learned much about the world of Islam.

Islam means "entering into a condition of peace and security with God through allegiance or surrender to him." The Koran is written in vivid rhyming prose and was mediated by the prophet Mohammed, its current form settled within thirty years of his death. In Muslim eyes, Mohammed completes a succession of prophets, including Abraham, Moses, and Jesus, each of whom refined and restated the message of God. I found it interesting to discover that the Koran, therefore, corroborates, updates, and expands the Old and New Testaments.

* * *

While in French Equatorial Africa, I became acquainted with the strange rituals of Vodou, as practiced in the Congo, Dahomey, and the Sudan. (In modern times, since I first contacted it here, I have called it Vodou.) My curiosity was instantly piqued about this very ancient religion—whose roots may go back ten thousand years—and I wanted to know more.

Vodun, as it was called in ancient times, is traceable to an African word for spirit. Although its essential wisdom originated in Africa long before Europeans started the slave trade, these slaves brought their religion with them when they were forcibly shipped to Haiti and other islands in the West Indies. Vodun was actively suppressed in colonial times; many Vodun priests were either killed or imprisoned, and underground societies were formed. Today over sixty million people practice Vodou in Haiti and other parts of the Caribbean, parts of Africa and South America, and in many large cities in North America.

On my return trip from Africa, I stopped in Paris, my favorite city, before boarding a steamship to cross the Atlantic. In Paris, at the *Musée de l'Homme* (Museum of Man) in the old Trocadero, I gave my first lecture—on my impression of Vodou as encountered in Africa. I was nervous, but when it was over, I felt I'd given my curious audience their money's worth; I'd even spent an additional forty minutes at the end, answering questions.

After my lecture, Professor Levy Bruhl, perhaps the world's leading anthropologist at that time, approached me. "Your talk was pleasing to your audience," he said. Then he cleared his throat. "Forgive me for being blunt, Ashton, but in my opinion your lecture was a bit superficial. When you return to America, you must go down to Haiti, where you will find a more interesting and far richer study of your subject."

He explained that in the early days of colonization the colonists were advised not to buy more than five slaves from any one tribe to work on their plantations. As the slaves already outnumbered the colonists about twenty to one, it was felt that differences in language and culture would help to prevent a revolt. What the colonists didn't know was that the slaves did have a means of communication— through their religion and through their Vodou priests and priestesses, who all spoke a common religious language, similar to the way Catholics used Latin.

"The evolution of Vodou in Haiti is most unique," Bruhl continued, his eyes flashing as he warmed to his topic. "There you will find all of the African Vodou rituals with Catholic Christianity superimposed."

The opportunity to follow his advice was soon to arise. It would send me down another fork in the path that would affect my life deeply and irrevocably.

CHAPTER 11

Strategy

Butch
April 5, 2001
2:04 p.m.

My kidnappers ignore me and keep driving, talking rapidly among themselves in Creole, a language they assume a *blanc* like me would not understand. Having lived in Haiti most of my life, I speak Creole as well as I speak English. I even think and dream in Creole. *They have no idea how well I understand their language, which gives me an advantage.*

I listen carefully, trying to figure out their next move. Reluctant to believe I don't have the one-and-a-half million, they aren't sure what to do next. It seems they might have been secretly tipped off about the sale of Villarosa but are reluctant to say too much. They don't seem to be aware that the sale hasn't happened yet. Again, I wonder about their connections.

I study them as they begin to argue in Creole. The speed-demon driver has the look of a hardened criminal, but as he'd found it difficult to put my car into reverse, I figure he is either extremely nervous or inexperienced behind the wheel. In the backseat, the fourth man is quiet and appears to be as frightened as I am. From what is being said, I surmise that he's embarking on his first such criminal venture.

My earlier assessment of the leader is correct. Despite their current discussion, it is obvious that the "intelligent" one who'd demanded the outrageous sum of money is in charge. I need to concentrate on him because he will make the decisions and conduct the negotiations.

However, it's clear to me that the sinister one sitting behind me with the Uzi is the one who will kill me. Earlier, I noticed his eyes looked wild, and now he is talking more rapidly and louder than the others. He seems high-strung and unpredictable, like he's high on crack cocaine—a very real problem in Haiti today.

The shocking realization hits me between the eyes. Not only have I been kidnapped, but I'm dealing with a crazy man with an itchy trigger finger who is holding a loaded automatic weapon against the back of my head. There's probably just as great a chance of his pulling the trigger on purpose as having it go off accidentally. *I wonder if I'll feel the bullet.*

* * *

As I sit in the passenger seat of my own car with a maniac driving and guns pointed at the back of my head, sweat rolls down my face, and seconds tick by at an agonizingly slow pace.

I find myself thinking about my life again . . . and about my father.

My father was fifty-seven years old when I was born on October 17, 1939. I imagine it wasn't easy for him to have a new baby around at that age. Although I was christened Marc, he nicknamed me "Butch" almost immediately.

A year after my birth, my father accepted the position of Cultural Attaché to the American Embassy in Haiti, an island he'd visited many times and loved. He moved our family to the island, where we led an exceptional, most unusual, and fascinating life.

As I mentioned earlier, as part of the diplomatic corps, my parents led an active social life, often hosting dinner parties or going out with other diplomats. My older brother and I were rarely included in this social world and remained at home with our help.

The great Horace Ashton loomed larger than life to me when I was a child, as he sometimes appears now in death. When I looked at him through the eyes of a young boy, I found myself fascinated and concerned at the same time. Half of me was bursting with pride, and the other half was angry that he wasn't like my friends' fathers.

When I was eight years old, my father, then sixty-five, had reached mandatory retirement age and chose to live out his life in the tropical island paradise he'd come to love so deeply. He'd found a spiritual connection here and related to the Haitian people because they were fun-loving and happy, with a passion for music and art. He loved boats and had a profound affinity for the sea and underwater life.

I understood why my father was so drawn to this island. Haiti was the only home I'd ever known, and I shared his passion for its dramatic beauty.

My favorite photo of my father

It was only after my father's retirement from diplomatic service that we spent time together and that our father/son relationship developed. My father built me my very own sailboat and taught me how to sail at the age of eight. At first I sailed my boat behind his, but soon I sailed all over the bay by myself. Dad gave me a lot of independence, not just in my sailing but also in my thinking. I didn't appreciate the value of it at the time.

When I was nine years old, he gave me my first spear gun and taught me how to spearfish. I was a good swimmer, and he took me spearfishing with his friends, Gustav Dalla Valle and Phil Nash, fellow pioneers of scuba diving in Haiti. Phil Nash recognized the close relationship I had with my father and later remembered me as "a bright kid who got out and did things."

Growing up with an older parent, I sometimes wondered what would happen to me and the rest of our family when my father passed away. When I tentatively expressed my concern, Dad gave me his typical response toward any problem: "Think positive, Butch. Everything will work out."

I had serious doubts about that. Even at a young age, I worried about money.

My father and I shared a strong connection to nature and the land, but he cared little about the ownership of it. He was fascinated by all things intellectual and spiritual but not material. My nature, in direct opposition to his, was to plan ahead for everything, especially finances. When I later became a father myself, one of my primary concerns was to provide my two daughters with a solid education and afford to send them to college in the United States. Yet in contrast, when I was growing up, my father had no real game plan or backup plan when it came to finances. He had set aside no money for my education, nor did he seem to care about it.

By the time I was ready to attend high school, my father could not afford to pay for my schooling. He had not worked enough years with the State Department to qualify for a pension and received little from Social Security. As there were no English-language high schools in Haiti, most of my friends were going off to high school and then on to college in the United States.

When I brought up the subject, my father said, "I didn't go to high school or college, and I did just fine. Go out in the world, son. You can accomplish whatever you put your mind to."

He never claimed a college education wasn't valuable, only that he had educated himself in a different way. Education was intensely important to him, but the school system held little significance. Thirsty for knowledge, he spent a lifetime reading everything he could get his hands on and exploring the world to learn about its many different religions and cultures. So just as Dad had taken on a lifelong responsibility for his own education, I was to be responsible for mine, and just as he'd left home at a young age to begin his adventures, I followed in his footsteps.

Thanks to a childless aunt and uncle who offered to pay for my high school education at the Virginia Episcopal School, my educational adventures began in Virginia at the age of fifteen. Unfortunately, during my second year, my uncle passed away and with him went my opportunity for a sponsored education. Without financial means to continue, many people would have given up. I was determined to finish school.

Several years earlier, my older brother, John Burdette Ashton, had left Haiti to attend school in Indianapolis. (Burdette was six years older than I. Our little brother, Todd, was eight years younger and still at home.) I moved to Indianapolis where I could live with Burdette and work my way through school.

By this time, he had completed his education and recently married. The three of us lived in a small rectory, where Burdette became caretaker of the church. I cleaned the church in the evenings to pay for my room and board.

I finally achieved my coveted high school diploma and then

went on to my first semester at the Indiana University Extension. For summer vacation that year, I traveled to Haiti to visit my parents, and my younger brother, Todd, planned to return to school the following semester. I'd even been offered a scholarship to Indiana University to become a buyer at the L. S. Ayres Department Store in Indianapolis. Hardworking, conscientious, and driven to succeed, I was excited about my future prospects.

What I didn't know then was just how driven I would have to be. My fateful summer visit to Haiti and my relationship with Villarosa would change the entire course of my life.

CHAPTER 12

Explorations Begin, 1905–1906

Horace

During my lengthy spiritual sojourn, I returned to the United States for work several times, beginning in 1905 when I sailed home from China to photograph the signing of the peace treaty aboard President Roosevelt's yacht. Not only did I need money to continue my travels and study of comparative religion, but I also wanted to boost my reputation as a talented photojournalist and strengthen my association with editors. In particular, my relationship with *Collier's Weekly* continued to grow. Early on, I decided to move from Washington, D. C. to New York City—the hub of the publishing industry and a better home base for a rising photojournalist who wanted to travel on assignment.

My spiritual travels had whetted my appetite for exploration and only made me yearn for more. Shortly after moving to New York, I joined the new Explorers Club (officially founded May 28, 1904) as one of its founding members,[11] along with Arctic explorers, Admiral Robert Peary and Captain Bartlett of the Arctic Club.[12]

The Explorers Club, "the strangest and most widely

---

11   "World's Adventurers Call the Explorers Club Home," in *Boston Herald*, 15 February 1925.

12   The Explorers Club has more than 3,000 members in thirty chapters spread across sixty countries. Its headquarters is located at 46 East 70th Street, New York City, New York. Visit www.explorers.org.

traveled organization in the world,"[13] was a gentlemen's club for adventurers and globe-trotting scientists, but it was far more than just a social club. Its goals were scientific in nature, and its members aimed to preserve the instinct to explore.

In the beginning the members numbered about three hundred when the older Arctic Club was incorporated into the Explorers Club, but at any given time more than two-thirds of them would be "away from home in northern snowfields, tropical jungles, or other little frequented places of the earth."[14] In its original clubhouse, an old brownstone just off Central Park at 47 West 76th Street, members gave lectures, swapped tales, and debated "who did what exploration first."

Over the years, members adorned the club walls with flags, maps, animal skins, and other trophies of many famous explorers, from Charles Lindbergh to Thor Heyerdahl to Edmund Hillary. The club's first president was Adolphus Greely, whose ill-fated expedition to Lady Franklin Bay in Greenland in 1881 began with twenty-six men and ended in 1884 with only four survivors.

I remember when the ship's bell used by Greely on his doomed voyage was hung in the club, and from that day on, tradition dictated that the bell must be rung at all club functions. An even bigger conversation piece was the sledge that Peary used on his successful trek to the North Pole.[15]

Many years later, the Explorers Club would be described in *National Geographic Traveler* as "a place where a polar explorer could rub elbows with a tropical tramp just back from a malarial-ridden jaunt through the

---

13   Merle Sumner, "The Strangest Club in the World," in *The Morning Telegraph* Sunday magazine, New York City, New York, 11 May 1924.

14   Ibid.

15   Franz Lidz, "Members Only," in *Sports Illustrated*, 22 March 2004.

jungle."[16] The founders also wanted to promote explorers' achievements and prove that exploration was a profession with exacting standards, not simply a brotherhood of hell-raising adventurers.

Explorers Enjoy Luxury of New $500,000 Home

SWAPPING STORIES OF ADVENT URES IN NEW LANDS

Left to right, seated: Dr. Franklin P. Lynch, John P. Holman, George D. Heye, president of the club; George K. niel, Captain Harold Noice, Francis Gow-Smith, S. H.

Explorers celebrated the opening of their new headquarters. Horace Ashton can be seen in the inset and at far right end of back row.

* * *

Initially, as a young photojournalist in New York, I wasn't as well known as I had been in Washington, but despite being assigned to cover sporting events, county fairs, and horse shows, I still found my share of thrills.

Hot-air balloon ascents were popular and often considered major attractions of county fairs. The concept

---

16   Patrick Kelly, "Life and Death at the Explorers Club" in *National Geographic Traveler*, April 2001.

of floating in the air and observing the earth below appealed to my sense of adventure and my desire to take pictures from a different vantage point. (Remember, these were the days before airplanes were a popular mode of transportation, and balloons still prevailed in air travel.) Like much of my life's experiences, my first trip in a hot-air balloon came about through serendipity, even if it did have an abrupt and surprising ending.

While covering local events, I had befriended two star hot-air balloon performers, Johnny and Dot Mack, who worked the fairs all over the eastern United States in the summers. Before one of their performances at a fair in White Plains, New York, I was talking to Johnny when a member of his troop announced he wasn't feeling well. This young man was to make history that day as the first person to drop from a hot-air balloon by parachute, and the spectacular feat had been publicized. Johnny and Dot were upset that the crowds would be disappointed. I offered to do the drop for them without charge, just for the fun of it.

Knowing that the stunt already had been announced and his credibility would be ruined if the jump wasn't made, but knowing it was risky, Johnny eyed me and hesitated. Finally, he said, "Okay, Horace. I'll let you jump, but first you'll have to sign a release, absolving us from all responsibility."

That should have served as adequate warning, but I was too excited by the possibility of flying to pay any heed. I signed the release and then underwent some briefing while the crew inflated the balloon and the pilot got ready. I was instructed to cruise to an altitude of about 3,000 feet. At that point, Johnny would fire a pistol. Upon hearing the shot, I'd pull a cord above my head that would release the parachute. Then I would descend slowly. Simple enough.

When the time came for my performance, I donned white coveralls and my parachute and then waited near the balloon. A large crowd had gathered to watch. After the signal was given, I ran forward and hopped aboard as the balloon was released, and then I climbed onto the trapeze, where I sat to await my jump signal. In a few seconds, we were airborne, rising rapidly over the fairgrounds and treetops. I felt no upward movement, just the strong impression that the earth was dropping away beneath me.

Because this was my first trip aloft, I became entranced by the scenery as the balloon rose miles above Westchester County with its beautiful estates. I could see the Hudson River, the Pocono Mountains in northern New Jersey to the west, Long Island Sound and beautiful Long Island to the east. In fact, I was so mesmerized by the sights I failed to hear the pistol. As I looked down and off to the southwest where the White Plains Fairgrounds and Race Track were no larger than a thumbnail, I realized we were far above 3,000 feet. Suddenly aware that we were drifting toward Long Island Sound, I decided to take action. I pulled the ripcord.

The parachute opened gently—without a jolt. I was free and began to glide toward the earth below. By pulling on the parachute's cords, much like one manipulates a marionette, I attempted to steer while looking for a favorable place to land.

Meanwhile, back at the fairgrounds Johnny and Dot had snapped into action as I made my descent. Seeing that I had taken no notice of his pistol–shot signal, Johnny had commandeered a car, and now they started out in the direction I was heading.

I spotted a beautiful pasture. As I neared the earth, a breeze snagged my parachute and pulled me off target. Within minutes I was being dragged on my back through a mucky, manure–filled barnyard, where it had rained only a few hours earlier. Finally, I came to an abrupt stop against a fence where I hauled in the lines and collapsed the chute.

Unfortunately,   while   being   dragged   backward

through the barnyard, enough fertilizer to grow a good-sized garden was scooped down my neck. Johnny and Dot reached me just after two stable hands from Whitelaw Reid's estate, where I had landed, had kindly turned a hose down my back and flushed out most of my slimy cargo.

My thrilling experience didn't deter me from ballooning. In fact, quite the contrary; it made me want to become a pilot. A few days later, I looked up Leo Stevens, a leading balloon pilot and instructor who owned a hot-air balloon center at Pittsfield, Massachusetts. He agreed to teach me the fine art of hot-air ballooning.

Stevens's center was the clubhouse for the American Aeronautical Society. I studied with him for several weeks and then prepared for the flight that would certify me with a license. According to the rules of the American Aeronautical Society, Leo would accompany me on my certification flight, but I would be in control of the balloon. He was not permitted to assist me in any way.

The start of our flight was not ideal. Just as the balloon was released, a gust of wind drove Leo and me against one of its great hydrogen gas tanks, causing the loss of a number of sandbags that had been attached to the outside of the basket. Since these bags were used for ballast, the balloon shot up to several thousand feet before I could level it off. When I finally did, I discovered we were heading south toward Long Island Sound instead of drifting to the northeast as planned. I released some gas to try to reduce our altitude and find a favorable wind in the opposite direction but had no success.

Leo concurred that I could do nothing more, but we were still approaching the Sound. Since daylight was fading quickly, we decided to make an emergency drop. Releasing gas alone for descent makes the balloon come down too fast. To arrest the drop, I knew we needed to release ballast, except that our ballast was almost gone. We released every weight that we had, even throwing over our shoes. Hoping to let the basket take the brunt of the impact, each of us chose an opposite side of the balloon's net and climbed the rigging, scrambling as fast as possible before it collapsed. The balloon fell rapidly, and I blacked out before we landed.

When I opened my eyes, I found that I was lodged high in a large tree. It was pitch–dark. I groped and felt a stout tree limb beneath me. I called to Leo and heard only a groan from below me. I slowly worked my way to the ground. The balloon bag and netting had snagged in the tree, breaking our fall, while the basket had evidently hit the ground. Leo was apparently still stuck in the tree, but I couldn't see him in the dark.

I spotted a light off in the distance and headed in its direction. Through the window of a small house, I saw a man and woman having supper in the kitchen, so I knocked on the door. When they opened it, they looked startled by my appearance. I explained what had happened, and they quickly lit a lantern and headed to the tree to help Leo down. He was bruised but able to walk. The couple took us in, fed us, and insisted we stay the night. In the morning they helped us salvage what parts of the balloon were worth saving—the basket was completely smashed—and then took us to the railroad station.

Even after that frightening experience, I remained undaunted and all the more eager to fly. I made several other ascents and received my balloon pilot's license in 1905.

* * *

Just as I was getting settled in New York and firmly entrenched in the Explorers Club, I heard from President Theodore Roosevelt's office. He offered me the position of "official White House photographer." I donned my cutaway coat, striped pants, and top hat and went to the White House to discuss the offer and to find out if I had to move back to Washington, D.C. Not a full–time job, the position depended on the president's schedule, which suited my lifestyle perfectly and allowed me time for my own travels along the way. I traveled with Roosevelt all over the United States and to other parts of the world, where I covered stories about America.

At first I photographed "important" people with the president. As my skill grew, I began to capture momentous events as well, sometimes for publication through the White House press contacts and sometimes directly for editors. I went wherever I was sent, wherever the American story happened. My lens became the world's window on the human condition, showing moments of joy, sorrow, pomp, circumstance, war, and peace.

Easter weekend, April 18, 1906, found me in Atlanta, Georgia, photographing the annual Easter Egg Hunt in Grant Park. I took delight in capturing this spectacular affair because it showed people at their best. Hundreds of children, black and white, hunted eggs together.

When I returned to my hotel in Atlanta that evening, I found a telegram waiting for me. It read: "Mr. Ashton, please take the first train to San Francisco. There has been a disastrous earthquake, and a great citywide fire is raging." Across the country, in California, a great earthquake had shattered the joy of that Easter weekend.

I boarded the next train out of Atlanta, but it took me three days to get to San Francisco. I arrived in time to take hundreds of human—interest pictures: people living in the open near where their houses had been destroyed; refugee camps established by the United States Army; the demolition of walls that were left standing but deemed dangerous; twisted cable—car tracks; great fissures in the earth, some as large as ten feet wide and forty to fifty feet deep. Some houses remained standing, but they were no longer attached to their foundations. Others had been pushed off their lots by the powerful movements of Mother Earth.

When I headed back to New York City after taking numerous rolls of film, I felt grateful. I was one of the lucky ones, able to leave a city that had to bury its dead and rebuild after such a devastating event.

* * *

In November 1906, I was scheduled to travel with President
Roosevelt to Panama, where Americans had just begun to
dig the Panama Canal, but I didn't have much work until
then.

Intrigued by what anthropologist Levy Bruhl had
told me about Haiti and urged by his suggestion that I
study the Vodou religion in depth, I yearned to visit the
exotic island. I realized my scheduled trip to Panama
would fit right in, so I made elaborate preparations to
travel on my own for six months before meeting up with
the president for my official duties in Panama. I even lined
up a photography assignment in South America that would
pay for the rest of my trip; I signed the contract before I
left and arranged to pick up additional instructions and
partial payment in advance in Panama.

Eagerly I made my way to Mayaguez, where I took
passage on a sailboat to Santo Domingo, the country
that shares the island of Hispaniola with Haiti. In Santo
Domingo I met an Episcopal bishop who was embarking on a
horseback trip to Haiti. He agreed to let me join him.

My anticipation built as we rode across this beautiful
tropical island, enjoying its majestic mountains, lush
greenery, fragrant flowers, and bright sunshine. On the
final day of our journey we mounted our horses and rode
across the Haitian border at Fond Parisien, near Gantier.
Having been on many spiritual journeys by now, I sensed
there was something special about this place. I could feel
it. The air felt more alive, or perhaps it was the perfume
of the flowers or the vibrant colors of their display on
our path as we rode. The climate, although hot, wasn't
oppressive but electric with promise . . . or was it I who
felt such sparks? I breathed deeply and closed my eyes
for a brief moment. I opened them to find an old man had
suddenly appeared in the road, holding up his hand to
stop us. He took hold of my bridle and said, "Welcome, Mr.
Ashton. I have been sent to meet you."

As a result of my experience in India, I again knew that something out of the ordinary was about to happen, and I embraced whatever it was to be with an open heart. I bade the bishop farewell and allowed the old man to lead me south from the main road through the great sugar cane fields toward the mountains.

After about a mile, we arrived at a large compound with many native houses. There I was ushered into the presence of a striking-looking, old black lady, dressed all in white. She was the *mambo*, or Vodou priestess, in charge of the compound.

"Welcome, Mr. Ashton," she said. "The Spirit has told me a great deal about you. After you left Africa, I knew you would be coming here, so I sent the old man to bring you to me. We have everything ready for you. Come and see the cabin we have prepared for you. It will be your home for as long as you care to stay."

It was obvious the old lady was clairvoyant. She appeared to be able to communicate mentally with other *houngans*, or Vodou priests, and *mambos* as she sent me from one to the other all over the country for several weeks. While in Africa, I had learned some of their religious language, called *langage*, so I was able to understand their rituals.

Throughout Haiti I was received like a long-lost son, although I'd never set foot on the island before. My hosts would not allow me to spend a centime. Once in a while, I passed through markets and purchased bits of cloth for dresses, silk scarves called *mouchoirs*, and other items used in Vodou services. I presented these modest gifts to my hosts whenever possible. Through the kindness of this amazing mambo and other practitioners I met, I traveled all over Haiti, contacted more than fifty houngans and mambos, and took part in many wonderful services.

Vodou practitioners believe that God is manifest through the spirits of ancestors, who can bring good or harm and must be honored in ceremonies. They believe there is a sacred cycle between the living and dead. Vodou is a practical religion, playing an important role in the family and the community.

Despite Vodou's noble status as one of the world's oldest religions, public perception of Vodou rites and rituals is often misguided, focusing on the evil or malicious side, the so-called black magic. This was not the kind of Vodou to which I was attracted or with which I became involved.

Vodou has healing spells, nature spells, purification spells, and even joyous celebration spells. Spirits may be invoked to bring harmony and peace, birth and rebirth, increased abundance of luck, material happiness, or renewed health. Music and dance are key elements of Vodou ceremonies, and the dance is not simply a prelude to sexual frenzy, as it has been erroneously portrayed, but an expression of spirituality, of connection with divinity and the spirit world.

Within the Vodou society, there are no accidents. Practitioners believe that nothing and no event has a life of its own. "The universe is all one and each thing affects something else." Scientists know that. Nature knows it. Many spiritualists agree that we are not separate but that we all serve as parts of one. So in essence, what you do unto another, you do unto you, because you are the other. "Voo-doo." View you. We are mirrors of each other's souls.

This made sense for me. I was a naturalist with a keen interest in science and a desire to make sense of the way the universe worked.

On that first visit I fell in love with Haiti in a way that haunted me for life. The breathtaking beauty of this island paradise rivaled that of anywhere in the world I had visited. I fell in love with its vivid colors and vibrant music; the rich green texture of its mountains beyond mountains; and its turquoise ocean, so clear I thought I could reach down and touch the bottom. I felt an immediate connection to this country and its people, culture, and religion that would ultimately become my home and final resting place.

CHAPTER 13

Scientific Endeavors, 1906

Horace

My career as a photographer was influenced by nature and science, as was my life and my religious studies. Looking back now, I see that my appreciation for nature began as a youth, growing up on the farm in the late 1800s. I'd learned a great deal working on the farm, and this knowledge and experience fueled a deep connection to nature that remained with me for life.

It was no wonder that I found myself with a natural talent for doctoring and a curiosity about the world of science, since my paternal grandfather was a noted surgeon and my three paternal uncles were also physicians. It also is not surprising that during my years of travel to remote places, I found occasions to use this talent.

It began early. At the age of seventeen, just prior to starting my career as a photographer with Clinedinst, I lived in a guesthouse in Washington, D.C., where most of the other tenants were government employees. One young man who worked in the Treasury Department studied medicine by taking night classes at Georgetown University Medical School. Knowing most of the men on my paternal side were doctors, he invited me to accompany him to some medical lectures on the current topic: gynecology. I found it intriguing but hardly thought I'd find an opportunity to use such skills.

One evening about three months after I'd attended

the lectures, I walked west on K Street, which bordered Franklyn Park. Suddenly I heard a loud scream coming from a Chinese laundry. I rushed into the laundry and almost collided with the owner, who was dashing about clutching a hot iron in his hand. "What's the matter?" I yelled in the midst of all the commotion.

He pointed behind the counter, where his wife lay on the floor screaming with the pains of labor. I ran behind the counter and instructed, "Get me some water and towels. Hurry!" Then I knelt to assist his frantic wife.

While I was on my knees delivering the baby, I heard a booming voice behind me. "What the hell's goin' on in here?"

I turned to face a big Irish cop, who was leaning over me. "Get out. I'm delivering a baby."

He shook his head in amazement and said, "Well, I'll be gawd damned." Then he left.

Mother and baby survived, and this experience would prove valuable to me several years later in Tunisia. While filming local rug-weaving, I quickly pushed my tripod out of the way of what I thought was a bundle of rugs. It turned out to be a pregnant woman giving birth, and I delivered a baby girl. Much later, in the Arctic, I would deliver another baby girl in an Eskimo igloo.

During my years of exploration, I set broken bones, patched up wounds, and routinely performed other acts of doctoring. While in Colombia on a photographic assignment following my trip to Haiti in 1906, I set the broken arm of an Indian who'd fallen off a ladder. He lived in the small village of Savanilla, and there was no doctor for miles. He was extremely grateful.

The next morning, I awoke to find a line of twenty men, women, and children outside the gate of the guesthouse where I was staying. Fearing the Indian had died during the night and the crowd had come to lynch me, I glanced around for my best escape route.

It turned out that he had sung my praises to his

neighbors, and the villagers with cuts, open sores, pains, and pregnancies had come asking for help. Drawing from what I had learned and being innovative, I was able to take care of most of them with what little material I had.

A few days later when word got out that I was about to leave, the villagers returned and begged me to stay. My host said, "Ashton, why don't you hang out your shingle and stay on? We could almost live on the presents these people bring each day."

I had other commitments, and true to the pattern now developing in my life, I bid farewell to the villagers and headed off on my next adventure. I'd been interested in exploring South America, and as was the case with most of my travels, my work once again provided the means for my exploration.

* * *

Before leaving for Haiti, I'd signed a contract with a reputable gentleman from California to re-create several hundred photographs his wife had taken on a South American expedition. She was a well-known travel lecturer who used slides to accompany her talks. During their expedition she'd shot about three hundred pictures, but unfortunately the undeveloped negatives were lost when a pack train fell over a precipice in the Andes Mountains.

After my amazing experience studying Vodou in Haiti, I sailed to Panama, where I picked up a substantial check and instructions from the Californian, as arranged. He assured me that another check would await me in a bank in Barranquilla, Colombia, a month later, after he'd received my photos in San Francisco. Had I known then that the man would go bankrupt and I would never receive the second check, I surely would not have accepted this job. But then I wouldn't have had the remarkable series of South American adventures that came my way.

I trekked into the Colombian Andes with a guide and pack donkeys to take the duplicate pictures and then returned to Barranquilla to communicate my success. While waiting for the second check to arrive, I explored northern Colombia. On one trip I took a small stern-wheel steamer with open decks up the Magdalena River and into the *canayo* (delta) of the Magdalena River on the way across to another photography job in Santa Marta. As the boat slowly navigated the brackish waters through the jungle, I heard rustling in the treetops as monkeys screamed to warn other animals of intruders. Squawking parrots flew overhead, and beautiful orchids surprised me at every turn of the river. This trip whetted my appetite for these rare, delicate flowers and for more rainforest and jungle exploration. I never once considered the hazards of such adventures.

One evening just before dark, our steamer arrived at a large open lagoon. Because the wind was strong and the waves were high, we could not continue, so we weighed anchor and wrapped some lines on the trees near shore. We bedded down in hammocks covered by mosquito nets, hoping to get some sleep. Instead we were kept awake by the howling wind that uncovered the nets, allowing the mosquitoes to feast on us.

While we were anchored, a Colombian gunboat joined us. To my surprise, I immediately recognized the commander, José Angulo, nephew of General Rafael Reyes, president of the Republic. A few years earlier General Reyes had been the Colombian foreign minister in Washington, D.C., and I had given photography lessons to José. We had become good friends.

José had been given the assignment to re-map the Magdalena River delta because all their maps had been destroyed during a recent revolution. As we talked, he confided that he didn't know the first thing about mapping. Having had previous mapping experience, I offered to help him after I returned from my assignment in Santa Marta. José was delighted, and we parted, promising to meet again in a week.

My boat continued east until it eventually arrived at a village that was the terminus of the narrow—gauge railway leading to Santa Marta. I was amazed by the magnificent scenery as we rattled through the tropical forest, one minute on flat ground, the next traversing deep gorges. When a heavy downpour began, I went inside and studied my Spanish book, so that I could communicate with the people I met. I lost track of time and didn't notice the rain had stopped until I was aroused by the screaming whistles of our locomotive. Looking out the window, I expected to see a cow or horse on the track. Instead, up ahead were many women gathering up their freshly washed laundry, which they had spread out on the tracks in the sun to dry. We had to stop the train and wait until they had it all in baskets before we could start up and continue on. When I looked back after we passed, the women were spreading the clothes out on the tracks again.

In Santa Marta, I engaged in my favorite pastime— photography. This particular assignment had come my way through a remarkable man who'd traveled Colombia a few years earlier as a mechanic on the new railway being built between Savanilla and Barranquilla. At that time, ships could not reach Barranquilla because of the sandbars and treacherous reefs at the mouth of the river. The railway job had earned him enough money to open his own import/ export business. He now owned a lovely home and a coffee plantation outside the city and supported himself through his various enterprises. He outfitted me with a horse and packsaddle and sent me up a steep trail into the Andes to photograph how coffee was grown.

After taking my photographs for the plantation owner, I headed back toward Barranquilla by boat. I met José Angulo at a refueling station in the forest, where Indians were cutting and stacking wood for the riverboats. I joined him on the gunboat, and we spent three weeks mapping the narrow jungle canals. The maps were printed in England shortly afterward, and, as a result, I was made a Fellow of the Royal Geographic Society in England.

* * *

Still awaiting the second check from the Californian, I found yet another diversion in South America that promised intrigue. I learned that a young American named William Burdette was in charge of a primitive gold mine owned by another American upcountry in the Antroquia region. Burdette was one of my family names, so I decided to pay him a visit, despite warnings that the Indians in that region were not friendly. The trip took a day and a half up the Magdalena by riverboat and two days' ride into the mountains on horseback.

When I reached the camp, I was told that Burdette was dying. I climbed inside the one-room, corrugated iron cabin set on three-foot stilts, which served as his house. There I found a young man, unconscious, with a raging fever, lying diagonally across the bed. I spent about an hour cleaning him up, took his temperature, which was 103 degrees, and tried to make him comfortable. I was exhausted from my journey, but there was no place in the cabin for me to sleep. I moved Burdette over to one side of the bed and lay down beside him, hanging my pistol and belt on the bedpost.

I awoke suddenly in the middle of the night. Half asleep, I instinctively grabbed my pistol. Then for no reason known to me, I climbed over Burdette and stood on the floor next to his side of the bed.

Moonlight lit the primitive room as I looked back across the bed. There I spotted the head of a large snake swaying above the floor where I would have stood, if I had climbed out of bed on my side. I was fully awake now!

I fired and decapitated the snake. The next morning I measured the intruder, a deadly bushmaster—about six-feet long, minus his head. When I recall this story, I can't help but believe my guardian angel was in the room that night.

I stayed at the gold mine with Burdette for several days, taking his temperature, ministering to his fever, and forcing liquids until he recovered. After I left, I never saw him again, but the success of my doctoring skills in South America was about to be seriously challenged.

* * *

Returning once more to Barranquilla, I moved into the Hotel Las Flores to await my long—overdue check. The hotel was the only building taller than one story in the city, and it had one shower in the cellar for all the guests. As I sat on the steps waiting for my turn to shower, I met two other young men in line ahead of me.

I introduced myself, and the young Englishmen introduced themselves, explaining they were just out of college. "We've been commissioned by a wealthy, titled Englishman, who has an extensive orchid collection, to come here and bring back the pure white cattleya," the skinny, fair—haired man named Ian said proudly.

"These rare orchids were reportedly spotted by a group of rubber gatherers in the Rio Negro Valley," added the darker fellow, who'd introduced himself as Richard.

In those days, only millionaires could afford orchids, so this sounded like a promising assignment. "Have you ever been in the jungle?" I asked.

"No," they replied in unison, shaking their heads, "but we're eager to take on this assignment. It's quite lucrative."

"Do you have any experience in the jungle or in the Rio Negro Valley?" Ian asked.

"Yes, I do. I just returned from two picture—taking adventures, and I mapped the delta of the Magdalena River with the president's nephew."

The young men looked at each other for a moment, silently communicating. Then Richard said, "Mr. Ashton, frankly, we don't know where to begin. Would you accompany us on our search? We've been offered a large sum to bring back several plants." Excitedly, he pulled out a map that showed the approximate area where the orchids had been seen. "We'll split the money three ways if you'll join us and show us the way."

Always looking for a new adventure—and especially one with serious financial benefits like this—I agreed. Their patron had provided money to organize the safari, so we reported to the British foreign minister in Bogotá and went about getting our outfit together. It consisted of seven porters, a guide, and the three of us. Our patron had made it clear that he would pay additionally for any other interesting orchid plants we found. At twenty-three years old, I knew nothing about orchids and neither did the young Englishmen, but we were all willing to give it a try.

It was a long, hard trip until we reached navigable water on the Rio Negro, named for its black water. On horseback, but mostly on foot, we trekked through dense, tropical rainforest knee-deep in rotting vegetation, often having to stop and hack a trail through the thick, wet growth with our machetes. There were millions of insects. Huge trees towered over a hundred feet tall; their vines were long, strong streamers rooted to the ground that formed lianas that men could climb.

The thick vegetation held hidden dangers for our small group. Deadly snakes lurked in the towering trees and the undergrowth. Two of our porters died from snakebites before we found our first white cattleya. My doctoring skills were no match for the deadly poison, which killed almost instantly.

Unwilling to give up, we pressed on. Two days later we finally discovered the orchid, high up in a tree that stood taller than the surrounding forest. A small group of Indians who knew the forest well dwelt nearby, and our guide managed to communicate with them. He asked one of them to climb up the high tree using the lianas, pry loose the delicate orchids with his machete, and bring them down carefully. The accomplished climber brought down three large white cattleya plants and a number of other varieties. We were elated.

Our good cheer did not last. On the way out of the rainforest, Ian was bitten by a snake and died. Again, I could do nothing to help. Richard and I wrapped our young friend's body tightly in a blanket and tied him to his horse. We then made a two-week march through the hot, humid jungle to bring his body back to the British foreign minister in Bogotá. Two more of our porters died from fever along the way and another from snake bite. Only five of us—less than half of our original group of eleven—returned from this deadly search for orchids. Our journey was sad and disheartening.

In Bogotá, the orchid plants were cleaned, wrapped dry in newspaper, and shipped to England by a steamship that took more than ten days to get there. Fortunately, they all lived to become the parents of the white cattleya that can be seen all over the world today.

As a result of this ill-fated adventure, I developed a great respect for orchids. Many years later, I would come to grow the white cattleya and many other orchid varieties at Villarosa in Haiti.

CHAPTER 14

Panic

Butch
April 5, 2001
2:06 p.m.

Having stopped arguing, my captors seem to be taking me somewhere specific. *To my grave?*

I focus my attention on their conversation in Creole. The leader is giving directions to the driver and mentions Zabeth. This is the name of a place far out in the country near the village of Ganthier, where Vodou worshipers come to cleanse themselves of evil spirits in a special, sacred spring. I know Haiti well from all my business ventures, and I am fairly familiar with this area.

My father, one of only two white men ever to become fully indoctrinated in the Vodou religion, took me to Source Zabeth as a child for one of the important ceremonies. All I remember about Zabeth is that the people dressed in white, and there was drumming and chanting and dancing. The sounds were strange to my young ears. I didn't feel comfortable there and had no desire to accompany my father again.

Perhaps his intense interest in Vodou was a strong factor pushing me in the opposite direction. I never understood or shared his fascination with it, although I must admit that simply by being his son I've been shown a lot of respect in Haiti all my life . . . until this moment as I am being held at gunpoint.

As an adult I had nothing to do with Vodou, except as a cultural tourist attraction when I was in the resort business. As an aside, wealthy Greek shipping magnate Stavros Niarchos made an overnight stopover on his magnificent yacht, the *Cristina*, in the early seventies, accompanied by a cousin of mine. During a lavish dinner on board, the conversation inevitably came to the subject of Vodou. Stavros was most interested in the subject, and he asked me to take him and his guests to observe a Vodou ceremony. To my surprise, as Horace Ashton's son I was honored at the ceremony and saluted by the *houngans* with much fanfare.

The only thing I know for sure about Zabeth is that I shouldn't let my captors take me to a remote location. As we continue to speed toward what will most likely be the place of my death—the ultimate irony for a nonbeliever like me is to die at a sacred Vodou site—I am helpless to change my circumstances.

Throughout my father's life, he escaped from many perilous situations. *What would he do now? Could he tell me a secret about this sacred site that would help me survive?*

Because frequently his guests were curious about the ceremonies and rituals, Dad talked openly about Vodou, and although he enjoyed playing to his audience and giving them the thrill they wanted, he was on a mission to correct their misconceptions about this ancient religion. He felt it was important to emphasize—because when people hear the word "voodoo" they think black magic—that Vodou is a religion older than Christianity. As in many religions, Christianity included, evil plays a part, but my father's involvement with Vodou was with the religious aspect, not black magic. He loved to remind people that Moses in the Bible was a Vodou practitioner. I wish I could remember what he told me about Zabeth.

The kidnappers are silent now as we drive through the city, and I cast my mind to my father again. I see his eyes light up in a deeper way and hear his voice swell with passion as he talks about his favorite subject—religion. He puffs on his pipe, frequently pausing to relight it, and I can't help but wonder how he manages to talk so clearly with a pipe in his mouth all the time.

The smooth aroma of my father's pipe tobacco and the smell of smoke is suddenly so strong that I glance furtively around the car to see if one of my captors has lit a pipe. I feel his presence and yearn to hear one of his stories.

CHAPTER 15

Candid Shots, 1906–1907

Horace

I arrived back in Panama just in time to spend three days visiting the construction of the Panama Canal with President Theodore Roosevelt. I had learned from traveling with the president that he was unpredictable, and I had to be prepared to grab candid pictures. On the day we arrived at the canal, one of the first things we saw was the huge sign that read "We'll do our best to help you build it!"

"Ah, that's bully!" Roosevelt exclaimed. At that moment, the president recognized an old friend operating the steam shovel. He strode up to the man and shook his dirty hand as if he were a long-lost brother. Naturally, I sprang into action with my camera. The president then hopped on and took over the steam shovel, giving me another terrific picture.

I was quoted about my trip to the Panama Canal with the president in a 1907 article in the *Norristown Register* titled "Roosevelt's Trail."[17]

It was November of 1906 and the president of the United States, Theodore Roosevelt, was at the Isthmus inspecting the digging of the Panama Canal and that herd of monsters (100-ton Bucyrus shovels) on the job. . . .'It was pouring rain,' said Horace Ashton, of New York, member of the Explorers' Club, who was accompanying Roosevelt on this trip,

---

17   Ethel Armes, "Roosevelt's Trail" in *Norristown Register*, Norristown, Pennsylvania, 25 May 1907.

taking photographs every seventy seconds. 'The entire three days Roosevelt was there it poured as it never did before. We were hip deep in wet and slimy clay every which way we turned every hour of every day!'"

**President Theodore Roosevelt oversees the construction
of the Panama Canal.
Photo by Horace Dade Ashton, 1906**

* * *

The president returned to Washington, and I went back to New York from Panama on a Royal Mail steamer that stopped at Jamaica. About an hour out to sea the captain heard an urgent appeal for help on the radio. Kingston had just been hit by a disastrous earthquake. We returned to find most of the business section of town had been flattened, and a few fires were burning. I immediately started snapping pictures.

Early that morning, I had purchased two rolls of film in Kingston. But that was all I had, and it didn't last long. Anxious to get good photographic coverage of this disaster, I raced to the shop where I'd bought the film. There, standing—or rather, in an upright position where a falling timber had crushed his head—was the young man who had sold me the film earlier in the day. There was nothing I could do but reach past his body and help myself to six rolls of film.

Word must have arrived in New York that we were the first ship from Kingston after the earthquake and that I was a passenger because two messages reached the ship before we docked in New York Harbor, asking me for first rights to the pictures. *The New York World* offered $500, and the *Journal* offered $800. I sold first publication to the *Journal*, and all the other papers had my pictures a few hours later, so I made over $1,000 for two hours work.

* * *

After that unexpected boost to my photojournalism career, I continued to seek interesting opportunities as a photographer. Plenty of excitement and travel came my way, but I stayed away from jungle explorations for several years after my sobering experience in South America.

Near the end of 1906, I was seeking a base of operations that would provide me with regular assignments, so I went to work for the country's first photo agency, Underwood & Underwood in New York City. I stayed with Underwood through 1911, traveling all over the world for them—photographing events, places, and people and capturing twentieth–century stories in a single shot.

I was even assigned to photograph the great American author Mark Twain (Samuel Clemens). Mr. Twain did not take kindly to reporters and photographers, and I was lucky to have been one of the few journalists he allowed into his home to photograph him.

Because Mr. Twain did much of his writing in bed using a fountain pen and a writing tablet, I asked to take his picture in bed. The result was a candid shot that captured the famed author doing what he did best—writing. I was fortunate to have the opportunity to take other unusually personal shots of Samuel Clemens, including one of the author with his wife and one with his sister.

My job at Underwood provided another opportunity to follow in the footsteps of Jesus. Just two years after my stay at the Tibetan monastery, I was sent to Palestine to make a series of stereoscopic pictures to be used in Sunday school lessons. My photos were used to complete the illustrations for an edition of the Douay version of the Bible, which had been authorized by Cardinal Gibbons of Baltimore.

I was thrilled that I would finally get to travel over the same territory Jesus had covered, as described in the Gospels. (I had not done that on my previous trip to Palestine to study the Talmud.) My time spent living in the same cell in the monastery where Jesus had stayed brought me closer to his spirit. Walking his path seemed like a perfectly natural extension of my spiritual quest.

Sadly, when I returned to Jerusalem after walking Jesus's path for six weeks taking pictures, I experienced the earthly side of this heavenly land. A woman who claimed

Mr. and Mrs. Mark Twain
Photo by Horace Dade Ashton

to be the wife of a local sheik tried to extort money from my employer in order to send my photographic plates back to the United States. I contacted my *dragoman* (traveler's guide, interpreter), and we packed up the plates in the middle of the night and had them sent out by pack camel. The next day, I left the country.

The plates, camels, and drivers were never heard from again. However, the attractive con artist's efforts were ultimately in vain, as I later returned and reproduced the pictures that were lost. Her behavior made me realize why there are so many problems in the world—few people practice their professed religious teachings in daily life.

While traveling all over the world for Underwood & Underwood, I packed a six-foot ladder with me that fit into a handy carrying case. It had a sliding extension on which I mounted the camera on a tripod. As I climbed the ladder, I'd raise the slide before me so that the camera would be ten to twelve feet above the ground. This was very practical for shooting in crowds, capturing parades, or photographing a speaker from the balcony of an auditorium. I used the ladder to shoot pictures of a ceremony in the lovely miniature garden of Count Okuma in Tokyo, and I used it when President Theodore Roosevelt spoke in the gymnasium of the naval academy in Annapolis over the remains of the great Admiral John Paul Jones.

Because I always enjoyed a challenge, I jumped at the chance to take the tough assignments at Underwood that I saw as more creative. One day, when the light was right in downtown Manhattan, I climbed up sixteen floors and out onto the girders near the top of the new Woolworth Building while it was under construction. But I didn't just take an ordinary shot of the skyline. I took what would become a black-and-white classic self-portrait—a picture of the photographer, perched high on a girder, shooting the skyline.

**Horace Ashton took big risks to get great shots. This epic self-portrait is now
on display in the Nelson-Atkins Museum of Art in Kansas City, Missouri.
Photo by Horace Dade Ashton, reproduced by and printed with
permission of the Nelson-Atkins Museum of Art, Kansas City, Missouri.**

Note: This photograph would later appear in a book published by Hallmark
called *An American Century of Photography: From Dry Plate to Digital* by

Keith F. Davis and the Hallmark Photographic Collection.[18] An excerpt from "About the Artist" on page 28 reads as follows:

> **Ashton, an employee of the Underwood & Underwood firm, typified the adventurous spirit of this first generation of news photographers. His varied subjects included the first public flights by the Wright Brothers, immigrants arriving at Ellis Island, life in New York City's slums and the upward growth of the city. Ashton's dizzying view of a news photographer high above New York (probably a self-portrait) exemplifies the era's notion of the cameraman as a daring and uniquely privileged observer of the vast spectacle of modern life.**
>
> **While Ashton continued his photographic work after 1910, he became even better known as an adventurer and author. Between 1924 and 1930, his exploits included ethnographic research in North Africa, a 4000-mile journey by dirigible, spelunking, an Arctic expedition, and a hunting trip with the King of Yugoslavia. If photographic history has a genuine counterpart to Hollywood's Indiana Jones, it might well be Horace Ashton.[19]**

While I was at Underwood and after I left, I had the pleasure of making many photographs of the great American actress Sarah Bernhardt. Her son would eventually engage me to travel with them on his mother's final tour of the United States in 1916. Much has been written about Bernhardt, so I will just say here that she was an angel. She was so kind and considerate of everyone in her troupe that her passing left many heartaches in those who knew her well.

* * *

18   Keith F. Davis and the Hallmark Photographic Collection, *An American Century of Photography: From Dry Plate to Digital*, March 1995. Keith F. Davis is an American photography curator, collector, and the author of several books on photography, who built the Hallmark Photographic Collection that spans the history of American photography. In December 2005, he donated the collection to the Nelson-Atkins Museum of Art in Kansas City, Missouri, where he serves as Senior Curator of Photography.

19   Ibid. 28.

Also during my time at Underwood, I became friendly with a colleague, Walter Gillam, and his family, who lived in Flushing, Long Island. Walter's brother, Arthur, was an amateur herpetologist in his spare time.

As evidenced by the elaborate dark green tattoos all along my right arm and down my left leg, I've always had a fascination with and affinity for reptiles. The tattooed creature winding around my arm is technically a dragon that I had done in my youth while sailing across the Pacific, but a snake tattoo is around my leg.

When Arthur discovered my keen interest in snakes, we became good friends. The sad loss of life on my first South American expedition reminded me that snakes can be deadly creatures, but it didn't dampen my interest in them.

Each spring, we ventured into the Pocono Mountains of northern New Jersey to collect snakes for the zoo. Equipped with forked sticks, knee boots, and cotton bags tied to our belts, we climbed around on the rocks where rattlesnakes came out to sun themselves after their winter's hibernation. After several expeditions, I became quite dexterous in this dangerous game.

A Pathé News cameraman learned of my hobby and asked if I would demonstrate my snake–catching prowess for a newsreel. Flattered by his request, I accepted. The following Sunday, Arthur and I took the photographer to the Poconos with us. We mounted his camera near a large rock and waited, knowing that once the sun shone on the rock the rattlers would crawl out of the cracks and crevices.

We didn't have to wait long. In a few minutes, a menacing–looking specimen slithered out. In studying snakes, I'd learned that a rattlesnake can strike only two–thirds of its length from a coiled position. After it strikes, its head again touches the ground and the snake quickly draws it back and coils for another strike. Wearing leather boots, I approached the snake from what

I considered to be a safe distance. It darted out to strike and missed me by a few inches. Its head then sunk to the ground in preparation for another strike.

At that moment I grabbed the snake by its rattle, whirled it around my head, swung it under my left arm, and quickly clamped its head between my arm and my body. Then I grasped it by the neck, just behind its jaws, and put it in my cotton bag.

Fortunately, everything worked as I had planned, and the film was perfect. We returned to Arthur's home in Flushing with our newly captured specimen and were about to call it a day when the photographer said, "Ashton, let's take one more shot of you handling the snake to make this newsreel even more convincing. How about if you hold the snake's head in your hand and squeeze it just behind the jaws so that its mouth opens wide, and we get a close-up of those fangs?"

"I can do that," I replied, "but I think my camera can better capture the close-up."

The cameraman agreed, so I rigged up my camera, preparing to manage the camera and the snake at the same time.

I took the snake out of the bag and held its head in my left hand with its body wrapped around my left arm and wrist. Holding the snake out in front of the camera as far as I could, I peered through the lens and squeezed the snake's jaws. As the rattler opened its mouth and extended its fangs, I turned the handle on the camera and made the film. I didn't realize, as I held the snake in my hand, that our prized specimen was shedding its skin.

Just after I began filming, the skin on the snake's neck slipped off, allowing the serpent to move its head. Sensing my hand nearby on the camera, the snake sunk its venom-filled fangs into my thumb. That persistent reptile was still dangling from my thumb when I placed it back in the bag.

Arthur quickly wrapped a tourniquet above my elbow.

Racing into the house, I grabbed a hypodermic needle filled with permanganate of potash, which I kept for emergencies such as this. I injected the needle into each fang mark, giving myself two big shots. Then I walked around the lawn for half an hour to keep my heartbeat up and the antidote pumping through my veins to counteract the poison.

The newsreel became one of the most convincing films ever made of a rattlesnake. Fortunately, I recovered in a few hours and continued my study of (and interest in) snakes. But my trouble with these fascinating reptiles was far from over.

* * *

A few months after the rattlesnake bit me, Arthur returned from Cuba with a new pet—a beautiful thirteen–foot boa constrictor. He was about to leave on a lecture tour and needed a place to keep his snake. Since there were no prohibitions about pets in my apartment and the boa constrictor was not poisonous, I gladly agreed to snake–sit.

When I started my job at Underwood, I had moved into a fabulous old house with dark wood floors and high ceilings on 34th Street at Madison Avenue. It had recently been converted to an apartment building, complete with a doorman, but the original house had been built by a wealthy New Yorker named La Baudie who called himself "Emperor of the Sahara." He was said to be a bit eccentric and had brought all the woodwork and interior trim from a palace in Andalusia.

I felt right at home. My room was a large studio about fifty feet long that contained a Steinway concert grand piano that a former tenant had left there temporarily. The windows along one side of my room looked over the lovely gardens of the other homes on the block, and beneath the windows sat a low steam radiator, covered by an ebony bench with red plush cushions.

One day I purchased two rabbits from the New York

Zoological Park as food for Arthur's snake. Before leaving for my office at Underwood, I locked the rabbits in the room with the snake and then let the snake loose to feed. It was late summer, and I was on the fourth floor, so I often left my window open.

When I arrived home, I couldn't find the snake, but neither could I find the rabbits. I looked under the furniture, and not spotting the snake, I lifted my gaze to the window, wondering if it could have crawled out. The lintel (horizontal support beam) over the entrance door was ten feet from the floor and extended about eighteen inches beyond the door. I looked up and spotted the snake folded gracefully on top of the lintel, where it stayed for about two weeks, contentedly digesting its meal. This became a pattern. Arthur's snake was a very quiet pet that came out to eat every two weeks and then found a new hiding place in which to happily absorb its food.

One morning, the building's doorman called me at my office. "Mr. Ashton, there's a nice young lady who has been studying opera in Milan, and she recently returned to New York. She needs a place to rehearse a couple of hours each day. Would you be willing to let her use your studio and piano for seventy-five cents an hour?" he asked.

"All right," I said, glad for the extra money. I had completely forgotten about the snake, since it had eaten a few days earlier and then disappeared under the radiator bench.

The opera singer came and went, used the piano, and practiced her arias. She liked the studio, and all went well for several days.

Later that week, I received another phone call at work. I was startled to hear a deep male voice on the line announce, "This is the New York City Police. We have an emergency at your apartment. Please come home immediately."

The caller didn't give any details, and I couldn't imagine what had happened. I ran out of the office and hailed a taxi. En route, I remembered my pet but dismissed the thought because I knew the snake was tame and harmless and had been recently fed.

The streetcars were stopped on the tracks from Broadway to the East River and the streets were jammed with cars (Ford's new Model T was becoming popular), horses and carriages, and people. Fearing there had been a fire, I jumped out of the taxi several blocks from my corner and charged through the crowd.

When I arrived at my building, I found a group of policemen standing on the sidewalk. "I'm Horace Ashton," I told them. "What seems to be the trouble?"

A husky sergeant launched into the story and didn't take a breath until he finished. "There's this dame up in your apartment sitting at the piano singing, and she strikes a high C. Just then, she sees this gawd–damned snake crawling out from under the radiator. It must be twenty–feet long! She dashes for the door, still holding the note, which is heard for blocks, runs downstairs, out the front door, and she faints on the cable car tracks, blocking traffic in the whole damn city."

Well, that explained the traffic jam. "I'm awfully sorry," I said, managing to sound contrite. "The snake is a pet, and he's perfectly harmless. Perhaps he liked the music."

"Liked the music, hell!" the sergeant roared. "He was going to eat her. Now you get that gawd–damned snake up to the zoo right away and come down to the station."

As soon as the traffic loosened up, I went to the station. The police made me pay a fifty–dollar fine for having a wild animal in my apartment without permission. For some time afterward, I visited my friend, the snake, in the zoo, and he was always glad to see me.

* * *

My interest in snakes stayed with me for the rest of my life. The serpent figures heavily in the Vodou faith. In fact, the word Vodou has been translated as "the snake under whose auspices gather all who share the faith." Perhaps my attraction to the symbol of the powerful Vodou snake spirit, Damballah Wedo, drew me to that religion.

Many years later, when I lived in Haiti, I would be asked by a professor at Florida State University to help him put together a complete collection of the species of snakes found on Hispaniola. It wasn't long before word got out, and I was being offered snakes for sale by the locals. I ended up purchasing many of the ones that weren't of interest to the university, just to keep them from being killed. I released them in the enclosed, heavily wooded acreage of my property, where they slithered happily through lush vegetation. Villarosa became a private refuge for my snakes, my orchids, and me.

CHAPTER 16

Survival

Butch
April 5, 2001
2:08 p.m.

Having learned that my kidnappers plan to take me to Zabeth and hold me there for an indeterminate time, I have serious doubts about being able to survive days in captivity. Five years earlier, I had undergone open-heart surgery to replace my aortic valve and need to take the blood thinner Coumadin every day. I do not have my medication with me.

I need to act now because my chances of attracting attention and getting help are better in the city. Regardless of the crack-head killer with the Uzi sitting behind me, I decide my best chance for survival is to escape before we reach remote Zabeth. The fear of having a paralyzing stroke for lack of medication is now paramount to my being shot while attempting to escape.

Perhaps it is the familiarity of the pipe smoke—even though no one is smoking in the car and I don't know where it is coming from—but a renewed sense of determination surges through me. We are still only ten minutes from Villarosa. If I can get out of the car alive, I can make it home.

As the leader continues to direct the driver, we bog down in one of the daily, horrific Port-au-Prince traffic jams. At a crawl we approach an intersection, one I normally cross several times a week.

There is a large girls' school at this intersection, *Les Soeurs de La Charité de St. Louis*, and I remember that at least two policemen are always directing traffic at peak times like this.

This is it—my one chance for escape. My body tenses in readiness. When the Land Cruiser stops at the intersection, I fling open the passenger door and jump out. I run about ten yards up the hill and then dive headfirst halfway through the open passenger window of a car that is starting to move ahead. "Go, go, go! Please go!" I yell.

The horrified driver panics and stalls the car.

I push myself back out the window and begin running again—up the hill to the gates of the school. Once inside, I slam the big iron gates, bolting them shut. Out of breath and dizzy, I lean against the locked gates of the school, frantically looking for help. *Where are the policemen? Where is anybody?*

"Help me! Somebody, please help me!" I cry out in desperation and fear, using up what little energy I still possess. I have no strength to run any farther. Grasping the cool iron bar of the gate with a slippery hand, my mind takes over again, reliving my life as if these few ragged breaths are guaranteed to be my last.

* * *

For most of my life, I was plagued by one fear—financial insecurity. After my father retired, I grew up feeling deprived of the material things my classmates were given by their fathers. I hated to watch my beautiful, refined mother struggle to make ends meet.

We'd eat rice and beans four days in a row while my friends ate chicken or steak. Typically, my mother never complained; she would joke about our lack of dessert by saying we were having "air pudding with wind sauce."

In my adolescence, I became increasingly more withdrawn and angry because I didn't see any tangible results of my father's work, such as more and better food on the table. When I expressed concern, he responded with tales of the time he spent as a monk in China and Tibet and had to beg for his one daily meal. I didn't understand or appreciate his spiritual ideas, yet at the same time, I found myself fascinated by my father's extraordinary way of not worrying about anything.

"Mind over matter," he'd repeatedly tell me. "Butch, I assure you that by thinking positively you will attract and realize a good outcome from any situation."

I didn't hold much stock in his assurance. Being more interested in the practical application and material manifestation of life's luxuries, I wanted better food on our table and better clothes on our backs. I didn't see how any amount of longing for these things could make them appear. How could just *thinking* positively make anything happen?

* * *

That fateful summer when I returned to Haiti shortly after I began college in Indianapolis, I discovered my father had fallen ill. He'd developed prostate cancer, and it was the first time I'd ever seen this physically fit, imposing man look so frail. It was painfully apparent that he was becoming an older man. I was eighteen and strong, while he was now seventy-five. Like any teenager on summer break, I had been looking forward to spending time with my friends at the beach. I was still a typical youth, prone to paying more attention to the good-looking girls in town than to mortgages and bills. A few days later I discovered my father was seven months in arrears on his mortgage payments and the mortgage lender was about to foreclose on our home.

This was the moment in my young existence that I was soundly hit between the eyes by what I now like to call the "realities of life." I was scared to death because I knew my parents had zero savings and very little income. My mind worked overtime, imagining the worst. *If our house is foreclosed on, where will my family live? We could lose everything, and we will be out on the streets!*

"We've managed so far, and we will continue to manage," my father stated with a quiet, unshakable belief that drove me crazy.

Manage how? I wanted to know exactly what concrete place the money was going to come from to make the mortgage payments and secure our family home. And I wanted to know now. Perhaps I was just as obsessive as my father but in the opposite way. I always wanted everything to be taken care of immediately. To this day, I can't stand to be even a day late on any payment. I obsess about promptness and money.

"Money, money, money. That's the problem with this world today," my father would always say. "There's a lot more to life than money."

I never openly challenged his beliefs, but now that Villarosa was about to be foreclosed on, I felt compelled to fight him. Knowing he wasn't feeling well, I held back my anger and tried to make my point calmly.

"I'm sorry, Dad, but I disagree. Money is important in life," I said and then tried to soften my tone. "Look, I understand money holds a lot more importance to me than it does to you, but we're talking about the dream house you built for Mom. You took out this mortgage with no way to pay it back, so you could make all those fancy renovations. If we want to continue living here, somebody's got to meet the responsibility and pay it off."

When the bill collector arrived at the front door with an ultimatum, demanding immediate payment of money due or calling for imminent foreclosure, I became terrified as I observed my father interact with this man.

"I'll pay you when I have the money. It will come," he said with a calm smile. His usual mind-over-matter approach to life remained firm. He didn't even glance at the paperwork the man handed him.

The man walked away, shaking his head. My family was in serious trouble.

The incident with the bill collector forced my hand. I adored my mother and couldn't bear to see her lose her beautiful home. At eighteen, I considered myself a man, so I determined that it was up to me to do whatever it took to save my family.

From this defining moment my entire life took on a new direction, and I took on a huge challenge. I decided not to return to college, and instead I chose to stay in Haiti and assume the financial responsibility for my parents, younger brother, *and* Villarosa, despite the political unrest that pervaded our island home.

* * *

Now, leaning against the gates of the girls' school, catching my breath for a few seconds, my determination and drive starts to return. Being held captive at gunpoint is about as hard as reality gets.

I have to do something. I have to save myself. What would my father do in this situation? I wish I had the chance to talk to him about it.

CHAPTER 17

World Tour with President-Elect Taft, 1908–1909

Horace

During the years I had traveled through the East studying religion, earned my balloon pilot's license, toured America and the Panama Canal with President Roosevelt, and traveled to Haiti and South America, much progress was being made in the field of aviation. My old friends Alexander Graham Bell and Glenn Curtiss formed an association of early flight pioneers that included President Roosevelt's personal representative, a young lieutenant in the United States Army Signal Corps named Thomas Selfridge.

The Wright brothers worked hard to build a plane for the United States Army. This prototype would have to pass several rigorous test flights before the army would agree to purchase it. A flight pattern was designated, taking the plane from Fort Meyer, Virginia (across the Potomac from Washington, D.C.), to Alexandria. The plane had to circle a small balloon before returning to land at Fort Meyer. The brothers spent five years perfecting their airplane and preparing it for test flights that would take place over a three-day period in September 1908. For two days their plane performed beautifully, rising to an altitude of about 1,000 feet, flying out across the river, rounding the balloon, and then landing gently back at its starting point.

That brisk September 17 morning was no different from the previous two days. Thousands of people streamed across the Potomac to watch the test plane perform again and cheer its pilots on. I was one of many photographers assembled on the parade ground, capturing these historic flights on film.

The awed anticipation of the crowd matched my own breathless excitement as I watched the plane take off with Orville Wright and Lieutenant Selfridge at the controls. They rose to the prescribed altitude and began their flight across the river, just as before. The sound of cheering swelled all around me. I held the camera ready and took my shots as they got closer, reached the balloon, rounded it, and began their flight back to Fort Meyer.

Just as they arrived over the field to land, at an altitude of about 150 feet, something appeared to fly off the plane. I heard the palpable intake of breath from the stunned crowd. From my vantage point it looked like one of the propellers, but I couldn't be sure.

The plane wobbled and then began to fall from the sky. There was nothing any of us on the ground could do to save it, so I snapped two pictures while it fell and one just as it hit the ground. (The dust from the crash hid the details of the second photograph, I later discovered, but I'd captured its plunge.)

I barely heard the cries of horror around me. Clutching my camera, I raced toward the crash site. A soldier clamored behind me, "Stop! Come back."

Doggedly, I kept on. The soldier jabbed his bayonet into my back.

I fell forward but managed to hang onto the camera. Scrambling to my feet, I continued to run. I arrived just in time to take pictures of men pulling Orville and the remains of poor Lieutenant Selfridge from the wreckage.

Fortunately, I wore a tough raincoat. Although my back bled a lot, the bayonet wound was not much more than a scratch. With blood trickling down my leg and into my shoe, I ran to the nearest street, looking for transportation to Pennsylvania Railroad Station. I needed to get to New York quickly and develop my pictures. I spotted a big black limousine with a uniformed chauffeur and cried out, "Please rush me to the railroad station."

A large man stepped up and asked, "Who are you?"

I introduced myself and explained what I had just witnessed.

"Get in," he said. I did, and we drove off at once. On the way, he said, "I'm the managing editor of *New York World*. I'd greatly appreciate it if my paper gets first publication rights to your pictures."

Naturally, I agreed.

That was a momentous afternoon for many reasons. I witnessed my first airplane crash, and I saw my first motion picture camera.

While waiting to photograph the flight, I became acquainted with the cameraman, and he was kind enough to show me the features of this novel device that could capture people in motion. I didn't realize then what a great influence these two events would have on my future.

A few months later, despite having witnessed the world's first fatal plane crash, I decided I wanted to learn how to fly an airplane. I had long been enamored with flight, and my recent interest in motion pictures presented new possibilities. I knew that learning to fly an airplane would offer me more work and travel opportunities, so I wanted to be ready.

In 1909, just four years after I'd become a balloon pilot, I learned to fly an airplane. Within a few months I was soaring aloft with a group of pilots who later became known as the "Early Birds," men who flew before 1910.

* * *

For the next few years my work kept me on the ground and at sea most of the time, but I was ready for what I knew would be big changes coming soon. I was keen on the idea of being a pilot, and I seized every opportunity to explore the skies. I truly was one of the "daring young men" later depicted in motion pictures. And on the occasional rainy day when I wasn't busy, I enjoyed sitting around the table at the Explorers Club, talking flight with the other Early Birds and explorers like me.

In the meantime, while I continued to work for Underwood & Underwood in New York, I still was considered the official White House photographer for President Roosevelt.

President William Howard Taft sits atop an elephant.
Photo by Horace Dade Ashton

In the fall of 1908, President Roosevelt assigned me to accompany president-elect William Howard Taft on a trip around the world before his inauguration in early 1909.

This journey opened new doors and led me into the company of many world leaders.

I photographed future President Taft with Emperor Meiji and the empress of Japan; the sultan of Sulu in the Philippines; Dowager Empress Tzu Hsi and young Emperor Pu Yi, the last emperor of China; Czar Nicholas and Czarina Alexandra of Russia; the kaiser of Germany; President Fallieres of France; and King Edward VII and the young Prince of Wales, David Windsor, in England's Buckingham Palace.

I could hardly believe my luck. Here I was, a young man from Virginia, traveling with the future United States president and photographing kings and queens. This whirlwind trip set the stage for future encounters with royalty that I will relate in later chapters, but now let me tell you about the most unique man I ever met.

While we were the guests of Czar Nicholas II and Czarina Alexandra in St. Petersburg, Russia, I visited with the czarina. "Your Majesty, I know that you were born Princess Hesse–Darmstadt. One of my ancestors was named Armstead, but only because his name was changed from Darmstadt when he arrived in America early in the seventeenth century," I said.

The czarina seemed most interested and began to ask many questions about my family. Finally, she asked, "How did such a young man become the press liaison officer with President Taft's party?"

"I was a war correspondent in the Russo–Japanese War. After that I entered a Buddhist monastery in China because I am intensely interested in comparative religion. Then I became President Roosevelt's official White House photographer, and he assigned me to accompany President Taft," I said, leaving out the part about my first meeting with President Roosevelt over the fake hurdle–jumping photo.

"Oh!" she exclaimed. "You are a student of comparative religion! You must meet and talk with our 'man of God,' Rasputin. Are you free tomorrow morning?"

"Of course, Your Excellency. I would love to meet your spiritual adviser."

At ten o'clock the next morning, I was summoned to the palace and immediately shown to the salon of the czarina. Her Majesty greeted me warmly. After exchanging pleasantries, I peered beyond this lovely lady and discovered one of the most spectacular men I had ever seen, standing across the room.

Rasputin looked older than I, and I later learned he was thirty-four years of age when we met. He stood taller than most men, and his long black hair fell wildly about his face and shaggy beard. He wore a light-blue silk embroidered shirt, a red and gold rope-like belt with large tassels, and baggy black velvet pants tucked into black riding boots. A gold chain with a large gold cross hung from his neck. His eyes were almost indescribable. Upon a closer look I could see the irises were gray-blue, but when he spoke, his dark pupils dilated until his eyes became great black orbs. His large hands were unwashed and bore long, dirty fingernails. My first impression was repulsion.

I could tell by his standoffish manner that he was not impressed with me either. However, when Her Majesty presented me as a student of comparative religion, his face and eyes were positively aglow. With the czarina acting as interpreter, he wanted to know all about my travels and my monastic life. His questions revealed a genuine interest in my experiences, and our conversation showed his profound understanding of the spiritual foundation of life. After half an hour, he asked, "What is your belief?"

"I was raised in the Episcopal Church of the Christian faith, and I believe in the real teachings of Jesus—not necessarily the way they have been interpreted by the various sects. When I read the original translations from the Aramaic, as Jesus taught, I learned that the Holy Spirit is in each of us and in every living thing in the universe. The only difference between people is our realization of that presence and our different rates of vibration."

He exclaimed, "You are right! It is the realization of that inner-dwelling spirit that gives us the power to heal."

Rasputin was quite curious about my experiences with some of the more primitive people who knew nothing of Christianity, and he listened intently. I shall never forget his eyes. This man of faith never took his eyes from me; they intermittently changed from blue to almost black and were somewhat hypnotic.

My audience with Rasputin lasted until noon. He was unlike anyone I had ever known. Aglow with the aura he emanated, I was convinced that I had just spent two hours of my life in the presence of a mystic. The experience was trance–like, but I would not call it hypnotism.

Since that unforgettable morning, I have read many books written by Rasputin's enemies, but there's no doubt in my mind that he was a man of faith and a great healer. Even though he may have sometimes allowed the animal side of his nature to predominate, I believe it was largely due to his uncultured, peasant background.

The nature of the women with whom he came in contact in the imperial household may also have contributed to his reputation. I saw many of those women myself. They were beautiful, fashionable, and avid for new experiences to relieve the boredom of court life. I'm sure that if some of them had made the same fuss over me that they did over Rasputin, I too might have succumbed to their charms.

When I formed my personal impression of Rasputin from this one meeting, I was a keen observer, an unprejudiced student of comparative religion, and a liberal–minded judge of character. At the time, I had read very little about the man, so I was uninfluenced by others. Since our meeting I have read a great deal about the so-called "Mad Monk" who was murdered in the Yusopov Palace a few years later. I am still convinced that he possessed unusual healing powers. Had he been exposed to culture in his early days, his life and influence would have been far different. Innately he was a "man of God."

* * *

Upon returning to the United States, my first assignment was to photograph President Taft's inauguration in Washington. The official ceremony was considerably more sedate than the Vodou rituals I'd witnessed in Haiti.

In addition to meeting with heads of state and religious leaders during my overseas trip with Taft, I was fortunate, through my ongoing work as a photojournalist in New York City, to make the acquaintance of prominent individuals in the arts. A few of these people became good friends, and over the years we shared wonderful times together.

I interviewed and photographed the great Russian ballerina Anna Pavlova before one of her last appearances in New York. Vaslav Nijinsky was appearing with her at the time, and she introduced me to Nijinsky and his wife. Mrs. Nijinsky asked, "Have you met Andre Oliveroff, one of our dancers? He's an American too."

"No, I haven't," I replied, not wanting to be rude by adding that not all Americans knew each other. In the course of my travels I was often asked this type of question.

Mrs. Nijinsky motioned to a handsome young man standing by Pavlova, and he came over to talk with us. I thought he stared at me in a strange manner. I later learned that Andre Oliveroff was really Oliver Grymes, a cousin of mine from Virginia who had studied at the Imperial Russian Ballet School in St. Petersburg. He recognized my name because my father's sister had married his uncle.

I made some beautiful photographs of Pavlova and Nijinsky. Some years later, after both had died, I was especially glad to have taken the pictures.

Much later I ran into Oliver's brother in Virginia, and he told me that Oliver had been Pavlova's favorite dancing partner. They had been inseparable for years. When she died in the Netherlands in 1931, a broken-hearted Oliver went into seclusion at a large estate on the eastern shore of Maryland. There he wrote an excellent biography of Pavlova titled *Flight of the Swan*, a worshipful memoir in which he told of setting sail with Pavlova's troupe for a year-long tour of Latin America in 1917.

CHAPTER 18

Escape

Butch
April 5, 2001
2:16 p.m.

With renewed strength I begin running again—I have to—down the long driveway of the girls' school. My escape isn't over yet, not by a long shot. *If I can just get to the building . . .*

All of a sudden I hear an unmistakable sound from behind; one all too familiar to those of us still living in the city—the staccato bark of automatic weapons. *Tonnerre!* My captors are shooting at me on a busy street through the gates of a Catholic girls' school.

Throngs of people and cars are still caught in the heavy traffic jam at the intersection, but nobody pays any attention to me or the gunman. It's just another day in Port-au-Prince. The police don't get involved. There are no heroes here.

I try to keep low as I run, almost stumbling, distraught, looking for a place to hide.

Hearing a loud crunch of metal, I glance behind me to see my kidnappers breaking open the gates. They charge toward me. Upright now, I run as fast as I can toward the building, knowing the safety of those brick walls are even too far away.

I feel a hand grab the back of my shirt and hear the fabric tear. My first instinct is to struggle. Then I remember that two months ago a nun was shot and killed *at this exact spot*. She'd been gunned down in cold blood while being robbed of her bank withdrawal for the school payroll.

Like her killers, my kidnappers want money. Unlike the poor nun, they need me *alive* to get their ransom. Rather than die on the same spot and hoping to buy myself more time, I make a split-second decision to stop struggling and abort my escape. Oddly calm, I raise my hands and await my fate as the sound of car horns and angry voices on the busy street recedes in my ears like the soundtrack of a dream sequence in a movie.

The killer with the Uzi stalks up and shoves his machine gun angrily into my face. By sheer reflex I push it away with my already raised hand.

He fires.

Looking down, I see a red stain spreading across my white shirt. I feel dizzy.

Why don't I feel the pain? Is my father's mind-over-matter philosophy at work here, like when he picked up the hot coals with his bare hands in a Vodou ceremony? But how can that be? I am a nonbeliever.

* * *

No matter what happened, my father truly believed that everything would always turn out all right. I remember a time when I was a boy in 1949, and my father sailed a friend's Bahamas schooner back to the beach after dark. The wind blew only a gentle whisper into the warm night air—not enough breeze to fill the sail, and the boat had no engine. This was a time before radar, and that night the lighthouse was not working. Typically, my father took none of these things as negative signs. "Mind over matter works. We'll soon be back at the beach," he assured us as he adjusted the sail.

As we grew closer to shore, our friends expressed concern

about striking a coral reef. I worried silently, knowing the bay was riddled with reefs.

"Don't be concerned," Dad told them. "I know every reef in this bay like the palm of my hands." He'd barely uttered those words when we heard a loud crunch. "See, there's one now," my father said calmly.

Dad was always that sure of himself. He believed without reservation that you can accomplish whatever you think. Sure enough, the boat wasn't damaged. That night when the tide rose, we made it safely off the reef and back to the beach.

In stark contrast to my dad, who lived by his beliefs every moment of the day, I've never been inclined to attach much importance to religion in my daily life. I resented my father's spiritual side because it seemed so impractical. It was not "mind over matter" that paid the mortgage on Villarosa. It was me.

While my father continued to study religion, I began to "study" entrepreneurship. At the age of eighteen I landed my first job, and after that I never stopped working.

I ran a lobster fishing company for Bud Spatola, an American businessman from Philadelphia. I spent over a year operating his sixty-five-foot sports-fisherman yacht with a Honduran captain and two Haitians I had recruited as crew.

I created and organized a network of over one hundred local fishermen who sold us their catch on a weekly basis. Soon we were shipping thousands of pounds of frozen lobster tails to the United States each week.

Bud was so impressed with the early success of the operation and its growth potential that he purchased a Grumman Seabee, a single-engine seaplane, and hired a former United States Navy pilot in order to speed up transporting the weekly catch.

I was accompanying a full load—about 1,000 pounds of lobster tails—on one of our journeys. Suddenly the plane's engine began to sputter, and the pilot quickly instructed me to manually pump the hydraulic landing gear back up so we could make an emergency landing in the bay of Port-au-Prince—a mile short of the airstrip. We had run out of gas!

You have not lived until you experience flying in a single-engine seaplane into Port-au-Prince Airport and run out of gas. The aerodynamics of that aircraft were like flying a lead balloon. The emergency landing in the bay felt as graceful as a belly-flop. Fortunately, I was able to befriend and hire a local fisherman that came to see what was going on. He took me in his row boat to get five gallons of fuel so the seaplane could make it back to the airstrip.

After more than a year of spending six days and nights each week at sea, I decided I'd had enough. Even though I had enjoyed long hours every day spearfishing and scuba diving in so many inaccessible, unspoiled reefs and bays while my staff was collecting and cleaning the catches of the day, I spent only twenty-four hours per week on land in Port-au-Prince. I missed all the pretty girls and the typical life of a young man my age. I carefully trained my replacement, and short of my nineteenth birthday I resigned and opened my first nightclub, La Fregate, in Port-au-Prince.

La Fregate was an immediate success with the young, well-off crowd in the late 1950s. I first met the very attractive Myriam Rivera there. She was home for the summer from school in the United States, out with her sister and cousins, and this was the "in" place to be. At our first meeting, I did not have the faintest idea that one day she would become my wife.

While my nightclub was successful, it was hard to sustain during those turbulent times. Due to Haiti's political unrest, frequent curfews were imposed between ten o'clock at night and five in the morning, hurting my business a great deal.

Having recently taken on the responsibility for Villarosa's mortgage, I needed a steady, reliable source of income. With my knowledge of the language, the culture, and the country in general,

I readily found a job as a translator/coordinator with General Vegetable Distributors, an American company recently established in the Haiti's "breadbasket," the Artibonite Valley. This well-established offshore fruit and vegetable grower/distributor was based in Pompano Beach, Florida.

My job required me to move to Saint Marc, about an hour-and-a-half drive northwest of Port-au-Prince, and thus began my financial and physical endeavors in the agro-industrial field for over thirty years.

A couple of years later, when a few of my closest friends and I were duck hunting in the Artibonite Valley, we were mistaken for part of a rebel-invasion force that had landed in the south of Haiti. We were unaware of this invasion but were arrested by the infamous *Tonton Macoutes*[20] and taken to a remote jail far out in the country.

While in jail, I was recognized by a member of the militia who had worked for me in one of my previous agricultural endeavors. I persuaded him to contact the father of two of my friends and tell him what had happened and where we were being held. There were no cellular phones back then, and this good fellow had to travel by bus to the closest city hours away—but he did.

It was all too common for people who found themselves in remote jails during that period to never be heard from or seen again. Needless to say, we were extremely fortunate to have made it out alive and unharmed. I knew too many who did not make it out of such remote jails during those times.

* * *

My budding career was placed on hold in 1963 when I was drafted into the United States Army. I was working as packing-plant manager at the same plant for Scott & Matson Farms, the successor to General Vegetable Distributors.

---

20   The *Tonton Macoutes* was a special operations unit within the Haitian paramilitary force created in 1959 by dictator François "Papa Doc" Duvalier.

The Vietnam War had just begun, and I had been dating Myriam for about two years. I promised her that we would discuss getting married *if and when* I returned from the military. Fortunately, after six months of active duty and just before being sent to Vietnam, I was granted a temporary hardship deferment after proving I was the primary source of income for my elderly parents. I was transferred to the U.S. Army Reserves and allowed to return to Haiti for the time being.

While my brothers were engaged in their lives, I call this period of my life "my character-building years." I adhered to the saying, "When the going gets tough, the tough get going," as I struggled to make ends meet. Like my father, I focused on my priorities, stuck to my principles, managed to keep the *status quo*, and provided for my parents.

Perhaps my father and I weren't so very different. We were both driven to succeed, and we each pursued money in our youth, although for different reasons. On the rare occasions when I really listened to his storytelling, I noticed there was money involved in most of his escapades. He traveled for jobs and got paid for his daredevil stunts, even if he focused more on the thrill.

My favorite Horace Ashton photograph hangs on the wall in my home. It is the famous black-and-white self-portrait he took from the top of the Woolworth Building in Manhattan. In the picture I have, he is standing on the girder high above the city. The photograph is my favorite for a number of reasons, certainly because it is a wonderful example of classic American art of the twentieth century, but mostly because it is so typical of Dad. I'm sure he enjoyed the thrill of it all that day.

Unlike me, my father placed little value on money. I suspect he only earned it to afford his next adventure. He was not one to plan ahead, as far as finances were concerned. He had gotten by this way since he was a boy, and he lived as if this lifestyle would continue forever.

SOLDIERS OF THE CAMERA—Adventures of the men who travel the world making pictures—See page 11—The illustrations on this page are from copyright photos of Underwood & Underwood.

HORACE D. ASHTON, ONE OF THE YOUNGER ADVENTURERS OF THE CAMERA, PHOTOGRAPHING NEW YORK CITY FROM A SLENDER STEEL SUPPORT PROJECTING FROM THE TOP OF A SKY-SCRAPER ABOVE FIFTH-AVENUE.

1907

As I struggled to make ends meet in various entrepreneurial ways, I doubt my father appreciated the financial benefits provided him by my own youthful adventures in business. In the 1960s before I ever owned a car dealership, I would buy older vehicles and fix them up to sell for a small profit. My father would borrow these cars and drive merrily along with a lit pipe in his mouth, oblivious to the sparks occasionally burning holes in the upholstery.

He seemed unaware how difficult it was for me to afford the car in the first place, let alone improve its condition so that I could sell it and make enough profit to pay the bills and buy the next car.

The polar differences in the beliefs of father and son continued to flow through our loving relationship and our entwined lives—sometimes like the trickle of a creek and sometimes like a raging river. Well into my adult life, I lived under the same roof with my father until he passed away. I provided for him and continually wondered how I could be so angry with a man I loved and respected so fervently.

He was always so positive and believed that things would work out. I am not about to consider positive thinking as a way out of my dilemma. I know that my father's philosophy hadn't always worked. Maybe it had for him personally but not for others around him.

His positive thoughts hadn't saved his companions from killer snake bites in South America. How did he reconcile his beliefs with those deaths? I wish I'd had the chance to talk to him about it.

Long after his death, I still wonder if I can ever reconcile the differences that were at the very core of our beliefs.

CHAPTER 19

Journeys Across the Americas, 1911–1913

Horace

Seeking a new challenge, I left Underwood & Underwood and went to work for the Raymond and Whitcomb Company in New York but not as a photographer. Because of my firsthand knowledge of travel, I was hired to act as an automobile tour operator, creating and promoting excursions in the United States and abroad. In 1911 I organized a few successful excursions, including automobile tours through New England, and then came up with the idea to lead the first passenger–carrying automobile tour across the continent.

My employer supplied five open eight–passenger Garford cars and a Prairie Schooner for baggage and spare parts. We booked eight passengers per car at $875 each, which more than covered all expenses to the coast, and hired Mr. Westgard of the American Automobile Association as our guide.

Our auto caravan traveled by easy stages from New York west via Buffalo and Niagara Falls and then on to Chicago, and westward across Iowa on a newly constructed road called the River–to–River, specially built for us and which had only opened upon our arrival. From there we went to Kansas City, Denver, Phoenix, and the Grand Canyon. We spent a short time in New Mexico and then drove through the Imperial Valley and on to San Diego and finally to Los Angeles. Where there were no roads, we had to remove the tires and run across deep canyons on the rims fitted over the rails of the railway.

I created a photographic documentary of the journey, and as we traveled through different cities, people lined the streets to watch the caravan pass by. I was very pleased with the publicity we received along the way. The *Albuquerque Evening Herald* wrote an article about the trip.

> After a most picturesque and interesting journey of practically 3,000 miles, the ocean-to-ocean touring party in the charge of H. D. Ashton, manager of the automobile touring department of the Raymond and Whitcomb Company, arrived in Albuquerque last night. . . . During the morning Manager Ashton was probably the busiest man in the city, outfitting for this week's trip . . . Manager Ashton is permanently stationed in New York and was assigned to manage this excursion because it was the first attempt of the kind to run a "pay-as-you-enter" automobile train across the continent. He was a war correspondent during the Japanese-Russian War and has been on various assignments in various parts of the world.
>
> "While this is my first experience in managing a trip of this kind," said Mr. Ashton, "I am certainly enjoying it. Of course it's a little different from following armies and writing war stories, but I am having new experiences every day that beat all the war business hollow."[21]

The trip was not without incident. In the mountains near Globe, Arizona, I tried to board our car while it was under way as I took a picture of the cars coming down the mountainside. My foot slipped off, and the 4,000-pound car ran over my instep as I fell. I staggered through a painful afternoon taking pictures, using a heavy cane that the chauffeur made for me.

That night in Phoenix, the x-ray film showed all the bones in my instep mashed flat. The doctor placed a plaster cast on my foot and told me not to walk on it for six weeks. To buy some time, I sent all the passengers up

---

21   "All Happy Despite Bad Weather," in *Albuquerque Evening Herald*, Albuquerque, New Mexico, 6 November 1911.

to the Grand Canyon by train and put the cars in garages for a complete overhaul.

After three days, we resumed our trip. My foot was most uncomfortable, so I broke off the plaster cast and walked with a cane. When we arrived in Southern California, we made our headquarters at the beautiful old Hotel Maryland in Pasadena and ran auto tours through California the following winter.

Excerpts from a large write-up in *Hotel Maryland Life*[22] were most complimentary:

> H. D. Ashton, representative of the Raymond and Whitcomb Company, and manager of the tour deserves much of the credit for its successful accomplishment. He has been pleasantly mentioned as "the brains of the party," and it is certain that he is responsible for much of the buoyancy of spirits, which made the trip a pleasant one. Even when a 4,000-pound car ran over his foot and broke all the ankle bones, he never lost heart, but was heard to remark: "I am thankful that I only broke one foot and that the party did not break my head."

After our cross-country auto caravan was so successful, I returned to New York and continued my work as a photojournalist. My foot eventually healed completely. The following year, I wrote a heartfelt article for *Sunset* magazine to accompany some of my photographs of the trip, titled "The Roosevelt Road."[23] It described our group's experience motoring through Arizona's Salt River Valley on "America's Finest Hundred Miles of Highway."

> For twenty miles across a desert of cacti and mesquite, an absolutely waterless plain, a broad highway was laid out to the foot of the mountains. For forty miles further into the most rugged mountain country in the West, the road was blasted from the rocks. This road

---

22   "The Manager's Story," in *Hotel Maryland Life*, Pasadena, California, 30 November 1911.

23   Horace D. Ashton, "The Roosevelt Road," in *Sunset* magazine, October 1912.

was continued for thirty-seven miles further, to the city of Globe, on the line of the Southern Pacific Railroad.

It is easily worth the trip from either coast to experience the wonderful sensations of a drive over that road. In scenic beauty and artistic, changing coloring, no highway in the world compares with it. The mountains are inspiring and the rocks are clothed in the richest colors. No language can describe the glories of the sunrise and sunset pictures on those crags and cliffs, or the witching beauty of the deep canyons veiled in purple shadows. It is a drive, once taken, never to be forgotten.

* * *

My love affair with film began when I took that first photography job with Clinedinst, and now I could only imagine the possibilities a motion picture camera offered. I began to study the motion picture industry and soon realized that moving pictures, as films were called back then, offered employment opportunities to thousands of people, from camera operators to extras. I was determined to become part of it, so I set about learning how to use a motion picture camera.

When I returned from the automobile trip across America, I went to work for the General Film Company, where I would ultimately realize my dream and combine my two great interests to become an aerial cinematographer. Whenever a rare opportunity to take to the skies came my way, I pursued aerial photography with a passion. Meanwhile, I enjoyed creating educational films and learning more about the art of cinematography.

During the summer of 1912, I was engaged to take a series of stereoscopic photographs of surgery. My workplace was the huge, sky-lit operating room of the old College of Physicians and Surgeons at Columbia University. These pictures were of the variations of an appendectomy, made under the direction of the famous surgeon Dr. Frank Hartley. These were used in many of the medical colleges in the United States for many years. In addition to photographing surgeries, I made a lot of anatomical photographs for medical studies.

* * *

I enjoyed working for General Films, and I learned a lot about motion pictures there, but travel and adventure always made my pulse quicken. Although I hadn't set out specifically to be an explorer, I was an explorer at heart and never one to stay still for very long. My teenage experiences at sea, combined with my natural curiosity and my work as a photojournalist, led me in that direction, and my quest for learning continued to feed my wanderlust. Being recognized as an explorer was yet another layer of the person I had become as I reached the age of thirty.

In 1913, I found myself in South America again, eager to learn more about that topographically diverse continent. As many explorers before me and many since, I too was curious about the mighty Amazon River.

A tall, handsome Englishman with prematurely gray hair—Captain J. Campbell Besley of the famous Campbell Highlanders—planned an expedition from the source to the mouth of the Amazon River. He asked me to join the party and record the trip, this time with a motion picture, using my newly acquired skills. Naturally I jumped at the chance to explore the Amazon and get paid to work with my new motion picture camera at the same time.

There was no aerial transportation at the time so our party traveled by ship to Lima, Peru. There Captain Besley hired Indians as guides and porters and added a penniless Harvard graduate to our party as our historian. The historian's job was to keep an accurate diary of the journey so that the notes could be referred to if lectures or a book were written later. Shortly after he joined us, the young man showed his true colors.

Beginning at the headwaters of the Putumayo, we had to make the first stages of the long, strenuous journey almost entirely on foot, which brought out the worst in our historian. He couldn't stand the insects, the noises in the rainforest kept him awake at night, and he was unable to carry his share of the equipment. Since it was too late to turn back, and we couldn't abandon him in the forest, we had to go on. Each of us took turns nursing him along and keeping him quiet at night so the rest of us could sleep. He made few, if any, notes, so he contributed nothing to the journey except misery for his companions.

The first two weeks we traveled on foot and by rafts that we constructed as needed, abandoning them when we encountered unnavigable waterfalls and rapids. On the upper Urubamba River, near Cuzco, we passed the ancient suspension bridge so vividly described in Thornton Wilder's exciting novel *The Bridge of San Luis Rey*. It looked exactly as Wilder described it, with priests and nuns and picturesque Indians crossing over the muddy rushing torrent below. Only the great carriage with the silver-mounted harness was missing.

We then spent three weeks navigating the river in canoes, a hazardous feat in those rushing waters. The Amazon was wider at Iquitos, near the Colombian border, and we were able to navigate by launch for about three hundred miles. When we reached the border of Brazil, we traveled by small steamer to Manaus, the headquarters of the United States Rubber Company's activities in Brazil before 1914.

In the upper reaches of the Amazon River, the forests and small islands teemed with bird and animal life. Monkeys screamed in trees overhead and bird calls rang through the jungle as the stench of rotting vegetation swelled in the steaming river mist. One night, as we traveled by launch, we spotted a large mound ahead, silhouetted against a moonlit stretch of water. Parts of this mound had a shiny surface that reflected the moonlight. We stopped, and several of us went ashore to investigate.

The shiny mound turned out to be an anaconda, one of the largest snakes in the world, coiled up and asleep on a sandbar. The monstrous snake made a conical mass about eight feet in diameter and six feet high, with a horse–size head.

We hoped to bring this gigantic specimen back to the United States, but we realized that it would take all of our resources to capture it. So we attached several strong ropes to a stout tree nearby. Creeping up on the snake, we passed the first loop over its head and tightened it at its throat. As the anaconda angrily uncoiled, two of our Indians crept up and passed ends of the rope under and over it until we could force it into a long, strong crate that we made from poles lashed together with roots. We constructed a special raft to bring the snake to Manaus. When we finally measured it, we were astonished to find that its length was thirty–eight feet, its greatest diameter was thirteen inches, and the length of its head was eighteen inches.

In Manaus we strapped the snake to a padded steel rail, so the creature would not be able to injure itself, and shipped it to the New York Zoological Park. Sadly, it was dead on arrival. I later learned that the anaconda had bent the steel rail into a loop in its quest for freedom. The skin and skeleton were given to the American Museum of Natural History as a record example of this species.

At the same time as we arranged shipping for the snake in Manaus, we shipped our useless historian home by steamer. By this time the trip had already consumed two months, but we decided to continue to the mouth of the river. The Amazon was so wide at this point that we were often out of sight of land; it felt like being on the ocean. We frequently encountered small floating islands, densely populated only by snakes and birds, where I captured many interesting species with my motion picture camera.

When the expedition ended, I turned all the films over to Captain Besley to take back to England. He told me that his next contract was to explore the great Western Desert in the Commonwealth of Australia and asked if I would go with him. I was eager, but the First World War changed our plans, and I never saw Captain Besley again. I did, however, return almost immediately to South America for another river exploration.

* * *

Shortly after I got back to New York, Caspar Whitney,[24] a rich New Yorker who owned and edited *Outing* magazine, contacted me at the Explorers Club. He'd planned an expedition to descend the Orinoco River from its source to its mouth, and having heard of my exploits on the Amazon, he asked me to join it. Of course, I agreed. This all–expenses–paid trip would place me precisely where I could pursue my interest in comparing the Indian tribes in Colombia and Venezuela with those I'd seen in Peru, Bolivia, and Brazil.

Our expedition did find what was called "The Source," a mountain stream that we reached at an altitude of over 12,000 feet. (I later learned that there were countless sources of these great rivers.) Our source was the upper waters of the Guaviare River, which rises in the high Andes just south of Bogota. It was known as the Duda River in its mountain torrent stage.

Following the Duda down through rugged, beautiful country, we reached Salto Angostura I, the first of three breathtaking waterfalls. Eight miles further, we reached Angostura II, and about 150 miles further, Angostura III, located where Meta Vichada and Guainia provinces meet. The Guaviare River forms the boundary between Vichada and Guainia provinces and some 250 miles beyond, just

---

24   Caspar William Whitney was an American author, editor, explorer, outdoorsman, and war correspondent. From 1900, he was an owner and editor in chief of *Outing* magazine, which promoted the outdoors and sporting pursuits.

where the Guaviare flows into the Ataeari, we crossed the border into Venezuela to rest for a couple of days in San Fernando do Atabapo. We had some difficulty with the officials at this remote post in Venezuela, but with Mr. Whitney's patience and my tales of previous experience in Venezuela, we got by.

After resting for a few days we navigated the wider Ataeari in small, uncomfortable, and not–too–clean motorboats down to Puerto Ayacucho, where the river is known as the Orinoco. We passed through Ciudad Bolivar and a few days later reached the town of Barrancas, where we chose the Manamo branch of the delta. At Pedernales we took another boat across the Gulf of Paria to Port–of–Spain, Trinidad.

Our journey was an unqualified success, as we'd found the source of the Orinoco. The first 750 miles of our journey took us through thinly populated forests and fertile plains that had few settlers. Then we encountered several different Indian tribes with whom we traded goods. In the highlands of Colombia, I saw many beautiful orchids in bloom. At the time I had no permanent home and no knowledge of the culture of orchids in captivity, so I left them undisturbed. Years later, when I cultivated orchids, I realized what treasures I'd left behind.

Caspar Whitney's story of the trip appeared in *Outing* magazine, and I heard that he wrote a book after that. Although I never saw either, I was told that the magazine story and the book featured many of my photographs.

* * *

After two exciting South American river expeditions, I remained stateside for more than a year, intent on pursuing opportunities in the burgeoning motion picture industry. Just as I began to establish my career as a serious documentary film producer and occasional madcap aerial cinematographer, I received a cable from my former employer, Major Burt Underwood, now of the United States

Army Signal Corps. It read, "Dear Mr. Ashton, please come to Washington, D.C., immediately. The United States Army requires your services."

I reported to Washington as soon as possible. Major Underwood greeted me and then said, "Horace, as an acclaimed photographer and a knowledgeable flyer, your skills are needed to instruct men in aerial photography for our nation's war efforts. We will make you a reserve officer in the United States Army Signal Corps. You can remain in New York and conduct a school at Columbia University."

I couldn't refuse, so I put my film career on hold to serve my country. At the time, I didn't realize that this would be the first of many times my country would enlist my service, and neither did I realize just what an important role aerial photography was to play in World War I.[25]

---

25   World War I was the first major conflict to use powered aircraft to observe and attack enemy forces from above. Established in 1860, the United States Army Signal Corps develops, tests, provides, and manages communications and information systems support for the command and control of combined armed forces.

CHAPTER **20**

Invisible

Butch
April 5, 2001
2:18 p.m.

I stare at the widening bloodstain on my shirt as I sink to the ground.

Literally hundreds of witnesses saw my shooting, but no one pays any attention. If they notice, they pretend not to see. No one tries to help me. These people are only concerned with their own safety, and I'm just another casualty of these horrific times in Port-au-Prince.

The leader berates the shooter. The sound of their voices only rings in my ears, and I can't make out the familiar Creole words.

* * *

For the last four years of his life my father spoke constantly to our children about how he would be their guardian angel after his death. He promised that we would never have anything to worry about; we would be safe because he would be looking after all of us. I was a skeptic, involved in the mad juggling act that was my life, and paid little heed. I had no time or patience for things I couldn't touch, see, or hear.

Am I a skeptic still?

I heave a sigh. At this moment, while my kidnappers pull me roughly to my feet and I begin to feel pain in my hand, I wish fervently that my father had been able to prove me wrong. I need a guardian angel now. Physically and mentally exhausted, I have never felt more alone in my life.

I look upward, and in silent desperation I call out to my father. *I need your help, Dad. Please help me. Where are you, Dad? Where are you now, when I really need you?*

No answer. *Did I really expect one?*

Blood soaks my shirt and pants, and shock threatens to overtake me again. With a gun pressed hard against the small of my back, my kidnapper forces me back up the sloping driveway through the school's broken gates to my car. It's still running, doors open, honking vehicles detouring around it.

Two of my captors shove me into the middle of the backseat and then climb in beside me and slam the doors. This time an armed man sits on either side of me to prevent my escape. I take comfort that the crack-head killer who had pushed the Uzi against the back of my head isn't one of them.

The driver maneuvers the car into the clogged, slow-moving flow of traffic, while I attempt to gather my wits. I raise my hand to my chest to feel for a wound and try to stop the bleeding. It's then I realize that only my hand is injured, and the wound bleeds profusely because of the blood thinners I take. I swallow giddy relief as I wrap my handkerchief around the bloody mess on my hand, wondering idly if a bullet or the gun slide mechanism actually caused the wound.

Now seated in the passenger seat, the Uzi resting against his shoulder, the shooter turns to glare at me. "What were you trying to do, you stupid *blanc*?" he accuses. "I told you I'd kill you if you try anything!"

"Well, you might as well kill me now," I reply, my bravado more from exhaustion than courage. I seriously wonder how I'm going to make it through this alive, especially if they still plan to take me to Zabeth, where I will find no help. "I'll be dead in twenty-four hours anyway."

"You may be," said the leader, now seated beside me, poking a gun in my ribcage. "I told you before; this is a simple business deal. You don't cooperate? We kill you."

"No, no, you don't understand, messieurs. Let me show you." Moving slowly and deliberately, I tear open my bloody shirt to reveal the unmistakable, ugly surgical scar on my chest. "Look, I need my medication to stay alive," I explain, making sure he notices the medical alert medal I wear around my neck. "And I don't have it with me."

"What kind of medicine?" he asks. "We will get it for you."

"It's for my heart. It can only be acquired in the United States."

The truth is that I do need daily medication, and I am very tired from all the blood loss. A new strategy suddenly hits me, and I am reminded that my father spoke of his good ideas as "brainstorms."

I'll play up my sick heart for all it's worth . . . and just maybe it will be worth my life.

* * *

My heart surgery was the only experience in my life I found difficult to understand without considering divine intervention. A routine checkup for insurance purposes revealed a potentially serious problem. My doctor, who happened to be a personal friend, insisted I seek further medical tests. After the results of diverse testing at two major heart centers in Miami over several months, my doctor, family, and friends eventually persuaded me to have the surgery that saved my life.

In 1996, after he completed the successful surgery to replace my aortic valve, the surgeon told me that my case was a medical mystery. My valve was so restricted that I should have had a massive heart attack and died. I'd had no symptoms.

Although I would never admit it to my wife and daughters, the experience gave me brief pause to consider my father's words about his being our guardian angel. More likely it was simply my fate to avoid a heart attack, I reasoned, so no explanation was really necessary.

* * *

Despite being extremely action-oriented, I am a fatalist in a certain way. I never questioned why I happened to be at home on the very day the bill collector arrived at Villarosa with his ultimatum, nor why I then saw so clearly what was meant to be my role in life. Taking care of my parents seemed absolutely normal to me. There was no doubt in my mind that it was my responsibility to shoulder because, of the three Ashton sons, I was the only one in a position to take it on. My older brother, Burdette, had his own family to take care of in the states, and my brother Todd was only ten at the time. He needed my help then, too.

The age differences between the three of us, which might have presented barriers to other brothers, were actually helpful while we were growing up. Because our father was so much older than our friends' fathers, we often turned to each other for guidance. Burdette had been my mentor, and I was Todd's. By the time Todd was sixteen, I was twenty-four, and our father was eighty-one.

That year the United States government placed a political embargo on Haiti, American investors were forced to cease operations, and all American citizens were instructed to leave Haiti immediately. As the United States Navy promptly began their evacuation, I was faced with a difficult decision: either follow my country's orders to evacuate or remain with my elderly parents, who chose to disregard the government's instructions. Since I had already made the decision to devote all my efforts toward the well-being of my elderly parents and my brother Todd, I knew what I had to do. I had Todd evacuated, and I remained with my parents.

In retrospect, I sometimes wonder what I might have become had I returned to the United States and graduated from college. What would my life have been like? But then, had I not stayed in Haiti, I would not have met my wife—and my daughters and my precious grandchildren would not exist.

I made my decision to stay and proposed to Myriam. She agreed to marry me, in spite of my warning that she was not only marrying me but my father and mother as well.

We were married in 1964. How lucky I was to be able to marry my best friend! She was what I needed to help me put my bachelor days behind me and settle down. She played the perfect devil's advocate, who always forced me to weigh the consequences of my decisions. I was the perpetual optimist, and she was not easy to convince. She was my counterweight, the voice of reason. Her high standards and high expectations were a new and constant challenge. Once I met her, the party was over. No more fast cars, fast motorcycles, fast boats, or fast women for me.

From the beginning Myriam developed strong relationships with my parents. I was amazed at how well she adapted to living under the same roof with her mother-in-law, never a small feat, and I was proud of how easily she fit into her new family and new life at Villarosa.

My parents accepted and loved Myriam. After we were married, on the first morning that my wife joined my family for breakfast, my mother ordered our butler, Justin, to place a flower on Myriam's plate at every breakfast. For the thirty-two years we lived under the same roof, there was a flower on Myriam's plate at breakfast every morning.

Living with my parents was very educational for both of us, and our children enjoyed wonderful relationships with their grandparents. My father was an intense man who knew everything, while my mother lightened things up and at the same time made it all seem fun and glamorous. They were both fascinating people in their own ways. Living with them was certainly never dull.

Myriam and I had different kinds of adventures than my father's early exploits, but they were just as full of risks—mostly financial. But we met challenges head-on and were not afraid of the risks involved. We never imagined that my life would one day be at risk because we had decided to sell our family home.

* * *

I have never been afraid of taking a risk. Even now as my kidnappers head for Zabeth, my life is already at risk. I feel I have nothing to lose. My best bet for now is to play up my sick heart. Perhaps my captors, thinking I am sick and weak and therefore no threat to them, will let their guard down and provide me with an opportunity to escape. Or better yet, they will release me because they are afraid they'll be charged with my murder if I should die of a heart attack.

I don't have to do much acting here because truthfully I am feeling tired and weak. Slumped uncomfortably against the backseat, I let my mind drift to more comforting thoughts of my father. He certainly took risks as an explorer and had many "brainstorms" along the way. He even worked as a movie actor in Paris for a while. When he captured bank robbers in Nevada and met other threats, he play-acted to survive or to save someone else. Whether it was a plane crash or a battle with a desert sandstorm, my father always managed to get himself out of it. He claimed his good luck was the result of positive thinking and his guardian angel—but I think he was especially quick-witted, resourceful, and even courageous.

I can just hear him disagreeing with me now.

CHAPTER 21

A New Focus, 1916–1920

Horace

After my stint serving my country in World War I as an aerial photography instructor, I—now Captain Ashton— remained in New York and continued making documentary films, this time for Pathé Productions. For almost four years I focused my filmmaking on earthly subjects, moving away from the heavens that offered such freedom—and so many risks—and turned my camera on the exploration of earth's smallest subjects: microscopic organisms.

The results became known as the Argus Pictorial, a series of documentaries that focused on science, art, and educational subjects. It was produced in conjunction with the Museum of Natural History in New York and made available in local theaters as newsreels and to schools for educational purposes.

Pathé Productions' Argus Pictorial was one of the first screen magazines, and I was the editor. The December 1917 issue of *The Moving Picture World*[26] had this to say:

> What a peculiar type of man must be required to produce a "screen
> magazine"! He must, first of all, be a lover of nature, have an unlimited
> fund of miscellaneous knowledge and know his audiences. Just such a
> one is H. D. Ashton, head of the Argus Laboratories, Inc. . . . Always
> a lover of nature, he has kept up his natural science studies and is

---

26   H. D. Ashton, "Editor of the Argus Pictorial, New Pathé Productions, a Lover of Nature," in *The Moving Picture World*, 1 December 1917.

Microscopic Movie Marvels

How Invisible Atoms are Made to Prance on the Screen Like Wild Animals

By HORACE D. ASHTON

ARGUS PICTORIAL

(Insert) Horace D. Ashton. At work in the studio, with ... *stage set, camera ready, his actors under the microscope.*

SO FAR as I know, mine is one of the few successful experiments in the taking of motion pictures of micro-organisms, and the first to follow a continuity in the scenarios. If audiences find the films a tithe as interesting as I have found the making of them, my efforts will have been worth while. And the undertaking is by no means simple, as you shall see.

I arrange a sort of scenario in which the species to be filmed is permitted to work out his life story. In each case the problem of sustenance seems to dominate. Take, if you please, a "Vorticella"; or bell anamalculæ, the bell, which resembles a lily-of-the-valley, swings at the end of a contractile stem with which it fastens itself to other objects. The edge of the bell is fringed with cilia—fine, hair-like projections—which create a current in the water, thus attracting its food.

To secure this and similar motion pictures, the ob-

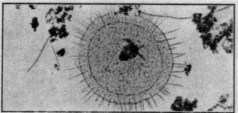

Beavers building a dam in the North woods.

Actino Sphaerium digesting young cyclops which he has devoured.

ject, magnified many diameters, plays its part in a field of action one-one-hundredths of an inch in width. The performer takes up a large portion of this space, and in one jump may move clear out of the field of observation. To manipulate the field with one hand while cranking the camera with the other is not an undertaking in which one can perfect himself in one lesson. When I am at work, the performer is magnified only two hundred, four hundred or eight hundred diameters, according to the power of the objective; but the motion picture projecting machine magnifies the film about one hundred and forty-four diameters, which must be multiplied by the four hundred or eight hundred aforesaid to get at the fact, and that is that the picture you see on the screen of microscopic life is magnified some thirty thousand diameters or more.

I have been fortunate in securing the friendly co-operation of men of high standing and authority, such as

Horace Ashton discovers the microscopic world.

affiliated with several of the leading scientific societies of America
. . . The Argus Pictorial, as presented by Pathé, will contain four or
five short educational subjects each fortnight, produced under his
direct supervision, assisted by a staff of men connected with some of
America's leading scientific institutions."

My work as the director of the Argus Pictorial was
fascinating, and I hoped to inspire others to become
interested in science. I spent my days in a glass–encased
studio on the roof of a New York City skyscraper (Chandler
Building on 42nd Street), studying microorganisms and
photographing them for the lay audience. Starting with
the amoeba, the simplest form of life, my assistants and
I worked in cooperation with the American Museum of
Natural History to make a progressive series of films that
represented all stages of animal life.

Rather than advertise an open casting call in the
newspaper, I tramped out into nature on the weekends
with my vials and test tubes to collect my performers
from the Bronx River or a particular pond near Flushing.
One Sunday, I walked for five miles along the Palisades in
search of stagnant, slimy water and found my biggest star
in a pool in the woods near Tenafly.

Back in the studio, the work was painstakingly slow.
I had to arrange my subjects on slides, focus them under
the microscope, replace the eyepiece with my motion
picture camera, and shoot the scene in about forty
seconds so as to not harm my subjects under the harsh
lights. I was occasionally confronted with a frivolous
performer, one that insisted on scampering about in the
most disconcerting manner, and as a director, I would have
to use my ingenuity to contain him. I don't know if it was
sentiment or gratitude for their performance that moved
me always to dismantle the "stage" very carefully and
return the microorganisms to their glass–bound habitat.
I could never bring myself to simply shake the droplet of
water onto the floor or wipe the slide clean with a towel.

The documentaries opened up a whole new world to me and to the general public, who had limited access to scientific knowledge at the time. My work was documented in the January 19, 1918, issue of *Scientific American*:[27]

A drop of water taken from a stagnant pond is rich in motion picture possibilities . . . To be sure, it does not present extraordinary promise when viewed with the naked eye, but under the critical gaze of the microscope, a new world is thrown open to the camera. For, with the drop of water as the "location," and with myriads of micro-organisms for the cast, there are comedies and dramas and educational features without end, for the motion picture screen. . . .

The first qualification of the micro-photoplay director is that he must be a born naturalist: he must not only be intensely interested in all forms of animal life, but must be intimately familiar with the subject. He must be ingenious, for the filming of the little performers calls for no mean ability at times. He must be a skilled photographer, for in the main, the work is one of photography. And, of course, he must know what is interesting to the public and know how to tell a story in pictures so that it will be instructive and entertaining. All of these qualifications are possessed by Horace D. Ashton. . . . Most important of all, his hobby is natural history.

My work received much acclaim, and I thoroughly enjoyed creating films that would make science come to life for students around the world. That same year, I wrote about my work in a magazine called *Reel and Slide*,[28] to explain its nature and make the public aware of its possibilities. I have always felt proud of my contributions to science and education in this pioneering phase of my career.

Even though I left school at age fifteen, I loved learning and continued to learn through my careers as a photojournalist, filmmaker, and explorer. I was taught

27   Austen Lescarboura, "Micro-Photoplays," in *Scientific American*, 19 January 1918.
28   H. D. Ashton, "Life Cycle of Micro-Organisms Animated for Classroom Work," in *Reel and Slide*, 1918.

that education is the great equalizer and knowledge is power. I prefer to think that knowledge is understanding; the more one knows, the less one fears.

December 1, 1917   THE MOVING PICTURE WORLD

H. D. Ashton

Editor of the Argus Pictorial, New Pathe Production, a Lover of Nature.

WHAT a peculiar type of man must be required to produce a "screen magazine!" He must, first of all, be a lover of nature, have an unlimited fund of miscellaneous knowledge and know his audiences.

Just such a one is H. D. Ashton, head of the Argus Laboratories, Inc., whose screen magazine, "Argus Pictorial," will first be presented to the public through Pathe Exchanges on November 18th.

Ashton was born and reared on a Virginia farm. Entering the newspaper business he went through the Japanese-Russian war for Collier's Weekly, and later with Underwood & Underwood visited many parts of the world. In 1910 he became an aviator, and in 1911 entered the motion picture business with the General Film Co., going into every branch of the industry.

Always a lover of nature, he has kept up his natural science studies—and is affiliated with several of the leading scientific societies of America.

The Argus Pictorial as presented by Pathe, will contain four or five short educational subjects each fortnight, produced under his direct supervision, assisted by a staff of men connected with some of America's leading scientific institutions.

H. D. Ashton.

No expense or effort will be spared to keep this Screen Magazine up to the high standard set by its creator. Already connections have been established in such far off lands as Australia, New Zealand, Africa, Japan and Alaska, and shortly we may expect to see interesting educationals and nature studies from these distant places among its features.

Newspaper article describes Horace Ashton's innovative screen magazine.

* * *

I decided to return to the world of mankind after investigating the microscopic world, but that venture was put on hold because of *another* call to serve my country. I could never refuse a request for help, especially when it came from my own government, and so I went to Haiti as a scout for the United States Marines.

From the moment I entered Haiti on horseback in 1906, I'd felt a great affinity with the land and its people. The Haitians must have recognized this because they welcomed me and treated me as one of their own. I returned to this beautiful nation as often as I could in the ensuing years. However, this was one time that I wished I was not there as an American because the United States occupied Haiti from 1915 to 1934.

In the early days of the American occupation, I believed this concept of occupation was the right thing to do. Haiti had two distinct classes—the small upper, or educated, class and the great majority non-educated, poor, subsistence-farming peasants. The educated Haitian preferred to concentrate on the intellectual world, leaving the hard labor to the masses. This led to the politico-military class, which had bled and tyrannized the masses for over one hundred years. Haitians had practically no civil rights.

This situation reached a critical stage in 1915, when a series of small revolutions followed Haiti's disputes of its foreign debts toward France. Political prisoners were executed; the president, who ordered the executions, was drawn and quartered; and arson, pillage, and rape followed. The first detachment of United States Marines landed and shortly thereafter restored order in the capital.

In 1919, while I was in Haiti acting as a scout for the marines and near the end of my stay, I wrote an article titled "Haiti To-Day," illustrated with my photographs,

Scribner's
Magazine
March 1920

entitled to the fruits of their labor, all
equally entitled to raise themselves as
high as possible, each in his own place,
without doing wrong to any of the rest.
It is the spirit of justice and fraternity
that must be our guide. And where are
we to look for leadership if not in institutions such as this—especially in this,
whose just and democratic spirit is its
most distinctive sign, the very hall-mark
by which it is and always has been known?

    Strong-hearted Mother of the North,
      Counting thy many-colored years,

And holding not the least in worth
    Those that were cast in want and fears—

Great Mother, thou art still the same,
    Whether in rags or purple drest—
To-day as when thine eaglets came
    To thy dark pines as to their nest.

We bid not *thee* to look abroad—
    Thine eyes have never sought the ground—
But us—oh, let our feet be shod
    Where *thy* thought flieth to be found!

Give *us* thy vision, us thy strength,
    To spread the truth which makes men free
And dying leave a land at length
    Worthy, O mighty heart, of thee!

HAITI TO-DAY

By Horace D. Ashton, F. A. G. S.

ILLUSTRATIONS FROM PHOTOGRAPHS BY THE AUTHOR

HAITI to-day is the scene of
the most interesting experiment in government that
may be found in this hemisphere. Strange as it may
seem, what the United
States is doing in Haiti and Santo Domingo is far better known throughout
South and Central America than here in
our own country. There isn't a doubt,
either, that, amidst all their talk of the
rights of small nations, those opponents
to the views of our representatives at the
Peace Conference were well posted on
every move we have made in that turbulent island.

This is due, in a great measure, to the
efficient work of the late Committee on
Public Information in giving wide publicity to those things which they deemed
it wise for the American public to know
and putting the "soft pedal" on activities which did not come under this cate-
gory. As a result, there are surprisingly
few Americans who know where Haiti and
Santo Domingo are, not to mention our
almost absolute control of the affairs of
both republics.

Lying between Cuba and Porto Rico,
directly in the path of steamers plying
between New York and the Canal Zone,
Haiti is at our very doors; so close, in

fact, that in March, 1919, three seaplanes alighted in the harbor of Port au
Prince, having left Charleston, S. C., the
same day. A moderately fast steamer
can make the run between New York and
Port au Prince in less than four days.

Although for a hundred years the country, torn by civil strife and bloody revolution, has gradually crumbled to financial ruin, it was formerly known as one of
the richest colonial possessions on the
globe.

To quote from the report of an expert
recently sent there to look into its agricultural and industrial possibilities:

"A conservative estimate of the total
value, at the present market prices, of the
products of Haiti in the year 1791 would
be not less than $30,000,000, as compared
with $12,000,000, the value of the exports
of Haiti for the fiscal year 1913–14."

While in 1914 there were only three or
four plantations in Haiti worthy of the
name, employing only a handful of
negroes under any semblance of intelligent supervision, the exports of the
French colony in the year 1791 were produced from over 7,000 plantations under
scientific management, and over half a
million blacks were actively employed,
under expert supervision, in these industries.

Council of war in front of the abandoned house of a Caco chief.
Left to right—Colonel Walter R. Hill, Captain Daggett, H. D. Ashton, and Lieutenant Powell. The three officers are the American officers of gendarmerie.

and confidence but their genuine affection as well. The children love him, and whenever he goes about the streets unofficially he can be seen with several little black kiddies trotting along by his side.

He is only one of a large number of young American officers of the gendarmerie who, by their keen insight into the psychology of the Haitian people, have won their respect, not only for themselves but for the American occupation. The educated and thinking Haitian cannot help but see that our intervention saved his country from utter ruin. Charles Moravia, Haitian minister to the United States, recently wrote:

"Now that the United States has extended its hand and offered to help the young republic, the hope may be entertained that its progress will be rapid, that the Haitian masses will be educated, their standards of life bettered, and that when the country becomes prosperous the American people will be doubly paid —in money, by an increase of their commerce, and in glory for having made another Cuba."

But there are exceptions to every rule. No plan for the reformation and betterment of any people has ever been attempted without its opponents. In the winter of 1918 a leader, with the traditional lust for political power, went about in the north and stirred up a small following, who openly declared themselves "Cacos," in opposition to what they termed "the white invasion." Marines were quickly despatched on his trail, and he and his followers were driven to the rugged, mountainous interior, where they are still giving us considerable trouble.

So brazen had the activities of these Cacos become by March, 1919, that Port au Prince began to show signs of unrest. The Cacos had ambushed a small detachment of gendarmes, all native soldiers,

333

These excerpts from the *Scribner's* magazine article detail Horace Ashton's presentation about Haiti.

for *Scribner's* magazine.[29] I also wrote another illustrated article for *The Nomad* about a night I spent alone in the ancient ruins of Citadel La Ferrier, Haitian ruler King Christophe's famous fortress near Cap Haitien on the north coast.

With the American occupation, the political situation in Haiti changed. A few months after the marines arrived, I happened to be present at a modern plantation—established with American capital—on payday, when several hundred Haitians received their first wages. It was curious to note the effect that actually receiving real money for their work had on these people. The workers could hardly believe their eyes; for many of them, it was the first money they had ever received for their labor.

It is safe to say that these men were in favor of the American occupation. Captain Homer Howell of Kentucky and his assistant, Lieutenant Stewart Taylor, a young Virginian, administered the military and civil affairs of the district at Port de Paix in a manner conforming to the highest American ideals. By their fair–mindedness, administration of impartial justice, and humanity, they won not only the people's confidence but their genuine affection as well.

Captain Howell and Lieutenant Taylor were only two of a large number of young American officers of the gendarmerie who, by their keen insight into the psychology of the Haitian people, won respect not only for themselves but for the American occupation. The gendarmes who served under them were loyal native Haitians who viewed the occupation favorably. The educated and thinking Haitian could not help but see that our intervention saved the country from utter ruin.

After a few years, a small group of people in the north, who called themselves Cacos, opposed the "white invasion" and promised to drive out the *blancs*, as the

---

29   Horace D. Ashton, "Haiti To-Day," in *Scribner's* magazine, Volume LXVII-22, March 1920.

Americans were called. The marines quickly reacted to the Cacos and drove them into hiding in Haiti's rugged mountainous interior—but not for long. This group became so bold and brazen that by March 1919 Port-au-Prince began to show signs of unrest. The Cacos ambushed a small detachment of gendarmes, all native soldiers, and killed all but one, who escaped and reported the fight. The Cacos adopted a policy of brutality that rivaled that of Attila the Hun. They hacked the bodies of any gendarme captured or killed with machetes and sent pieces of their victim to his friends as warnings. Rumors of their strength filtered into Port-au-Prince, as they captured villages, forced the men inhabiting them into service, and torched whatever was left behind.

Colonel Walter N. Hill, of the gendarmerie, declared martial law, and messengers were dispatched to the interior to inform citizens to come in and report. Following this ultimatum, patrols were sent into the interior and ordered to open fire on any bodies of armed men encountered in the countryside. The patrols consisted of two white officers, three or four marines, and about twenty gendarmes. No supplies could be carried, so the patrols had to live off the country. This proved serious in areas where the Cacos had burned all the houses, destroyed the gardens and cane fields, and driven off the cattle and horses. In fact, they swept the country as clean as did Sherman in his famous march to the sea.

I was allowed to accompany Colonel Hill and Captain Daggett on one of these patrols, which lasted for ten days. During that time we traveled several hundred miles through the most rugged and desolate—but most beautiful—regions in all the West Indies. Our food consisted of the flesh of an occasional stray beef cow, which we would shoot; our bed was the hard ground.

In Las Cahobas we were surrounded by Cacos. We could see their campfires in the surrounding hills and hear the weird call of their conch shells at night as they echoed down the valleys. Twice reports reached us that we were to be attacked and the town burned, but the Cacos didn't come.

When we started out, there was some conjecture as to what might happen if one of our patrols ran into a really strong body of Cacos. Would the gendarmes stand by their white officers? Weren't they, after all, really fighting their own kind? To observe these men closely, one could not help but think of their dark history, and wonder.

As the days went by, we had frequent encounters with the enemy, but the gendarmes still stood by. Our skirmishes with the Cacos were always running fights. They'd gather on the crest of a hill some distance away, blow their conch shells, and yell defiance at us. When we'd get near, they would appear on the next ridge, some distance away. They never actually confronted us until one day when they ambushed a young lieutenant who had gone to an outpost to inspect his gendarmes. He was shot under the right arm, severing his spine. His men surrounded him and fought off the Cacos until the marines arrived.

A second detachment of marines was sent from Cuba to assist the occupying forces. Eventually the Cacos were captured or killed. Most were found to be of the poor, uneducated class.

One serious consequence of this Caco warfare, among many, was its paralyzing effect on the interior's commerce. The market women were afraid to risk robbery and bodily injury on the roads and did not bring their produce to market. Famine threatened some localities as a result.

In my March 1920 article for *Scribner's* magazine, I made a plea for foreign investors. "Although the Caco troubles have died down, they are not at an end. Haiti needs to reorganize her finances and interest foreign governments in investments. Since the new constitution of June 19, 1918, was adopted, foreigners can now own land in Haiti."[30]

---

30   Ibid.

The American occupation raised concerns at home. As James M. Callahan, a professor of history and political science at West Virginia University, said, "The new American responsibility in Haiti—whose government is an engine without a flywheel, threatening its owns destruction by its own energy—is far greater than that assumed over other weak governments in the Caribbean region, and may raise problems far different from those of the other territories in which the American government exercises supervisory control."[31]

* * *

The Great War, as World War I was then known, was over by the time I returned to New York after my year in Haiti. The world had changed. New frontiers had been created, and I was eager to explore them.

In this time before television and sound films, there was a great demand from the postwar audience for public lectures, particularly travel lectures with accompanying film. Some years earlier, my lecture in Paris about Vodou had been well received, and since I'd held my own with the best of them around the table at the Explorers Club, I fancied myself an amusing storyteller. That talent, combined with my skill with a motion picture camera and my flying ability, would provide me a good living as a lecturer and allow me to pursue my passion for exploration.

To obtain material for my lectures, I decided to take a yearly journey to some interesting place off the beaten track. Over the next ten years I traveled extensively, learning about different civilizations, making motion pictures, and lecturing. The 1920s was my period of intense travel and exploration, and through my journeys I became a social scientist.

---

31   James M. Callahan, Ph.D. taught at West Virginia University in the early twentieth century and wrote many books and articles on history and government. The source of this quote cannot be located.

But before I took off to exotic locales and began my career as a lecturer, a couple of other jobs came my way, so I headed to Nevada. In 1920, I was engaged by the city of Reno to make motion pictures to publicize their first great rodeo, and as part of the promotion, I hired actress Norma Shearer to be the rodeo queen. It was a great success, and the rodeo became a well–attended annual event.

While in Nevada, I was paid well by a Hollywood studio, first to shoot rodeo footage and then to cast and produce what turned out to be an excellent western called *Black Steve of the Sierras*, later released by Universal. It took us only a month to make this western, and I considered the experience more of a picnic than a job because I had so much fun doing it. When the picture was finished, we debuted it at Reno's largest theater as a benefit performance. That night, a blown fuse plunged the theater into total darkness for half an hour and forced us to scramble for kerosene lanterns. It added an exciting twist to our wrap party.

That wasn't the only plot twist for me, and what happened next would make a good scene in a western movie.

I have always felt a strong sense of responsibility toward my fellow human beings. Doing the right thing has always been important to me, and I had an opportunity to do just that in Nevada. While in Reno, I was appointed deputy sheriff and instructed to keep an eye on local property because trouble had been reported by the Union Pacific Railroad. My title required powers of observation, and mine were keen, but it also gave me an opportunity to take action.

One day when I heard that two young masked men had robbed the bank in Carson City and had been seen traveling toward the mountains, I had one of my "brainstorms," as I liked to call my regular moments of inspiration. I dashed to my room, put on some old clothes, loaded up my small car with supplies—coffee, bacon, eggs, pancake flour, axes, a shovel, a pair of handcuffs, blankets, and a pup tent— and then drove toward Lake Tahoe. Since the mountains led to the California border, a logical place for them to run, this seemed the most likely route they'd take.

When I stopped for gas, I asked the beefy attendant if he'd been busy. "No, sir. Been pretty quiet up here except for two strangers passin' through a few hours ago. Headed north towards Fallen Leaf Lake, they was," he said, wiping his greasy hand on the front of his overalls before taking my money.

I drove through the woods, along the lake road covered in pine needles. I didn't see anyone. Further on, the narrow road wound through a valley of rich pastures, and in the distance I glimpsed snow-covered mountains reaching up over forest-clad foothills. The only sounds I heard were bird songs and cow bells. When nightfall came, I spotted a small campfire and parked near it. There was no one in sight, so I walked into the camp, sat down, and put another piece of wood on the fire.

A short time later, a man approached. "Are you up here all by yourself?" he asked.

"Yes, I'm looking to set up my campsite, and I happened to see your fire. I love this area and was lucky to have a few days off work," I added casually.

"Well, why don't you join us?" he asked. "My friend and I came up here to fish."

I went to my car and got out the food and my gear and then cooked a fine supper for my newfound "friends." They were grateful, as they explained they'd become lost and had brought nothing to eat. I found that odd, considering they were on a fishing trip, but kept my thoughts to myself. Another odd thing about their so-called fishing trip was that their only camping equipment appeared to be a couple of ragged old blankets and a scratched metal flask containing some kind of foul-smelling liquor. I saw no evidence of fishing gear. What I did see, however, were suspicious-looking bulges in their clothing!

We sat around the campfire telling stories and getting along famously until the stars grew thick overhead and the cool of the Lake Tahoe night made us draw closer to the fire. When they passed me the flask, I only pretended to take a nip. It was well after midnight when the two finally decided to bed down for the night, and I went to my nearby tent and crawled inside. I lay still in the darkness, fully dressed with my boots on, listening to the hooting of owls and the wind in the trees, waiting for the sound of snoring, which soon reached my ears.

About three in the morning, I crept out of my tent as soundlessly as a cat stalking prey. The two men lay wrapped in their blankets, sound asleep near the embers of the dying fire. Reaching dangerously close to one of the snoring men, I carefully slipped his gun from his jacket pocket and then checked to make sure it was loaded. He grunted but didn't wake up. I let out my breath.

I managed to grab the second man's gun a fraction of a second before he awoke, sputtering and rubbing his eyes as if he didn't know where he was. When they tried to reach for their weapons, they cursed loudly at the shock of discovering they had been disarmed. Then, seeing me standing there with one of their own guns pointed at them, they began to bargain with me. They offered to give me half the booty and even told me where they'd hidden it in a hole in the trunk of a nearby tree.

I informed them that I was a deputy sheriff, and they were under arrest. Without taking my eyes off the two men, I tossed them the handcuffs and then forced them at gunpoint to handcuff themselves together. I put the handcuffed bank robbers in my car before retrieving a khaki knapsack full of money from the tree trunk and then we all drove to the sheriff's office in Truckee.

As it turned out, the authorities had been trying to catch these two criminals for a long time. Before they robbed the Carson City bank, they had robbed two Union Pacific stations. The bank gave me a $500 reward for my work, and the railroad also sent a check to express its gratitude.

* * *

My decade as a lecturer/explorer really began when the Compagnie Generale Transatlantique, having just inaugurated a chain of tourist hotels from Morocco to Tunisia, hired me to create motion pictures that would attract American tourists to these exotic locations. The hotels were first—rate, and the company a very cooperative employer. It was a perfect job for me because not only would I get to explore unusual places and learn about different cultures, but the all—expenses—paid trips would provide me with new material for my travel lectures. During the early 1920s, through photography assignments like this one, I was offered a number of paid opportunities to explore North Africa and study the people and their customs, dwellings, and religion.

In 1920 flight was not yet an option for international travel, so I departed New York Harbor on a ship bound for Spain. From there, I planned to make my way by car and train to southern Italy, where I would board another ship for North Africa.

While driving an open Buick from Barcelona toward Madrid near sunset, I got my second flat tire that day. I had no means of repairing it on the road, so I sat there hoping someone would come along whom I could persuade to take me into the city.

A few minutes later, a large, sleek Hispano—Suiza came along, driven by a good—looking young man with a snap—brim hat. Surprisingly, a uniformed chauffeur sat beside him. They stopped and asked if I was in trouble.

I explained my sad situation, and the driver responded by telling his chauffeur to remain with my car. Then he invited me to get in beside him. Once inside, I immediately recognized my Good Samaritan as King Alfonso of Spain. He was very kind, and we talked a great deal on the way into Madrid. When he learned that I had been one of the founders of the Explorers Club, he insisted that I accept his hospitality in the palace.

I stayed with King Alfonso for several days, during which I met his cousin "Jimmy," the Duke de Alba. When they asked me if I liked bullfights, I answered honestly that like most Americans I did not. "I have seen bullfights in Mexico and Colombia, and I think it is a cruel sport," I told them.

The king replied, "But Ashton, you missed the real beauty of the sport, the delicate grace and precision of every movement of the matador. It is equal to the finest ballet. We have at present perhaps the most wonderful of all our great matadors—Joselito. Jimmy, take Ashton down to Seville on Sunday, and let him see a real matador at work."

Reluctantly, I accompanied Jimmy to the bullfight, but as I watched the remarkable choreography of this great matador, I had to admit the king had been right. The enthusiasm of the crowd was so contagious that I joined in, yelling as loudly as the others. I had changed my mind about bullfights, but I didn't realize how deeply it had affected me until many years later when I dreamed—and painted in full color—every detail of this bullfight

At the time, Spain affected me deeply in another way. As I traveled through Andalusia, heard its native music, breathed its perfumed air, and studied its colorful and ravishing Moorish architecture, the country awakened memories in me that reinforced my belief in reincarnation. I would later trace these memories to events in the march of Hannibal's invading forces that had crossed from Carthage in Africa to Europe at the "Pillars of Hercules," now Gibraltar. In this other life, I became convinced that I had apparently headed eastward with them across Europe toward the ill—fated siege of Rome.

CHAPTER 22

Contact

Butch
April 5, 2001
2:24 p.m.

As my captors wind through the intimidating snarl of traffic in Port-au-Prince, my breathing grows labored, and I close my eyes, feigning drowsiness. I blink them open and glance at the leader. "Honestly, I'm not doing very well here. I must have lots of fresh water to drink, and I need air."

Apparently I make my point. The kidnappers stop brazenly at a store in one of the busiest sections of town and buy me several plastic pouches of drinking water. But they leave me no opportunity to attract attention or attempt escape. The water helps a little, but I continue to feign signs of weakness, making my body limp and my breathing shallow.

Although they seem somewhat concerned about my medical problems, my captors continue on to Source Zabeth. During the more than half-hour journey, I continue to pretend to grow weaker and less coherent. This isn't much of a stretch, since I've lost a lot of blood and am exhausted.

As we leave the city, heading toward the sacred site, I hear my cell phone ring again and again from inside the glove compartment, but I am helpless to answer it. Through the whole ordeal my cell phone rings practically nonstop, and my business band radio (walkie-talkie) continues to call my name. The four hoodlums holding me captive ignore the insistent sounds, but I can tell by the way the leader presses his gun into my ribs at each interruption that he is rattled by all the ringing and radio traffic. I wonder why he doesn't answer the call and make ransom demands or else toss the phone out the window.

Just then, radio static cuts through the momentary silence in the car. "Butch, for God's sake, where are you?" Myriam's voice demands. She is still unsure of what has happened to me.

"Who *is* that?" the leader finally asks.

"It's my wife. She's worried about me," I say feebly, still keeping up the act.

He reaches into the front seat and picks up the radio. "Madame Ashton, we have your husband. If you ever want to see him alive again, you will have to pay us one-point-five million U.S. dollars."

Now she knows! My wife's worst fear is realized. The radio is quiet for a second.

"Prove to me that he's still alive," Myriam says in a shocked but amazingly controlled voice.

Good for you, Myriam. You tell them.

"Careful what you say," the leader hisses at me in good English and then holds the radio up to my mouth.

"I'm okay," I say weakly.

He snatches the receiver away. "There you go, madame; your husband is alive. Now let's talk about how he is going to stay that way." The leader discusses finances with Myriam on the radio, and I can hear both sides of the conversation.

My dear wife is showing as much bravado as I had shown, and knowing how terrified she must be, I am proud of her. She confirms what I told them about my health and needing medication, and then she makes them the same offer of $20,000 to $30,000. It really is all the money we readily could have available.

* * *

Myriam and I are both hard workers, and together we make a strong team. We found ways to make a living, to educate our children, and to take care of my parents until their last days, and we managed to have fun doing it. We faced many challenges, but we had an unbelievably fantastic life in Haiti and a series of successful business ventures. You name it; we did it—fishing company, plantations, nightclubs, restaurants, resorts, travel agency, airline, assembly factories, and a car dealership. With each new enterprise, we learned valuable skills and came up with new ideas. The friendships we made along the way were the biggest treasure of all. Life was nonstop—one entrepreneurial adventure after another. They were different kinds of adventures than my father's early exploits, but they were just as full of risks.

About a year into our marriage—with both of us working and bringing in small salaries—we were having a hard time financially, due to the burden of paying my parents' mortgage. But we were clever and devised a plan to solve the problem. We decided to rent Villarosa to the German ambassador at a good price and rent a more affordable home for three years. Together we convinced my parents of our idea. We found a comfortable house to rent and moved our family into it.

I took a job with Myriam's uncle on Plantation Dauphin, a 33,000-acre American-owned plantation that produced and exported sisal for the upholstery and twine industry. Plantation Dauphin was a six-hour drive from Port-au-Prince, but my salary alone could pay for a rental house. We moved there, began saving, and thought we were doing well.

Approximately one year later, Nebojsa Dimovic, my mother's brother—an uncle I had never met—arrived in Haiti on a cruise ship from London. After World War II he had made a substantial fortune in real estate in London and still owned considerable property there. His daughter, an only child, had married someone with whom he didn't get along. He treated me like a long-lost son and asked me to join his business, because his daughter and son-in-law were not interested.

Uncle Nebojsa flew me to London, began to teach me about the real estate business, and showed me around London and his company, Chesham Properties Ltd. He refused to address me as Butch because he said it sounded like an American gangster. Instead, he called me Marc, the "beautiful name" I had been given.

During the five days in London together, he made an amazing offer for me to go into business with him. He deposited 150,000 pounds sterling (about half a million dollars in 1965, equivalent to roughly $7.5 million today) into a bank account in Nassau, Bahamas, with the conditions that I invest and manage this money. My share of the profits would be 50 percent. I could invest the money in anything, anywhere I chose within the pound sterling area, but I could not exchange the money for another currency. For example, I could not invest it in Haiti or the United States— because we would lose too much on the currency exchange.

Overnight Myriam and I went from being two kids struggling to make ends meet and wondering how we'd pay the next bill to investors with substantial capital. Excitedly we traveled around the Caribbean, looking for prospects in the British-sterling area. After three months, we decided on Freeport in the Bahamas. We spent another two months in Freeport, setting up our business, and began negotiations to buy a newly built, twenty-apartment complex known as the Racquet Club.

All the while, my uncle's strict accountant, or "bean counter," from Chesham Properties questioned every charge we made on our expense account. I would submit weekly expense reports, and I'd get letters back from him weekly, which asked questions like "Marc, we need to know why Myriam spent two dollars for her hair. Why did you spend three dollars for a taxi when you can take the bus?" After the third month I began to get frustrated with the constant questions, explaining that there was no public transportation in Freeport, we were on an undeveloped island, and the only way to get from Point A to Point B was either to walk, take a taxi, or rent a car.

Just as we were about to close the deal on the Racquet Club complex, I began to think I was chasing the wrong rainbow. Once we acquired the Racquet Club, we would be committed to living in the Bahamas.

I had second thoughts. Once again I realized I was the one who had chosen to be responsible for taking care of my mother and father as they aged.

I talked this over with Myriam and reminded her that she had agreed to marry my parents when she married me. "What are we doing in Freeport, putting up with all this nitpicking?" I asked, frustrated. Then I admitted, "I got sidetracked chasing a buck and abandoned my primary objective." That realization made us decide to return to Haiti.

I called my uncle that afternoon, told him the deal was off, and returned his money. We walked away from half a million dollars, a small fortune, to go back to an uncertain future. We returned to Haiti with literally no money to our name. Myriam's father had to meet us at the airport to pay the airport tax upon our arrival.

* * *

Nearly forty years after walking away from such a fortune, now that Myriam and I earned everything we have through hard work, I realize that my life has come down to money—the almighty dollar—once more.

Doubt and fear register on the face of the novice sitting beside me, and I hear the driver and the killer muttering in Creole in the front seat. Obviously the leader doesn't believe Myriam. "If you want to see your husband alive, take as long as you need to get the one-point-five million dollars ready," he demands. "I will call you back with instructions."

Before she can protest again, he cuts off the conversation and tosses the radio back into the front seat.

* * *

There is no reasoning with the leader. I must be losing my mind under stress, but his stubbornness reminds me of my father, or maybe it's just that my mind wants to escape to familiar thoughts.

Dad did whatever he wanted to do *his* way, and often made decisions for others. He expected his sons to unquestioningly embrace all he'd learned from his studies and experience over the years and to thirst for knowledge as much as he did. He expected we would understand the importance of prayer and meditation and embrace that too.

My days were too short already, and I worked long and hard to make ends meet. Stopping to meditate—to do nothing— seemed a waste of time to me. I would often return home from work at one or two o'clock in the morning to find Dad in his chair in the studio, his dog dozing at his feet, still studying religion or meditating. "It's late, Dad. Why don't you go to bed and get some sleep?" I would gently suggest.

"There will be plenty of time to sleep when I die, but for now, I need to learn more," he always said, looking up at me with a peaceful gaze. "You need to meditate, son. You spend far too much time on the day-to-day things. Practice disconnecting like I've taught you. Learn how to get your head in the right place."

Whenever he attempted to encourage me to meditate, I would challenge his reasoning but never his beliefs. "Dad, before I can get my head in the right place, I need to get my pocket in the right condition. Somebody needs to put food on the table."

He would sigh softly but without judgment. "Butch, you don't understand. That is all part of the meditation process. If you clear your mind and think positively, then things will work out positively."

"I understand that you believe that, Dad." At this point in the conversation I would have to make an effort to keep my anger in check. "But for me there's got to be action . . . more than just praying or meditating. Somebody's got to get out there and do it."

Our familiar conversation served no purpose. While our two lives overlapped and we enriched each other in many ways, we processed life differently, often in direct opposition. Typically, Dad would turn back to his books, and I would go upstairs to my bedroom to get some sleep. I don't know when he rested, but he was always up, and dressed—bow tie and all—when Myriam and I joined him for breakfast early the next morning, before leaving for work again.

Myriam and I are a team; we're both visionaries with the stamina to work hard and accomplish our dreams. We worked side by side for many years, mostly in agreement, but just for fun I love to tell the story of the time I fired my wife.

We had our travel agency then, and one day we had a little spat about the way something was supposed to be done. I told her I was the boss of the business and the one to make the final decisions. She wouldn't back down, so I fired her and told her to go home.

When I returned home later, she met me at the door, hands on her hips, demanding to know what I was doing there. "Uh . . . I've come home from work." I stated the obvious.

"Well, I'm the boss of the house and the one to make the final decisions here. You're fired!" she said.

Fortunately, we worked things out and had a good laugh about it, so I wasn't forced to find a new place to live.

Now, during the worst moment of our lives, Myriam and I are still working as a team. Hearing her brave voice on the radio reminds me of all the reasons I want to live. Besides hugging my daughters and spoiling my grandchildren, there are still many things I want to do. After having heart surgery and getting another chance at life, I am not about to give up without a fight and die alone in the back woods of a country I grew up in and love, all because my captors consider me a rich *blanc*.

* * *

I would often ask my father for advice when I had a problem or concern, because I valued his wisdom and knowledge. While his perspective and beliefs were different from mine, he had so much experience and many acquaintances in many areas. Even after his retirement from diplomatic life, he still knew many of the political players. It was natural for me to come to him.

There were times I'd be considering a particular investment or considered changing investments I already held that might be affected by the political situation. In this volatile economy and changing governments, it was important for Myriam and me to know how political changes might affect our livelihood. For instance, I might say, "Dad, you know so-and-so, and he has now been made minister of commerce. I'm trying to make an honest living, and I need to know what I'm up against. Are these people responsible? You always talk about integrity. Is his family known for its integrity?"

"Sit down, son," Dad would usually say. "Listen to the *Daily Word*. You need to take time to read this and come to greater understanding. This message we read today will help you tomorrow."

His abstract responses were frustrating, but occasionally, he did share valuable information with me. In retrospect, I wonder if he wasn't being obtuse on purpose, to teach me how to stand on my own two feet. I understand now that there was much more to the man than what I saw on the surface. He rarely said anything without purpose.

Horace Ashton met the world and the people in it on his own terms. It had always worked out for him, and he attributed his success to the positive frame of mind, which he achieved through meditation. He was only trying to teach his sons to handle life in the same manner he had handled it.

As I've said, our priorities were different, but we were similar in several important ways. My father and I both lived life *actively*. We did things, whether it was diving, or painting, or climbing mountains in search of orchids, or building a boat, or renovating a house, or building a resort, or negotiating a business deal, or managing a citrus grove, a travel agency, an airline, a car dealership—we were fully engaged. Even in his later years, Dad was constantly occupied, creating or studying or meditating or reading his *Daily Word*.

Not only did he participate in life actively, but Dad had passion for what he did. Later on, his passion for his experiences and his desire to educate others came through in the telling of tales on that tropical Haitian island. I admired these traits in him, and I like to think he passed them on to me, even if I manifested them in different ways.

Unlike me, my father could never stay in one place for long. Adventures awaited.

CHAPTER 23

North African Explorations, Early 1920s

Horace

After my experiences in Spain, I boarded a ship and sailed across the Mediterranean to French North Africa (Morocco, Algeria, and Tunisia), anxious to explore new frontiers. What I couldn't know then was that I would eventually find a place that would touch my heart almost as deeply as Haiti—the Sahara Desert.

I was enamored of an interesting theory about North Africa: the Celtic people had originated in Asia and trekked to Ireland and Scotland by way of Arabia, Africa, and Spain, leaving behind them the troglodytes and the Basques on the march of Tuaregs, who are of Berber origin. Before I left to explore this theory, I was quoted in the *New York Evening Post*: "The most fascinating discoveries in this field are those which have to do with the arts of the African peoples as compared to the Scottish and Irish. Their languages are entirely different. They are alike in physical characteristics to a certain extent. But their greatest likeness is to be found in their music and their jewelry."[32]

Travel to Morocco had been restricted before 1919, and tourism in the region was just opening up. However, Christians were given limited access to certain areas

---

32   Mann Hatton, "This Enchanted Isle," in *New York Evening Post*, New York City, New York, 22 July 1926.

of these heavily Muslim countries. In the city of Fez,[33] Christians were not permitted to enter certain streets that bordered on important mosques.

As a student of world religions, I was fascinated by the rituals the Muslims practiced on a daily basis. While staying in Fez, each night I enjoyed the harmonious calls of the *muezzins* (Muslim criers that called the faithful to prayer) that rang from the balconies of minarets (slender towers attached to mosques). These melodious sounds that filled the nighttime streets touched me in a spiritual way and added to the exotic atmosphere of the city. I learned that there is a league of muezzins, and they are trained to call harmoniously in beautiful tenor, baritone, and bass voices each hour during the night. Their cries do not disturb those who are sleeping, but I can attest that they leave a lasting spiritual and emotional impression on those who are awake.

In the daytime, the maze of winding, narrow alleyways, where one could easily get lost, was lined with market stalls, noisy with the bustle of people and full of colorful fabrics and rugs. The sound of tinkling chimes seemed to follow me everywhere. While in Morocco, I enjoyed touring different cities, but it wasn't always easy to make motion pictures. The Koran prohibits the reproduction of any living thing, so the Moors were reluctant to be photographed.

I used a specially designed camera that was not only different in appearance from the usual moving picture camera but also was noiseless. Most of the time I kept my camera hidden and attempted to shoot on the sly. If asked what I was doing, I replied, "I'm surveying." An American newspaper headline later credited me with being the "first to put the Moors on movie film." I believe I was the first photographer to take any pictures of the interior of Morocco.

* * *

---

33   Known as Fés on today's maps.

Seeking adventure and spurred on by my desire to learn more about local culture and religious practices, I decided to travel away from the cities that had been civilized by the French. I left Fez and headed east toward the Algerian border town of Oujda. At the time, the French were having great difficulty with the Riff mountaineers, a fiercely independent Berber tribe that descended and murdered travelers who were on the road at night. I arranged to spend the night in Taza, a fortified post on the main route, so that I could avoid these cutthroats.

During my visit to Taza, I was allowed to go outside the walls and wander about until sunset. As I sat on the ground near the gate watching the setting sun, I could touch ten or fifteen varieties of tiny, multicolored wild flowers that grew in abundance. The nearby hills were aglow with yellow flowers interspersed with blood—red poppies—a veritable artist's palette.

When the guard closed the gates for the night, I came inside and met a colonel of the French Tank Corps who had been enjoying some wine and became quite talkative. As we conversed and he learned that I was there to make motion pictures, he said, "I have something wonderful for you. Come back to Fez with me tomorrow morning, and I'll arrange for you to fly over a battle that will take place between Arab horsemen and French tanks in a few days!"

I took him at his word and agreed to accompany him, although I could not imagine such an unusual battle. A few days later, we flew out to a point in the desert where the mismatched opponents stood opposite each other—a large troop of Riff horsemen holding their guns in the air, and a number of light French tanks lined up on the road. As the signal was given, the tanks started up a steep, rugged hill while the horsemen galloped down the hill directly toward them.

Apparently the Riff mountaineers had never seen tanks, and they did not know to be afraid of them. They charged at the tanks, shooting into the gun ports and waving to me from their saddles between shots. I flew above this unbelievable scene, standing in the plane's cockpit while turning the camera's crank. The Riffs did succeed in putting three of the tanks out of commission before they galloped off, but they left their dead and wounded on the battlefield to reap their rewards in paradise. When we returned to Fez, the general reprimanded the colonel and confiscated my film, which was the most novel footage I ever shot.

* * *

A few days later, I witnessed another strange and deadly ritual during the fête of Sidi Aissa, a Muslim saint, near Meknes, a town just west of Fez. The saint was alleged to have been born on a low conical mountain that now held his shrine, about 1,000 feet up. Centuries ago, a wide road was constructed straight up the side of the mountain to the shrine.

For this celebration, spectators and the faithful lined both sides of the road all the way to the top, where more than fifty of the sect's fanatical devotees had assembled. They were lined up in formation, row upon row of them, ready to charge. The men in the front row were armed with broad, short-handled battle-axes that flashed in the sun. As they started down the hill, the devotees screamed a chant. The men in the front line took their battle-axes and began to chop at their own foreheads until their white robes were crimson with blood. When they became blinded or weakened by the loss of blood, they fell and rolled for some distance. Then a man from the second row dashed forward, grabbed the fallen ax, and began chopping at his own forehead. This pattern continued. As one line fell, men from the next line rushed in to take their places. The smell of blood and the sound of screaming cries cut through the horrific chaos on the hot, dusty hillside. Only a few reached the base of the hill under their own power, while the fallen were carried down by their companions who had not had a go with the axes.

To complete this gruesome ritual, these fanatics marched thirty kilometers into town. At midnight the group entered the town square on hands and knees, driving a full−grown sheep before them. When they were all inside, they attacked the sheep, killing it with their knives and devoured the entire carcass, bloody and raw.

The next day in the new hotel in Fez, I dined with a French officer at a quiet table covered with clean white linen and set with silver and crystal, while ceiling fans turned lazily overhead and ruffled the fronds of the potted palms.

* * *

After witnessing these rituals in northern Morocco, I traveled to Marrakech in the south to watch the storytellers and snake charmers in the great square. I was allowed to watch, but I was not allowed to make motion pictures.

Anxious to film exotic Moroccan culture that would promote tourism, I contacted my good friend Walter Harris, an Englishman I'd met earlier who had worked for the *London Times* in Tangiers. Well connected in Morocco, Walter now lived in Marrakech. He persuaded a group of Schleaur dancers to perform for me in his courtyard.

I made a contract with their leader, agreeing to pay him a certain amount for one hour's dancing. Before the dance began, they spied my camera and left. I was upset, but Walter intervened on my behalf and took me to visit El Glaoui, the ruler of South Morocco. After Walter explained the situation, El Glaoui summoned the troupe and told them if they didn't carry out their part of the contract at once, they would all be put to death.

El Glaoui was a most remarkable man. He had been a powerful bandit chief, collecting tribute from all the caravans that passed through the Atlas Mountains with their cargoes of ivory, ostrich plumes, wool, and other products from Central Africa to the markets of Morocco and the outside world. When the French took over Morocco, they made him vice sultan—in essence, the ruler of the south—and gave him the authority to collect all taxes for the French government. Since El Glaoui's daughter had married a son of the sultan, it was a cozy arrangement.

El Glaoui had a magnificent palace in Marrakech, whose palm-fringed garden pools reflected the snow-covered peaks of the Atlas Mountains. He also owned a mountain stronghold a great distance from the city where he invited me to take part in a falcon hunt for the moufflon, or mountain sheep, and gazelles. I journeyed with him in a royal caravan, winding our way up dizzying heights to this ancient fortress, where I witnessed the power he had over the people of these mountains. He was constantly being summoned for a conference with chiefs from neighboring regions.

When we went out into the hills to hunt with the falcons, I was amazed at how well trained these wild birds were. To see them circle around far up in the air and then dive like an arrow on their prey below and kill with one stroke of their deadly claws was unbelievable. Afterward they'd always return to the wrist from which they'd flown.

A strong, proud man, El Glaoui enjoyed the power he held in south Morocco for a number of years after I met him. His charmed life ended eventually, after he was forced to apologize to an exiled sultan who had been pardoned and then returned to power. Apparently, the sultan had been told that El Glaoui had said something against him while he was in exile. The French forced El Glaoui to apologize to the sultan publicly—to get down on his knees, kiss the sultan's feet, and swear his allegiance.

El Glaoui died a few days later. Many believed he had become disconsolate and died from a broken heart.

* * *

Wanting to explore North Africa further and gather more material for my lectures, I bid farewell to the very much alive–and–well El Glaoui and my friend Walter Harris in Marrakech.

Then I returned briefly to Fez, where I prepared to continue my journey eastward. Crossing the border into Algeria, I headed to Sidi–bel–Abbes, the headquarters of the famous French Foreign Legion. I reported to the commandant and was assigned a room in the officers' quarters for the few nights I was expected to stay.

The first evening I spent in town, talking with several Arabs in the coffeehouses. When I returned, the gate to the legion's compound was locked. I knocked loudly, but there was no response. I then walked several blocks to another gate but still couldn't raise anyone. So I climbed the wall, dropped over inside, walked through alleys past several men, and made my way to my quarters.

One of the officers asked how I got in so late. When I told him, he said, "*Mon dieu*, the sentries have orders to shoot anyone entering after hours without permission. In the case of anyone climbing the gates or wall, they have orders to shoot first and ask questions later. You are one lucky man!" I smiled, believing he was right.

Several days later, I hitched a plane ride from the headquarters with a French Foreign Legion pilot to the Mediterranean coastal city of Algiers (Alger); the view out toward that azure sea was magnificent, and I got some wonderful aerial footage en route, including a view of the waterfront hotel that would surely attract tourists.

In the bustling port of Algiers, I continued to look for interesting subjects to film. One Sunday I found a bonanza. It had been a quiet morning, and I was in my hotel room overhauling and cleaning my motion picture camera. I had just reassembled and loaded it when I heard a great commotion in the street below. Rushing out to the balcony, I looked down to discover that a ship carrying a large group of pilgrims returning from Mecca had just docked. Passengers disembarked as cargo was unloaded.

Excited, I dashed down three flights with my heavy

camera and tripod on my shoulder, and ran up the street ahead of the oncoming procession. I set up my tripod and camera and waited out of sight until they drew near, knowing they would object if they saw my intention. As they approached, I stepped in front of them and cranked the camera.

The pilgrim leaders screamed at me, gathering rocks to stone me as they began to run at me. I grabbed the camera by the tripod and swung it in an arc to protect myself.

A man in the crowd ordered, "Run for your hotel. I'll save the camera."

Recognizing him as a porter whom I'd employed several times, I handed him the camera. Stones flying, I took off at top speed down the street to the hotel without looking back. I sprinted through the lobby and up the three flights to my room, where I collapsed on my bed, breathless but unhurt.

Within the hour, the porter appeared with the camera. I paid him well for his rescue. Privately I gave thanks that I hadn't been torn to pieces by the fanatical throng as a friend of mine had in Turkey, while doing the same thing.

* * *

From Algiers, I toured by road along the beautiful Mediterranean coast to Tunisia. Along the way, I stopped at a small hotel for lunch, sitting on the outside terrace, where I noticed all the tables and chairs were chained to the ground. When I asked why, the manager explained that the forest around the hotel was infested with a tribe of large green monkeys, like those of Gibraltar. During the summer, families from nearby Algiers would come to the restaurant and bring loaves of bread to lure the monkeys down from the trees to be fed. The monkeys had become so used to it that they would grab anything they could get their hands on, including the tables and chairs. Tourists were warned to keep handbags and cameras out of sight.

That day, I unexpectedly managed to get some remarkable films of monkey life. One old monkey made the most wonderful and grotesque faces to amuse the pink baby in his care. I imagined they were grandfather and grandson. It caused me to wonder if I would one day tell this story to my grandchildren.

I made it to Tunisia without having my camera stolen by monkeys and headed to the coastal city of Kairouan, where I planned to visit the famous dervishes. These dervishes were one of a number of various Muslim orders dedicated to a life of poverty and chastity. Some dervish orders practiced howling; others were fond of spinning around until they fainted from exhaustion or dizziness.[34] Curious as usual, I wanted to learn more about the religious rituals of the dervish orders.

In Kairouan I found an amazing ceremony at one of the *tekkas*, as the dervishes' mosques were called. Thirty dervishes sat in a great circle on the tekkas's highly polished marble floor, bare headed, with their long hair flowing down their backs. Their arms were locked around each other as they swayed from side to side in unison, chanting wildly. A green—turbaned mullah, who had been to Mecca, stood in the center of the circle watching his charges as they worked themselves into a spiritual frenzy.

A spectacle followed that one might question, even after observing it firsthand. Several large wooden shields hung on the wall, and each contained a number of steel skewers inserted in a fan—like manner. Each skewer was about three—eighths of an inch in diameter and three feet long, with a large wooden ball on the dull end.

From time to time the mullah selected one of the swaying dervishes, placing him in the center of the circle. The mullah grabbed a large, rusty skewer and used a heavy wooden mallet to drive it several inches into the dervish's neck, just above the middle of the collarbone. I watched in amazement as he'd leave the skewer dangling from the

---

34   The term "whirling dervishes" comes from this practice.

neck of the dervish by the weight of its wooden ball and grab another. This one he passed through the abdomen from side to side, so that at least six inches extended out each side. Then the mullah passed several smaller skewers, resembling large hat pins, through the nostrils, the cheeks, and the throat directly below the chin.

No blood poured from any of these wounds. The human pin cushion, who appeared to be in a trance, showed no reaction to pain. After a few moments, the mullah placed a cheek against his, murmured a prayer, and then withdrew the skewers, one by one, without a single drop of blood, just as though the skewers had been inserted in rubber.

The next day I had the coincidental opportunity to meet this very dervish. I went for a haircut and recognized the barber as the dervish who had been skewered. There were no marks anywhere on his body!

* * *

Years earlier, while driving across the Sonora and Mojave deserts of the United States, I had become enamored of the desert. But I didn't realize how much I loved this unforgiving climate zone until I was enticed by the charms of the Sahara. I yearned to know this particular desert more intimately, and as I traveled closer to the heart of the Sahara, I found others who felt the same way.

Continuing my journey southward along the coast of Tunisia, I met a Frenchman in Gabes who so loved the desert that he built a hotel there. When sandstorms prevailed and other Europeans left during the summer's heat, he would remain with a skeleton staff. He'd lived on the edge of the desert for more than thirty years, and when I met him, he was totally blind. He was still able to share the city he loved from memory, acting as my tour guide in Gabes.

My first night in his hotel, I was awakened about midnight by the sound of the most unusual music. I climbed out of bed and stood on my balcony overlooking the square. It was filled with camels, as a caravan had arrived after

I retired. The camels slept beside their loads, but two elderly men sat against opposite columns in the arched arcades around the square. One sang in a beautiful, clear falsetto, while the other played an obbligato on a flute, creating beautiful melodies. It was mesmerizing, and I think this moment marked the beginning of my courtship with the Sahara.

Intrigued by my guide and his desert city, I decided to spend a few more days in Gabes before venturing seventy-five miles farther south to Douirat, home of the cave-dwelling troglodytes.[35]

---

35   Troglodyte refers to a primitive person who dwells in caves.

CHAPTER 24

Living Among the Troglodytes, Early 1920s

Horace

I'd named the Berber tribe who lived in the cliffside village of Douirat "troglodytes" because they were primitive cave–dwellers. The word can also mean recluse. Tucked away in a corner of Tunisia that few, if any, Westerners had visited, the troglodytes were certainly reclusive from the rest of the world.

I raised myself up on one elbow to survey the dim, vault–like room, where, nearly blinded by the glare of the African desert, I had thrown myself down to sleep three hours earlier. The only light in the windowless chamber filtered its way through the cracks of the low, ill–fitting door, but I could see my rock dwelling was bare, except for the mat on which I had slept and my saddle and effects dumped in one corner. Feeling rested, I rose and padded across the rough floor and then threw open the door. A beam of sunlight, weaker now as the day waned, fell across the stone.

Looking out, I found Douirat to be one of the strangest places on earth. Located in the mountainous region of the Ourghamma plateau, near the Sahara's Great Eastern Erg, the city was built entirely into the sides of a cliff. The dwellings were laid out on shelves for hundreds of feet, and above and below me I could see rows and rows of doorways in the rock. The shelf outside my door was the main street of Douirat. Before me stretched a great valley, bathed in a deep blue haze, and far across it towered a barrier of red sandstone mesa—like hills, tipped with the last flame—colored rays of a setting sun, under an opal sky flecked with shell—pink clouds.

The sound of goats bleating echoed in the valley as children drove the numerous herds up the steep grade and through various cliff—side doorways. As I stood in my own doorway, stooping slightly, a tall, gray—haired man with a weathered face and kindness in his eyes addressed me in the Berber language and then simply beckoned me to follow him. We walked along the shelf—like street, made a turn, and entered one of the walled courtyards, where we found several men squatted on the ground. To my relief one of them spoke a little French and introduced me to my host, the sheik of Douirat.

The sheik bade me welcome and asked me what the land I came from was like. I described a nation far to the west, across a great ocean, and told of modern cities where millions lived in buildings that pierced the sky to a height of fifty stories or more. When the sheik asked about our religious beliefs, and I admitted that they were somewhat neglected in our struggle for the material, he smiled and said, "I'd rather be here."

I presented the sheik with gifts of tea, fresh mint leaves, and vegetables I had wrapped in wet papers and brought by mule from the oasis at Gabes. He was so grateful that he invited me to visit his house later to share his evening tea.

Returning to my room, I spread a blanket on the ground before the door and settled down to watch the curtain of darkness draw itself gently over the valley. Stars blinked forth, one by one, like specks of gold in a great inverted bowl of soft violet.

A short while later, the sheik appeared at my door, followed by a boy carrying a huge dish about the size of a wash basin, covered with a two—foot—high conical "hat" of woven grass. He placed the dish before me, lifted the cover, and the delicious aroma of steaming couscous reminded me that I was hungry. Two bowelled fowls were entirely covered with a great heap of steamed barley, cooked with bits of mutton and an ample supply of olive oil, with green olives sprinkled over the top. The lack of utensils didn't bother me, as I had traveled extensively in North Africa and previously had enjoyed their savory *plat-du-jour* with my fingers.

Being unable to express my profound gratitude to my host except by sign, I began to eat. The sheik politely walked away, as it is a breach of desert etiquette to watch another eat. When I finished, I clapped my hands, at which time the boy reappeared and took the remainder away. Sufficient to feed six or eight people, the remainder would constitute the evening meal for the women of the household who had prepared it.

That night, as I sat on rugs laid on the floor of the sheik's house with several tribal elders and an interpreter, I was told that I was welcome in the village as long as I chose to stay. I thanked my hosts and explained my plan to penetrate farther into the mountains to visit some of the other cave towns. My hosts recounted their traditions from the days before the French arrived, when the feudal towns were at perpetual war with their neighbors, and the swift-riding Tuareg robbers from the heart of the Sahara swooped down upon them, carrying off their herds and sometimes their women. As I sat listening to their stories, I surveyed the whitewashed room.

The sheik's chamber, like all the others, was twenty feet long, eight feet wide, and eight feet high, with ceilings that formed perfect vaulted arches. Crude lamps had been created by cutting a niche into the wall and placing olive oil and a wick in a depression at the bottom. Large pillows lined one wall, and the bed at the far end of the room was a stone shelf three feet above the floor covered with layers of heavy woven blankets. A small, plain table—the only traditional furniture I saw anywhere in the village—sat against the rear wall. Upon it the sheik had arranged his papers, a framed lithograph of the prophet Mohammed on a winged horse, and some photographs left by another visitor. Curiously, a large club about the size of a baseball bat, shiny and bearing the marks of long use, hung on the wall.

I asked what this strange club was used for, and the sheik explained that it was the "marriage stick," an implement used in a troglodyte ritual, thousands of years old, that reminded me of the Stone Age, when cavemen used clubs to drag their brides home. When a young man reaches fifteen, the marriageable age, the older women of his family seek a wife for him, a girl of about twelve who lives in the same village. The women of the boy's and girl's families enter into extensive negotiations until a bargain is made regarding the number of goats and sheep and other livestock the boy's family will exchange for the girl's hand in marriage. All this is carried out before the boy or girl has even seen the other, for the troglodyte girls and women are jealously guarded from the gaze of any male, save an immediate family member.

On the marriage day, the young girl is dressed in all her finery and secretly removed to an unoccupied cave, where she bars the door and remains alone. Meanwhile, the bridegroom gathers several of his comrades and locates her hiding place for a night raid. Under cover of darkness, the bridegroom breaks down the door with the "marriage stick," lent to him by the sheik. The bride greets her betrothed with a fierce onslaught, fighting him off, using teeth and nails. After a struggle, he grabs her, holds her at arm's length, delivers one heavy blow to the head with the stick, and drags her out. Then he swings her in front of him in the saddle, amid the yells and gunshots of her family members who have come to her rescue, and makes off with her to their new home. The "marriage stick" is returned to the sheik and again takes its place on the wall as a fitting emblem of the mastery of man.[36]

---

36   Horace D. Ashton, "Cave Men of the Desert," in *ASIA* magazine, December 1924.

The ritual was also intended to encourage the woman, through screaming and fighting, to get out all her anger in one go before marriage, rather than nagging her husband later. While the marriage ritual may be hard for outsiders to understand, divorce was practically nonexistent in this culture, and everyday life in Douirat was simple.

Every morning I watched veiled women and girls, in endless procession, thread their way down the steep hillsides, carrying large earthen vessels upon their heads and driving diminutive donkeys before them, laden with goat skins and other clay jars to be filled at some distant well. I was amazed at what adept climbers they were, but this was the closest I got to any of the women, because the men were fiercely protective. Each house had a walled courtyard that served several purposes: the women could go outside and still have privacy, for they are veiled and secluded from childhood; the livestock slept there; and the courtyard served as a fortress in times of siege.

A few days later, I bid my generous hosts good-bye, packed my belongings, and loaded the mules. Then I departed to learn more about the troglodyte culture in other villages. The other villages were also dug into the conical mesa—like hills and composed of a similar succession of strata—sometimes to a height of a thousand feet or more—with the streets arranged like terraces or giant steps. These steps mounted to a *ksar*, or citadel, and on my way I stopped at one of the citadels for another look across the vast intervening valleys toward the mountains, marveling again at how much the view reminded me of the Grand Canyon.

I pushed on through the hills for days, riding over trails so steep that the mules would lose their footing at times and slide down the slippery, time—worn rocks until checked by heaps of broken stones. Frequently we disturbed great desert lizards warming themselves in the morning sun and sent them scampering noisily for their holes beneath some rock. There was little animal life to be encountered here, though pet gazelles were quite common in the towns.

A tribal people of the white race with olive skin and dark eyes, the Berbers were not barbarians, as the meaning of their name suggested and their brutal wars had characterized. They may be uncivilized in that they have few implements and no modern conveniences, but I found them to be loyal, courteous friends. As did all the Berber tribes, the troglodytes held certain rules of hospitality that allowed me safe travel. A stranger who approached one of their towns with good intentions was kindly received.

As word of the American explorer spread, I was met at each outpost and escorted into the village, where I was presented to the sheik and officially welcomed. There was always a vacant whitewashed cave for the welcomed stranger to reside that had been dug like all the others between the shelves of limestone and comparatively soft marl. No sooner had I unpacked my blankets than men appeared with gifts of live chickens and eggs, later prepared by the women for my meals, and the sheik always made a ceremonial call with the large washbasin piled high with couscous. But unless I was invited by the sheik to stay longer, I learned I had better be prepared to move on in three days.

These sheiks of the desert were nothing like the romantic Hollywood sheiks that drew flocks of American women to popular motion pictures. A real sheik, as the oldest and most revered man in the *douar*, or clan, was an elderly man with leathery skin, greasy whiskers, smallish eyes that were likely sore from the sands and heat of the desert, and an emanating odor due to lack of bathing.[37]

As I traveled, I learned that within a radius of a hundred miles of the troglodyte district lived several other branches of the same tribe, whose dwellings differed

---

37   Claire B. Donaldson, "Sheik Far From Romantic Figure," in *St. Petersburg Times*, St. Petersburg, Florida, 17 January 1926.

greatly. I was amazed by the persistence with which all the desert tribes clung to their unfriendly habitations. The curious houses they built, their laborious methods of irrigation, and their sunken date groves were all a part of their stubborn effort to survive.

In Medenine, houses were built on the level plain, like huge loaves of bread. They were arranged in the shape of horseshoes or long, straight rows, and five or six houses were stacked on top of each, originally as defense against the Tuareg marauders. The single—room houses, known as *rhorfas*, were used principally as storehouses, although sometimes they sheltered the older, feeble tribe members. At least 80 percent of the people spent nine months a year roaming the desert with their herds, planting and harvesting their meager crops as they went. The old folks stayed behind and acted as caretakers, awaiting the autumn homecoming, when the town was surrounded with thousands of nomad tents for three months.[38]

When I arrived at the village of Medenine, I found only the elders at home, but they welcomed me like the other tribes had done and offered me lodging for the night in a rhorfa. The next morning, I climbed to the top and viewed the concrete vaults, spread out across the vast sun—baked plain. No stairs led to the houses' upper rows, and access came from climbing slight projections on the front walls, using hands and feet. I was amazed that even the elderly tribe members seemed to experience no great difficulty reaching the top story.

On my journey I encountered a third type of Sahara cliff—dweller that I called a well—dweller.[39] These people dug deep round pits at high elevation and then made slanting tunnels through to the bottom of the pits. The only means of entering was many yards from the edge of the pit. The rooms within were square caves aligned around

---

38   Horace D. Ashton, "The Troglodytes of Southern Tunisia," in *Le Voyageur en France*, February 1924.

39   H. F. Manchester, "Finds Moral 'Barbarians' Living in the Desert," in *The Sunday Herald*, Boston, Massachusetts, 18 January 1925.

the edge of the pit, which acted as a sort of courtyard or roofless living room. The women, children, and goats were then housed in this subterranean dwelling. When a sheik is wealthy enough to possess a harem, it, too, is maintained in one of these well-dwellings. Practically all their lives are spent underground, and when they die, they are brought up and placed in shallow graves on the surface.

Woe to any man who approaches the edge of the well, as he will be shot immediately. Thankfully I was informed of this when the sheik welcomed me shortly after my arrival, but that didn't stop me from wishing privately that I could one day photograph the harem women. I didn't know it then, but that day would be my honeymoon.

* * *

Having spent thirteen months exploring North Africa, from Morocco to the desert cave-dwellers, I had filmed some amazing sights—practices and customs unknown to the Western world. During the trip, I was fortunate to have had gracious hosts who were willing to share the daily aspects of their lives and include me in their rituals. Perhaps they welcomed me because I'd studied their religion. I don't know, but I knew I was blessed to have been granted a unique opportunity to shed light on areas of the "Dark Continent."

The hotel chain that employed me was pleased with my work, and I now had more than enough footage to accompany a travel lecture. Enthusiastic to share what I'd learned, I returned to New York to prepare my first lecture. Not long after I arrived—and quite naturally—I dropped in at the Explorers Club to see an old friend. There I got a call from the manager of a famous Broadway theater, inviting me to give my first lecture.

Appearing on Broadway was about to be an adventure of a different kind, in many ways more terrifying than any I'd had yet.

CHAPTER 25

Lifeline

Butch
April 5, 2001
5:00 p.m.

Three hours have passed since my kidnapping, and I am still alive. Time seems eternal at a time like this; each second feels like an hour. I think of the times my father spent in the desert—his awareness of slowing down, of thinking, of mindfulness.

Now the leader contacts Myriam again and begins more negotiations that get nowhere. On several occasions she states emphatically that she is not interested in paying for a dead body and warns them they had better keep me alive if they want to collect any ransom. I also try repeatedly to negotiate with the leader, but he seems convinced my wife will come up with the amount he demands.

I trust Myriam is working with the authorities and doing everything in her power to get me home alive. I also need to do everything in my power to ensure my survival. More than any other time in my life, I realize that I need to trust my instincts and be prepared to risk everything, if and when the moment presents itself. The thought of escape gives me a momentary spark of hope. I know how hard she works and recall her perseverance when she wants to accomplish something.

* * *

I remember that after we gave up the investment business in the Bahamas, we returned to Haiti without any money and moved back into the little rented house with my parents, while the German ambassador remained at Villarosa for another three years.

Determined and undeterred by our losses, we signed a five-year lease on an oceanfront beach resort about two hours from Port-au-Prince and planned to develop it on weekends. We also bought a travel agency shortly afterward, which would provide us with steady work Monday through Friday. We were visionaries who each valued hard work and recognized that it was the only way to earn money.

However, Kyona Beach was not a typical deluxe resort on a tropical island. The previous owner had tried to make it a tourist destination, but visitors were subjected to harsh security measures by the feared *Tonton Macoutes*. They had to go through seven different checkpoints en route to the beach, get out of the car with their hands in the air, reveal any items that might be considered weapons, and often be patted down while guards stood nearby with guns.

Haiti had experienced several invasions by exiles and occasionally foreign mercenaries who wanted to overthrow the government. Papa Doc vowed to defend his government at any cost, and he trusted no one. Innocent people were frequently rounded up, questioned, arrested, and shot—or simply disappeared. People didn't go anywhere unless they absolutely had to go, and the same nightly curfews that hurt my nightclub were still enforced. Anyone on the streets during curfew risked being shot, no questions asked.

When we first arrived, the beach property was nearly abandoned. It had only a few bare buildings and lacked dishes, equipment, electricity, water, an office, supplies. There was nothing except a beautiful beach. These things did not dampen our spirits. With all the friends we had, Myriam and I felt we could create a thriving business to serve the locals.

Each Friday, after working all week at our travel agency, Myriam and I made the two-hour drive to the beach resort to spend the weekend there, fixing it up. Our many friends were very supportive during this process, and they eventually became our first guests.

Once the resort was habitable, our friends who enjoyed the sea and sand arrived. We regularly rented out all six rooms, which meant that Myriam and I wound up sleeping in our car almost every weekend for about three years.

Myriam worked the kitchen; I worked the bar and also gave waterskiing and scuba diving lessons. More and more people began to come and have a good time, and the resort became very popular. We hired a little band to play on Sundays, and by the second year we served more than two hundred meals on Sunday evenings, in addition to having a full house on Friday and Saturday nights. Despite the heavy security and Draconian curfew, word spread about our resort.

In fact, it became so popular that members of the Duvalier family unexpectedly arrived as guests one Sunday. Luc-Albert, a fellow who had worked for me on an agricultural project and went on to marry one of Papa Doc's three daughters, had become Minister of Tourism. He showed up at Kyona Beach in this capacity with his wife and her young brother, Jean Claude Duvalier, who was then sixteen years old and would later become known as Baby Doc when he assumed Haiti's presidency.

They arrived unannounced with forty to fifty security guards, including members of the notorious *Tonton Macoutes* and the elite Palace Guard. Since Baby Doc had been the object of an assassination attempt when he was only six years old, he rarely went anywhere in the intervening ten years. When he did, he always had a heavily armed security force accompany him. This day was no exception because there were two Duvaliers to protect. We found the guards intimidating, but after our initial feelings of fear and concern wore off, we realized this was a pleasure visit orchestrated by my former employee and friend, Luc-Albert. He introduced Myriam and me to his wife, Nicole, and to Baby Doc.

By this time, I had built the reputation of being a good water skier, scuba diver, and sailor who was very knowledgeable about boats. Baby Doc asked if he could ride in my ski boat while I taught guests to water ski. His request created a security issue, and I had to allow two heavily armed Palace Guard officers to accompany us in my small ski boat. Baby Doc immediately fell in love with the sea and boats, which he continued to enjoy through his years as President for Life.

As president of Haiti, Baby Doc occasionally called me to ask for advice. During his presidency, he always called me *Capitaine* and was very respectful, well mannered, and correct.

When our five-year lease expired, Myriam and I had to give up the resort after building it into a successful business. The original owners wanted to return and run the resort themselves. We left Kyona feeling very disappointed and sad. But Myriam stood by me, as she always did, and I knew today would not be any different. *She* would find a way to save me.

* * *

I must do my part, and I continue to feign illness, pretending to grow weaker. They'll lose everything if their hostage dies before they get their hands on the money, so I'll try to rattle them. Listening to the Creole discussion en route, there is disagreement and doubt among the ranks. The leader is still in charge, but his plan seems to be shifting.

When we finally arrive at Zabeth, the driver attempts to take us deeper into the bush toward the town of Thomazeau but is forced to abandon the plan when the Land Cruiser bogs down in the thick mud. From the backseat, I must explain how to get the vehicle out of the mud. They elect to stay in Zabeth until nightfall.

In true Haitian character, my kidnappers invite me to go swimming and pass the time with them in the cool, magical, mystical spring waters of Source Zabeth. I smile inwardly. This is a prime example of what I call *facteur H* (the H factor). It's similar to Murphy's Law, and something we often joke about around the dinner table at Villarosa. Facteur H is an expression I developed after years of experience. It means ***that anything involving Haiti*** or Haitians will probably not have the expected outcome due to circumstances and cultural differences.

Facteur H could save me! I unclench my stomach as I consider this unique cultural characteristic. Hope surges through me, holding me up like a life preserver. My instincts tell me that if I can just stay alive long enough, *something* or *someone* will be bound to screw up, and I will get the opportunity I need.

* * *

Having employed more than 2,000 Haitians at one time or another in my numerous business endeavors, I have experienced facteur H on many occasions. Superstition and religion are greatly involved with this characteristic and play a big part in Haitian culture.

For example, one day at the travel agency, I got a call from our butler, Justin, who said, "Mr. Ashton, you'd better come home right away. Brunette is dead."

Shocked by the news that our maid, who was like a member of the family, was dead, I asked, "What happened?"

"I don't know," he said, "but she ran in here, completely white, screaming, 'I'm dead! I'm dead!' I'm calling you to tell you she's dead."

I drove home and found Brunette lying on the ground outside, groaning, looking as white as a wall, crying, but very much alive. I assured her that she was not dead.

"Oh yes, sir, I'm dead. I'm dead," she said, shaking her head and groaning again.

Knowing it wouldn't be easy to convince her otherwise, I sought to uncover the logic. She had been cleaning behind the bed. I kept a sawed-off shotgun, which was covered by a curtain panel, behind the headboard for security reasons. After thinking about what might have happened, I surmised that over the course of daily cleanings, Brunette must have accidentally loaded a shell into the chamber of the shotgun. This day, as she cleaned, the shotgun discharged with a terrifying bang. The pellets must have hit the ceiling and broken the plaster, showering white dust all over her. The poor girl was scared to death, thinking she had shot herself. Her ears rang from the shotgun blast in a confined room, and she glanced at her completely white reflection in the mirror over the dresser. She looked like a ghost and concluded she was dead. This was not atypical of life in Haiti.

While looking behind the other curtain, I was surprised to find the cross my father had carved. I discovered my wife had hidden it there without my knowledge. My father's quest to study religion took him from being a monk in Tibet, to being a Vodou expert, to writing papers, to exploring the Rosicrucian philosophy based on religious beliefs. He described himself as a "student of comparative religion." During his studies, he sculpted a sample of his thesis by carving an elaborate wooden cross, putting into it all the power of his spiritual beliefs and the sum of his knowledge of religions. This was the cross now behind our bed. Many people believed that the cross my father had carved held great powers.

Although most people in Haiti are superstitious—my wife and daughter Daska are somewhat superstitious—I am not. Unlike them and unlike my father, I do not consider myself a spiritual person.

Sometime after my father's death, as things began to grow worse in Haiti, Myriam hid this cross behind our headboard, convinced of its power. For about six years, I remained unaware that my father's wooden cross rested behind my head every night.

As I've said, I am a pragmatist who feels all things can be explained logically. I am not superstitious, and I don't believe that a piece of wood can hold spiritual powers, no matter what its shape, what religious symbols were carved on it, or who carved it.

* * *

5:25 p.m.

Although deadly in their purpose, my kidnappers are surprisingly childish in their manner. I can hardly believe it, but they really are serious about all of us pausing in the middle of a crime to take a refreshing swim. My refusal to join them fuels my strategy.

"I'll die if I go swimming in that cold water now," I gasp. "I need to rest, and I need cool, fresh air. It's difficult for me to breathe. Please turn the air conditioning back on. I cannot survive in the heat."

The car, which has been turned off, is stiflingly hot. Feeling as if I am about to suffocate, I have a new admiration for how my father bore the desert heat in Africa.

The leader barks an order, and the driver starts the car and turns on the air conditioning. Two remain in the car to guard me— the killer, who moves into the backseat beside me, and the driver— and sure enough, the leader and the novice go for a swim as if they are on a carefree Sunday afternoon outing.

The driver flips on the commercial radio and dials the popular local station, Radio Metropole, to listen to their mix of Haitian, American, and Latin music. The heat brings back the panic in my gut and a whirlwind of thoughts race through my mind. *Will I be killed in this remote spot, miles from the city? Who will find me way out here?*

Thankfully, the air in the car grows cooler. Turning inward,

I tune out the music and practice meditating as my father taught me. At this moment, all I can do is pray. I tell myself that even though I don't hold much faith in achieving a tangible result, the process will help to calm me down.

Like a true monk, my dad remained unflustered, completely confident he would overcome any obstacle thrown at him throughout his life, whatever it might be. He never learned to speak Creole fluently like I had, yet he communicated perfectly with everyone he encountered, even on a New York stage.

I never saw my father lecture in a theater, but I can imagine how he charmed his audiences with his adventures. Broadway must have been something in the 1920s. According to the scrapbook articles and playbills, the name *Horace Dade Ashton* flashed on several marquees and drew sold-out crowds and rave reviews. I can easily picture him standing in front of a cheering audience, because I know he would have enjoyed that. He loved to tell stories and jokes and took great joy in making people laugh or in seeing the looks on their faces when he surprised or educated them. He wouldn't tolerate vulgar language, especially from his sons. Even when he told a "dirty joke," he found a way to make it funny without the use of vulgar language.

My father was six foot one but appeared more imposing because of his athletic build and excellent posture. In my mind's eye I see him clearly, standing larger than life, illuminated in the spotlight at the front of a Broadway theater. A hushed silence descends over the packed rows of seats, anticipation spreading and perhaps more than a little awe. Listen now. I hear him announce in his lively, confident way, "Good afternoon, ladies and gentlemen. Hang onto your hats because you're about to see some remarkable footage that no one has ever seen . . ."

CHAPTER 26

Sharing My Adventures, Early 1920s

Horace

My lecturing career started with a bang. The manager of the Capitol Theater on Broadway in New York City, Rothapfel, or "Roxy," as he was known, requested that I let them show *Strange Cities of the Sahara*, my film about the troglodytes, while I stood to one side of the screen and gave a talk as it ran. He offered me $850 if I'd appear three times daily for fifteen minutes each time for a week, and I agreed.

My lecturing career almost ended before it began when Roxy told me I had to appear in an Arab costume: burnoose, turban, and all, including prayer beads. He assured me that the bright spotlight would shine on me only for a few seconds at the beginning of my talk and then it would be made smaller and fade to yellow, while the audience focused on the screen. Reluctantly, I agreed to go through with the costume.

Broadway's Capitol Theater, an entire city block long in size and seating nearly 5,000 people, was sold out for my debut of *Strange Cities of the Sahara*. I even received top billing over Will Rogers on the marquee for the week.

This was in the era before sound films, and to my horror I learned that the theater didn't even have a public address system. A few days before my first show, I stood in the great empty auditorium and wondered how I could possibly project my voice to the back of the gallery.

A friend sent me to see a gentleman at Carnegie Hall, who managed to teach me the essentials of voice placement with three lessons. His best advice was "Mentally enclose your audience in a great eggshell with your voice." I practiced doing this in the empty theater and had my friend stand in different locations and flash a light when he could hear me clearly.

Opening night arrived. Dressed in full Arab garb, I braved the bright spotlight and the cheering of the excited crowd and then, as butterflies beat their wings against the insides of my stomach, I began.

Suddenly, a man at the rear of the main floor stood up and yelled, "Use a calling tone!"

I raised my pitch slightly and heard no more from him or anyone else, except appropriate laughter at my commentary, "oohs" and "aahs" as the motion picture ran, and thundering applause at the end. My first lecture was a raving success, and the reviews in the papers the next day were extremely favorable.

A write-up in *The Sun* on April 8, 1922, included many details from my presentation:

> Mr. Ashton has just returned from a thirteen months' trip through the Sahara Desert and French North Africa, covering some of the most unusual parts of the Mohammedan world . . . His expeditions are further distinguished by their exclusive character, since they always consist of only one member, himself, accompanied by his trusty camera.
>
> The troglodyte cities are habitations that have been built entirely underground. "History shows these habitations to be at least 2,000 years old," says Mr. Ashton, "although they probably existed long before that. It is believed that they originated during the Roman invasion from the north, at the same time that the Tuareg tribes came up to attack the country from the south. The distracted and frightened inhabitants, in desperation as to how to protect themselves, frantically dug holes into the tops of the hills and settled into

them with all their worldly goods. This custom seems to have been carried down through the generations and these particular tribes have been cave-dwellers ever since." [40]

The review in the April 22, 1922, edition of *The New York Times* positively glowed, saying my *Strange Cities of the Sahara* was "exceptionally entertaining" and "one of the most interesting films that has been shown on Broadway in a long time." It praised my skill with the camera by saying "the photography is excellent and credited my subject matter as strange and fascinating as anything photographed by Martin Johnson in the South Seas."[41]

The Evening Mail, another New York newspaper, stated it was "the best screen number on the bill. Both the pictures and Mr. Ashton's address are intensely absorbing, bringing a decidedly unusual glimpse of desert life."

Immediately after my week at the Capitol, I was invited to do the same in the Fox Theater in Philadelphia, but I accepted only on condition that I could appear clad normally. This was followed by a return to Broadway by public demand, this time in the Criterion Theater, where they wanted me to wear the Arab costume. I refused but finally compromised by wearing high laced boots, khaki shirt, riding breeches, and a pith helmet.

On the first night of that engagement, I thanked my lucky stars for the helmet. While in the men's room I heard the buzzer announcing my appearance and rushed to the stage, stepping into the spotlight just in time. A man seated in the orchestra frantically signaled me, and I looked down to discover I'd forgotten to close my zipper. I grabbed the pith helmet off my head, held it strategically in front of me, and began my lecture. Illuminated by a spotlight and standing before a crowd, this was certainly the most embarrassing moment of my life.

---

40   *The Sun*, New York City, New York, 8 April 1922. (This newspaper was published from 1833 to 1950.)

41   *The New York Times*, New York City, New York, 9 April 1922.

HORACE ASHTON-F.R.G.S.
ILLUSTRATED NARRATIVES
management of
150 Lafayette St.   Nomad Lecture Bureau   New York City
1925

**Horace Ashton wears his pith helmet for a speaking
engagement on Africa.**

I was proud of the films I created and pleased to attract
an audience on Broadway. I got such good press notices
that my career as a lecturer immediately took off, and
soon I was contacted by the big lecture bureaus that
began to book me into all the top venues. For the next ten

years I gave travel lectures all over the United States and in South America and England, where I spoke before members of the Royal Geographical Society and at Oxford and Cambridge.

My experiences in North Africa were written about in many publications, including the *Buffalo Express*, the *Buffalo News*, and *The Evening Star* in Washington, D.C., after I presented my North African films and lectures.[42] Some even quoted my opinion that since there were so many different Moslem[43] sects that I felt there was no danger of a Holy War, as it would be impossible for them all to coordinate their efforts.[44]

Ambush Camera Gets Unique Moslem Views

Incongruities of Christian civilization introduced almost overnight into a Moslem community were shown in motion pictures before the National Geographic Society last evening, when Horace D. Ashton exhibited films of Arab tents pitched against radio towers, of brass bedsteads and grandfather clocks against backgrounds of mosaic and arabesque interiors, and veiled women riding in automobiles. "Only a decade ago Morocco virtually was untouched by occidental influence," the lecturer said. "Before that it was unsafe for a Christian to travel there. Even now most of the home life is forbidden to the observer . . ."[45]

★ ★ ★

---

42   "First Man to Put Moors on Movie Film," in the *Buffalo Express*, Buffalo, New York, 23 December 1922.

43   Muslim is used to describe the followers of Islam today.

44   "Need Not Fear Another Holy War, He Thinks," in the *Buffalo News*, Buffalo, New York, 23 December 1922.

45   "Ambush Camera Gets Unique Moslem Views," in *The Evening Star*, Washington, D.C., 2 December 1922.

From THE SUN

New York, Saturday, April 8th 1922

Horace Ashton, explorer and lecturer, who presents his illustrated narrative, "Strange Cities of the Sahara" at the Capitol Theatre this week, in all of his travels to almost every corner of the globe, extending over a period of over twenty years, has never had a mishap of a serious or minor nature. His expeditions are further distinguished by their exclusive character, since they always consist of only one member, himself, accompanied by his trusty camera.

Mr. Ashton has just returned from a thirteen months' trip through the Sahara Desert and French North Africa, covering some of the most unusual parts of the Mohammedan world. The first picture of the series, "Strange Cities of the Sahara," which is being presented by Messmore Kendall and W. G. Clark, records for the first time in motion pictures three of the most curious cities in all Africa—the Troglodyte cities of Medenine and Matmata and the Touareg city of El Oued-Souf.

The Troglodyte cities are habitations that have been built entirely underground. "History shows these habitations to be at least 2,000 years old," says Mr. Ashton, "although they probably existed long before that. It is believed that they originated during the Roman invasion from the north, at the same time that the Touareg tribes came up to attack the country from the south. The distracted and frightened inhabitants, in desperation as to how to protect themselves, frantically dug holes into the tops of the hills and settled into them with all their worldly goods. This custom seems to have been carried down through the generations and these particular tribes have been cave-dwellers ever since.

"There is a curious custom among these people. In each of the communities there is a guest house which is placed at the disposal of any visiting foreigner. Each day another family undertakes the duty of feeding and acting as host to the visitor. They provide him with water, dates and a generous supply of the native dish, a mixture of dates and greens."

Mr. Ashton is a member of the Explorers Club of New York, the American Academy of Sciences and many other scientific societies all over the world. He adds interest to the presentation of "Strange Cities of the Sahara" at the Capitol by accompanying the pictures with a running narrative.

From THE N. Y. TIMES

Sunday, April 9th 1922

For many followers of the screen travel pictures are more enjoyable, as a rule, than the customary photoplays and comedies, and the number of such who went to the Capitol Theatre last week, as well as many others who are afraid of anything branded "educational" but do not run away when a good film is thrust upon them must have found H. D. Ashton's "Strange Cities of the Sahara" exceptionally entertaining. Mr. Ashton penetrated the great desert to the remote abodes of its troglodytes and brought back one of the most interesting films that has been shown on Broadway for a long time. Considering the difficulties under which his pictures were made in this hot, sandy region, their photography is excellent, and in subject matter they are as strange and fascinating as anything photographed by Martin Johnson in the South Seas. The spectator is amazed by the persistence with which the desert cave-dwellers and the tribes more or less akin to them cling to their unfriendly habitations. The curious houses some of them build, their laborious methods of irrigation, their sunken date groves, are a part of their stubborn effort to survive. Those who sat on the cushioned seats at the Capitol with all New York and its conveniences outside must have wondered at people who could live the life they saw pictured on the screen and heard Mr. Ashton talk about. So, then, in causing this wonder, and arousing the keen interest that went with it, the film accomplished its object and performed one of the best services of the screen.

Address all communications to
H. D. ASHTON, 451 West End Ave., N. Y. C.
Telephone: Schuyler 9935

**Newspapers praise Horace Ashton's presentation on the
Sahara Desert.**

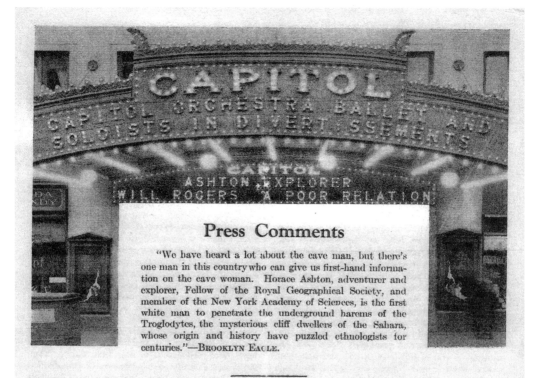

Press Comments

"We have heard a lot about the cave man, but there's one man in this country who can give us first-hand information on the cave woman. Horace Ashton, adventurer and explorer, Fellow of the Royal Geographical Society, and member of the New York Academy of Sciences, is the first white man to penetrate the underground harems of the Troglodytes, the mysterious cliff dwellers of the Sahara, whose origin and history have puzzled ethnologists for centuries."—BROOKLYN EAGLE.

"Incongruities of Christian civilization introduced almost overnight into a Moslem community, were shown in motion pictures before the National Geographic Society last evening, when Horace Ashton exhibited films of Arab tents pitched against radio towers, of brass bedsteads and grandfather clocks against backgrounds of mosaic and arabesque, and veiled women riding in automobiles."—WASHINGTON STAR.

"Horace Ashton, the explorer and lecturer, stands to one side while his marvellous films of the overseas flight of the airship 'Los Angeles' are being shown, and as the amazing views are being unrolled he tells the whole story. Every question arising in the minds of the audience is anticipated and the travelogue, delivered by this man who saw it all and made it possible for others to feel most of the excitement and none of the annoyance, is a most satisfying performance."—PHILADELPHIA RECORD.

"Horace Ashton, F.R.G.S., has travelled much in South and Central America, Haiti, the Near and Far East, and is pretty much at home all over the world, but it is in Northern Africa on the sand-swept Sahara and among the strange cities and oases of this mysterious region that he has made his most fascinating and exotic discoveries. He has, himself, photographed these places with splendid artistic results. He gives much more than a travel lecture, it is an entertainment with motion pictures as a background."—NEW YORK BULLETIN.

The press loves Horace Ashton's talk on the Sahara Desert.

National Geographic Society

WASHINGTON, D. C.

GILBERT GROSVENOR, PRESIDENT

December 2, 1922

Mr. Horace D. Ashton,
451 West End Avenue,
New York City

My dear Mr. Ashton:

I wish to express the sincere appreciation of the members
of the National Geographic Society for the admirable lecture which
you gave before our organization on December 1st.   I have heard many
enthusiastic comments on your entertaining and instructive address and
remarkable and fascinating motion pictures and slides, and only regret
that absence from Washington prevented my having the pleasure of hearing
the address also.

With best wishes for the success of your lecture tour,

I am

Yours very sincerely,

Gilbert Grosvenor
President

The National Geographic Society thanks Horace Ashton.

While I was in New York lecturing and showing my films of North Africa, I received a telephone call asking me to do some aerial filming for a picture with Leon Errol, aptly titled *A Lunatic at Large*.

I hired a friend to fly the plane while I filmed the

scene. The plan was that he would barrel–roll the plane from the Battery up over Fifth Avenue to Central Park and back down to the Statue of Liberty, leveling off so that I could change films, and then he would repeat the barrel–roll. I would sit behind him, shooting footage.

While we were upside down on our second trip, the motor conked out and failed to restart. We had to make a forced landing. As we passed over New York City on this bright November Sunday morning searching for a spot to land, we could see Central Park filled with children and skaters, streets crowded with traffic, and the East River jammed with floating ice. We glided toward Long Island but ruled out the Sound because we were not equipped for a water splashdown. In Long Island City, we saw that the tennis courts were full, the streets crowded, and the Long Island Railway tracks were impossible because of overhead high–tension wires.

Running out of time, the pilot spotted a small vacant lot behind some apartment houses and headed for it. As he steered the aircraft, I hurriedly detached my expensive movie camera from its mount on the fuselage. Then I pulled up the cushion from the bucket seat I occupied and wrapped it around the camera, forgetting to refasten my safety belt. I looked up just as we passed under some electric wires. Just then, the plane hit a pile of rocks on the ground.

I was thrown out, and everything went black. I regained consciousness a few moments later, stunned to see the plane engulfed in flames. Sitting on the ground, clear of the wreckage, I was still clutching my camera, which was still wrapped in the seat cushion. My only injury was that I broke my nose again.

To my great regret, my friend, the pilot, burned with the plane. If I had refastened my seat belt, I would have perished with him.

CHAPTER 27

Into the Sahara, Early 1920s

Horace

My curiosity about the Sahara had been sparked in Morocco when I read the books written by Isabelle Eberhardt, whose profound love for the desert transcended the pages. Born in Russia, she attended school in Switzerland, where a love affair with a fellow student ended in tragedy. Nursing a broken heart she ventured to the Sahara, where the life of the desert Arabs gave her the background and material for her first novel.

As a horsewoman, Isabelle was fascinated by the thrilling spectacle the locals called Fantasia, where a large group of horsemen, standing in their saddles and screaming at the top of their lungs, charged forward, holding their guns overhead and firing in the air. Determined to join the charge, Isabelle cut off her hair and adopted the native costume of burnoose and turban. She learned to speak the language, and with her skilled horsemanship she soon was accepted by a group who believed her to be an Arab youth. She rode and lived with the tribe for a number of years until she was injured when her horse fell in a Fantasia. Her secret was discovered when they treated her injuries, but she had endeared herself so deeply to her companions that her closest friend insisted they become man and wife. She had no choice and accepted his offer. She lived the remainder of her life in a small hut with her husband, writing novels about desert life.

When I visited their hut, the two shared their love of the desert with me and gave me valuable information about the life and habits of the nomadic tribes. Sadly, on a future trip to the area, I learned of the tragic end to their romantic life in the desert. Their little mud hut on the banks of a normally dry river was washed away in a sudden flash flood. When Isabelle tried in vain to save the life of her husband, who couldn't swim, they perished together. A tomb now sits at the site, commemorating the heroic life of author Isabelle Eberhardt, whose books had awakened my desire to explore the Sahara.

* * *

My first intimate journey into the Sahara began at Biskra, an Algerian city bordering the eastern side of the desert, where I visited writer Robert Hichens in his handsome villa. He'd recently sold the motion picture rights to his novel, *The Garden of Allah*. In those days, the great wind machines now used to create sandstorms in the movies had not yet been invented, so I was hired by the producer to make a series of films of a genuine sandstorm, something that had never been attempted.

Before I left the United States, I'd had a special camera constructed to keep out the sand. At Biskra I paid an exorbitant price for a camel caravan and local tribesmen willing to venture into the desert during sandstorm season. Our caravan headed southeast for several days into the Eastern Erg, where the sand dunes were sometimes six or seven hundred feet high. Despite the hardships of riding on a camel in the hot sun and blowing sand, I was instantly won over by the charm of the desert.

On the one hand, the power of the desert presented great risk, but on the other, it offered the most blessed peace I've ever experienced. Caravan life was basic, focused on survival. Every day our drinking water would be almost boiling hot by the time the sun set, and every night we'd wrap the water jug in a woolen blanket covered by a wet goat skin to cool it. As I drifted off to sleep, the occasional groaning of the camels after they had traveled long distances without grazing was the only sound I heard. This—my first experience sleeping in an Arab tent in the open desert—was the beginning of my love affair with the Sahara, whose lure, like a siren's song, would repeatedly call me back.

Among the sand dunes, we pitched a camp. Feeling as if not only Hollywood but the desert itself had challenged me to film an actual sandstorm, I was determined. It took several days of endless waiting for nature to accommodate me.

One morning, I woke up coughing, half−smothered by the flying sand. I quickly veiled myself and then roused my troupe. With great difficulty, I persuaded them to get underway. The storm was a humdinger that lasted for three days. We got sand in our eyes, ears, and noses. Every mouthful of food was full of sand; grains even managed to find their way into sealed water bottles!

I got several thousand feet of film without scratches and considered that a miracle. It was also a miracle that the entire caravan made it safely through the storm. For three days and nights we dared not rest for more than fifteen minutes at a time for fear of being buried alive.

Later, my remarkable desert sandstorm film, *By Caravan Through the Garden of Allah*, caught the world's attention. The *Westport Standard* said it was "one of the best examples of motion picture photography in existence." An excerpt from the same review stated, "During the trip Mr. Ashton and his caravan were caught in a severe storm, which raged for three days and nights, yet he stuck to his job of securing pictures that would show faithfully what a real sandstorm looked like."[46]

After that experience I never hesitated to go

---

46   "Ashton to Tell of Caravan Trip," in *The Westport Standard*, Westport, Connecticut, 7 February 1924.

anywhere in the Sahara, because nothing worse could ever happen. Or could it?

* * *

My next caravan journey into the Sahara, which also involved shooting desert scenes for a Hollywood production, happened to fall during the ninth calendar month when Ramadan, the annual religious fast, occurs. Ramadan is a period when devout Muslims will not travel because they are not permitted to eat or drink between sunrise and sunset. So I engaged a group of Berbers to lead my expedition.

For three days all went well, but on the fourth day I developed agonizing pains in my side and called one of the Berbers to help me. He pulled up my shirt, revealing a greenish—blue patch about eight inches in diameter on my right side. As I knew little of their language and we didn't communicate well, my guides did not reveal the source of my discomfort to me. Immediately they changed course, but I was in such agony that I hardly noticed what they were doing. When we arrived at a couple of stunted date palms in a small depression in the sand an hour later, they helped me dismount. A few minutes later, I lost consciousness.

I awoke a day or two later and raised my head. It hit the ceiling. I was in a confined dark place, but I noticed a dim light beyond my feet. After my eyes adjusted, I discovered I was stuck head first in a tunnel—like hole in the side of one of their wells. A coarse cloth curtain covered the opening. When I called out, one of the Berbers lifted the curtain and pulled me out feet first. I noticed my pain was nearly gone, and I felt much better. My guides gave me a drink of water, fed me some chicken and an orange, and placed me back in my small tunnel to rest. After I recovered about a week later, I learned that my appendix had burst.

These nomads recognized my symptoms and knew

what to do. One of the men had ridden off to a nearby encampment and obtained some herbs and other provisions. I was dosed with an herb that made me sleep and a second that dissolved my ruptured appendix. Then they buried me alive to escape the hordes of desert flies. Talk about folk medicine! I never learned what the herbs were, but the Berbers' cure worked like a charm. Within a few days of awakening, I was able to continue the journey and film the desert footage I needed to complete my assignment.

On our way out of the desert, we passed through part of the Eastern Erg with its great sand dunes. There I learned to catch and eat sandfish.

Between the sand dunes the ground is hard and flat-caked gypsum. As we traveled over it, I noticed that it vibrated and sounded hollow. The Berbers told me that a subterranean river ran twenty feet below the desert's surface. Just then, one of the men dashed to the face of the dune, shoved his hand in quickly, and pulled out a wriggling white lizard about eight inches long. He quickly cut off its head and placed it in a small sack. I watched while the men caught several more, and then I tried my hand. It wasn't difficult at all. As we passed, the vibration disturbed the lizards that slept buried in the sand on the side of the dunes during the day. They wriggled slightly to cover themselves better, revealing their locations. Sandfish, as the lizards are called, are skinned and fried, and the meat tastes exactly like tender chicken.

Sandfish was just one of the desert delicacies I learned to enjoy. As my caravan journeys into the Sahara continued, I made friends and recognized the importance of sharing a meal in desert hospitality.

By

CARAVAN

through the

GARDEN

of

ALLAH

I N MR. ASHTON'S thrilling account of his long caravan journey into the fastnesses of the treacherous Sahara we are introduced to another side of this versatile traveller, for here we see him as a true naturalist, ever alert to each new surprise which nature presents to him. He tells us of strange creatures which the natives call "sand fish," caught in the early morning in the sand of the great dunes; of curious beasts with disjointed eyes, which wandered into his encampments to look him over; of scorpions and poisonous vipers and the myriads of insects which swarm in the great dry wastes of the desert. That side, which long ago won for him a fellowship in the Royal Geographical Society of London, is revealed in his able presentation of geographical knowledge, as he pictures for us oases of waving green, vast salt schotts which lie below the level of the sea and where, shimmering in an almost unbelievable heat, dance the most fantastic and convincing mirages. We are taken into the Erg, that most forbidding and yet most beautiful region of the earth, where, like huge storm-tossed waves the mountainous dunes of fine wind-blown sand stretch out for hundreds of burning miles. Into this land of thirst Horace Ashton forced his way, not in winter as the average traveller would go, but during the hot months of the Sirocco or south wind, so that he could bring back to you the first authentic pictures of a real desert sand-storm and describe to you as an eye-witness one of those great natural phenomena which, to most of us, must remain throughout life as mythical as the great flood. For pictorial charm and strangeness these motion pictures rival any that have ever been made. They depict not only the natural beauty of this alluring region, but bring to us an intimate view of the lives of its little-known inhabitants in their life-long struggle with sand. This lecture, though describing one great journey, is the result of many, and has brought the lecturer the distinction of being America's leading authority on the Sahara. Mr. Ashton is the author of many notable contributions on this subject which have appeared in America's leading periodicals and the press.

* * *

Several years later, I assembled a caravan to travel into the desert to make scenes for my film *Gofla* (distributed by United Artists). Just before I left Algiers, General Meynier, commander of the military territories, asked me to deliver a letter to Pasha Boaziz ben Ghana, religious leader of all the Muslims in the Sahara. Several of the nomadic tribes were fighting over grazing lands, and word from the Pasha would help the French Arab Bureau bring peace to the conflict. I didn't tell the general that I had met the pasha during an earlier trip, and we were old friends. I looked forward to seeing him again.

I was warmly welcomed when my caravan arrived at the encampment of Pasha Boaziz ben Ghana. A special banquet was prepared in my honor, and many sheiks were present. Women served great ceramic dishes—about fifty centimeters in diameter with towering conical straw covers—filled with steaming aromatic couscous. Two men came in bearing an entire sheep that had been slaughtered for the occasion and then slowly barbecued in a pit. Thankful that I had already been initiated into desert etiquette, I was not surprised when the pasha dug out one glaring eyeball and popped it into my open mouth. He took the other eyeball for himself. It was a great honor, and since I didn't flinch, all the men grunted their approval. After I passed the examination, so to speak, I enjoyed the remainder of the banquet, which ended with a delightful performance by a skilled and very pretty belly dancer.

* * *

I returned to the Sahara again, this time on a map–making expedition for the French, but my curious nature led me to explore a new corner of the desert. I wanted to see the mountainous region known then as the Hoggar (listed on today's maps as Ahaggar), where I hoped to photograph the illusive and notorious robbers of the desert, the Tuaregs. A nomadic Berber tribe with a bloody history, the Tuaregs roamed the western and central Sahara and the Hoggar area, where elevations rose up to 10,000 feet.

The commanding general at Fez kindly lent me an open–cockpit plane and a pilot. The plane was a Farman, and the machine gun mount on the cockpit's front was ideal for my camera. We took off from Fez, passed Taza, crossed into Algeria, and headed southeast. As we flew over oases and sandstorms, I could see for fifty or sixty miles in every direction. In the distance I could see the dim outline of the mountains of the Hoggar.

I was enjoying the scenery as I filmed sandstorms below, when the pilot leaned forward and tapped me on the shoulder, pointing down. I could see nothing but bare desert—not a tree, an oasis, or any sign of life. I shook my head. Had he seen the desert robbers? To get a closer look, the pilot began to descend. We reached an altitude of about 2,000 feet when the motor suddenly stopped. I quickly dismounted my camera and prepared for a crash-landing.

The pilot managed to land, but the plane made a ground loop and one wheel struck a rock, destroying the landing gear. There would be no chance to take off again. We were stranded in the middle of the open desert in the blazing sun, equipped with only a small canteen, some chocolate, and a few biscuits.

Under these circumstances, all I could do was pray. I've always been a great one for prayer, and fortunately my prayers have always been answered.

Neither of us was seriously hurt, and we climbed out of the plane. The terrified pilot did not look well, and I directed him to sit under the shade of a wing. In less than an hour, he became delirious. Because my French was limited and his English was worse, I had a difficult time with him. I waited until he fell asleep and then tied him up so he couldn't wander away.

Believing we were more than a hundred miles from anywhere, I waited until sunset to climb a nearby sand dune and read the stars. They were so bright and beautiful that they calmed me as I sat there looking upward. Then I heard a dog bark.

Hearing the bark again, I began walking in the direction of the sound. I crossed several large dunes until I came to a black tent filled with desert nomads. As I approached, two fierce-looking dogs ran at me. A tall man crawled out of the tent, and I held up my hand in a friendly salute.

Despite all my travels, I never developed a talent for learning languages. I could not communicate well in Berber, so he took me to the tent where there was an old man who spoke French. I explained what had happened in my limited French, but the Berbers didn't seem to know what an airplane was. I finally persuaded the first man to come with me to the plane. There we found the pilot, still lying quietly on the ground. I turned him loose and tried to explain that this nomad was part of a caravan heading northeast. We could accompany them as far as Gabes.

The next day we dismounted the motor and instruments from the plane and loaded them on camels for our journey. Crossing the desert took us two weeks to reach the first town, Ouargla, and it took another week to Gabes. Although the intense heat of daytime desert travel can be almost unbearable—relieved occasionally by the refreshing cool of the great oases, like gardens of Eden, scattered here and there over vast distances—there's always the compensation of those chilled and eerily silent nights.

I believe that accidents—even plane crashes—do not happen without reason. My unplanned caravan journey across the desert, which covered the same distance in six weeks that it had taken us to fly in eleven hours, was an unexpected gift that only deepened my love for the Sahara.

I've often wished I were a poet so I could do justice to those desert nights. The surge of emotion I felt each evening as I watched the sun slide quickly under the distant line of sand, leaving a vermillion-hued trail, was my reward; I had survived another day in the desert to experience the cool, life-saving silence of its night air. My sleep at the end of this day would not be death.[47]

---

47   Horace D. Ashton, "Explorer Describes Sahara Expedition," in Washington, D.C.-area newspaper, 1922.

CHAPTER **28**

Tunisia, Turkey, and the Troglodytes, Early 1920s–1925

Horace

One Sunday in Tunisia, I sat on the dusty ground under the shade of an olive tree, overlooking a barren, pasture–like hill that sloped down to the glistening Mediterranean Sea. Neither the calls of gulls swooping to catch fish below nor the dry heat of the late afternoon sun distracted me from quiet contemplation.

The mystical experiences I'd had in my early twenties while studying the world's religions and my immersion in other cultures since had opened my eyes to reincarnation, and I often wondered if I might have lived before.

Earlier that day, I'd talked briefly with one of the "white" brothers, two white–bearded elders known locally for their wisdom. He'd told me something of the tragic history of ancient Carthage, which had been located on the peninsula that jutted out from the North African coast in present–day Tunisia.

Ancient Carthage was founded in 800 B.C. as a colony of the Phoenicians, ancient sailors and traders who lived in the northern part of Palestine along the Mediterranean coast. The Phoenicians made Carthage a center of North African trade, and over time it became a powerful colony.

More than six hundred years later, the Romans dominated most of the Mediterranean but did not control Carthage. Rome initiated a series of wars known as the

Punic Wars[48] to place Carthage under Roman rule. Over nearly one hundred years, three wars were fought. During the Second Punic War, the great Carthaginian general Hannibal decided to bring the war home to the Romans. It was reported that he crossed the Alps with a large contingent of men, horses, and elephants but was soundly defeated by the Romans. Carthage was completely destroyed after the Third Punic War in 146 B.C.

As I gazed upon the Mediterranean vista, I noticed an unusual—looking, horseshoe—shaped body of water with an island in the center of the horseshoe. I must have been dreaming as I sat on the slope with my back against the olive tree, because the scene suddenly came to life. Before me lay the ancient city spread out in all its glory.

The horseshoe—shaped lagoon became a small harbor once again, and several galleons returned to port through the entrance by the island. Men in shining armor seated upon elephants passed up and down the ramp of the city's great fort. The place where I sat was no longer a dry pasture but the lush terrace of some rich man's palace. There was a sunken garden below me in the foreground where I could see a beautiful bath, and through the clear water I glimpsed the signs of the zodiac laid out in mosaic tile on the bottom. The strange noises of the city echoed in my ears, as they were very different from the traffic and bustle of the cities in our day.

The vision lasted only a few minutes, but it was so real to me. Afterward I hurried to the elder at the museum, whom I had met earlier, and explained to the brother what had happened. He took down a very old book from a shelf in the library and opened it to a drawing of ancient Carthage. I had never seen this picture, but it was almost exactly what I had envisioned earlier. I was amazed at my own vision.

The brother did not seem surprised. Smiling, he showed me a cable he had received two days earlier that

---

48   *Punicus* is the Latin word for Phoenician.

anyone else might have thought to be a coincidence. The cable read: "Sir, please be advised that Mr. Byron Kuhn de Prorok, a member of the Explorers Club, will arrive with a small group of archaeology students from Harvard. They request permission to spend a few weeks excavating the site of ancient Carthage."

I knew Byron, as I enjoyed camaraderie with other adventurers at the Explorers Club whenever I was in New York, sharing lively conversations and thrilling stories together. I was delighted to learn he was leading an expedition to this area. However, as I was scheduled to depart for Paris the next morning, I could not wait in Tunisia to greet my fellow club member. Before I left, the brother asked me to take him to the exact olive tree where my vision occurred, and when I did so, he marked the spot.

Several years later, I returned to Tunisia to take my second wife on a honeymoon to the troglodyte caves (another story). En route, I stopped at the museum to visit my old friend, the "white" brother and elder. He took me to the same spot where I'd sat under the olive tree and had the vision that Sunday afternoon. Before me now was a large pit about thirty feet deep, surrounded by a railing and covered by a roof. When I looked down, I saw the exact mosaic floor of the bath that I had seen in my vision. The Harvard expedition had uncovered it precisely under the spot where I had been sitting years earlier. How had I known? Had I lived during the time of ancient Carthage?

The experience brought to mind my studies of Buddhism and Hinduism in the Orient, where I had learned a great deal about reincarnation. The question of reincarnation was one I would return to consider often. I openly discussed this subject with Bishop Leadbeater of Australia, a prominent member of the Theosophical Society. He told me that he too had clear memories of exact events from at least two previous lives on earth.

* * *

I'd barely arrived in Paris when I received an urgent cable from Pathé News in New York with an exciting new assignment. I was to charter a plane and fly to Italy to film the latest eruption of Mount Vesuvius—one of the dozen eruptions from 1913 to 1944 that were all part of the same ongoing geological disturbance—from the air.

I quickly arranged insurance for the plane and pilot, and packed up my camera equipment. The next day dawned clear and sunny, and we took off on a beautiful flight across France to the Cote d'Azur; then we headed south along the Italian coast to Naples. When we flew over the bay, it wasn't hard to spot the huge mushroom cloud of smoke billowing from Vesuvius. I filmed it first from a distance.

As we approached and circled the volcano, I ordered the pilot to fly in under the cloud of smoke so I could photograph the crater. About halfway around it, a sudden rush of hot sulfur gas hit one wing. We rolled and slid down into the crater.

As the plane descended, I struggled to dismount my valuable camera. When we crashed, one wing stuck into a crack in the black, hardened lava. The pilot and I scrambled out and ran toward the side of the crater. Within seconds the plane burst into flames.

Our greatest difficulty was that in running over the hot lava we burned off the soles of our shoes and blistered our feet. I discovered I'd broken my nose again. Having repaired my own broken nose the first time as a teenager after a baseball accident—and several times since—I was by now becoming somewhat of an amateur nasal surgeon.

Fortunately, I managed to save the camera, and the films were later shown worldwide. The audience never knew that I had broken my nose and burned the soles off a new pair of shoes.

* * *

On my frequent trips to North Africa in the early 1920s, I often stopped in Europe. One country that I was eager to explore was Turkey, which had changed a great deal since the world war ended. Toward the end of 1923, I went to Turkey to take photographs and observe firsthand the many changes that had taken place since the country was no longer the center of the Ottoman Empire. I also hoped to visit with its first president, Mustafa Kemal Pasha, who later became known as Kemal Ataturk, the founder of modern Turkey.

During my stay in Constantinople (now Istanbul), I noticed that all the taxicabs were driven by former officers from the late czar of Russia's Imperial Guard. The city was crowded with Russian refugees, mostly of the aristocracy. The wives spent their days selling their jewels, wonderful old silver, furs, and other valuables with which they had escaped. Some of the men and women performed as singers in nightclubs, and some of the women made dresses for the ladies of the diplomatic corps. These were people who had lived in luxury all their lives, with many servants waiting on them, and now they had joined the working class.

At the time, the new Republic of Turkey was being administered by the United States, England, and France, since it had fought on the side of Germany and Austria during the Great War. Our acting United States ambassador was Admiral Bristol of the United States Navy, whom I knew well, and he requested that I make some aerial motion pictures of Constantinople. Admiral Bristol arranged with the British to fly me over the city. We fitted my camera to the edge of the open cockpit and flew quite low over the city for ten or fifteen minutes while I got some great footage. All of a sudden, something went wrong with our fuel line, and the motor conked out.

The only place that looked fairly safe for a forced landing within the range of our descent was the vaulted roof of the Turkish bazaars. The expert pilot managed the landing, and remarkably the only damage was a demolished landing gear and a gaping hole in the roof. Fortunately, no one was hurt.

I climbed out of the plane and walked to the edge of the roof. Peering down, I saw the rug merchant and his neighbors busily cleaning up the mess below as though a plane dropped onto their roof every day. Signaling them to stand aside, the pilot and I let ourselves down into the bazaar by hanging from the roof by our hands and dropping about ten feet onto a pile of brightly colored rugs. The rug merchants welcomed us warmly and insisted that we have a cup of strong Turkish coffee.

With great pride they showed us their beautiful hand-woven rugs with intricate designs in rich reds, oranges, and blues. Examining the unique designs on each, I noticed they weren't uniform all the way around. I could imagine an entire Turkish family, from children to grandparents, each working on his or her own section and crafting one rug together. When we departed, the merchants thanked us for "dropping in."

A few days later, I would experience another miracle healing. I explored more of Turkey by taking a trip up the Bosporus on one of those small boats that stop at all the landings as far as the Black Sea. The Bosporus is a very beautiful and historic strait, through which the water of the Black Sea flows into the Sea of Marmora and the Dardanelles, connecting the Black Sea with the Aegean arm of the Mediterranean. Along its shores there are magnificent palaces and luxurious villas of the rich, all with dreamlike gardens. From the boat I watched flocks of small black and white birds flying very close to the water in both directions. It was the oddest thing; when they'd meet, one flock would fly up and over the others and then descend to their former level and continue on their way.

In the garden of a mosque on the Golden Horn, which separates Para from Constantinople, I found a mullah sitting with a small board across his knees and a box of small nails and a hammer in his hand. Seated before him was an elderly man who gazed at the board as he held his index finger on the side of his knee. I learned that the mullah was a healer. Anyone with a pain could give him a small fee, sit down, and place his own finger on the pain while the mullah, praying all the while, slowly tapped a small nail into the board. When the head of the nail was all the way into the board, the patient was always cured.

Watching this healing ceremony reminded me of similar religious healing ceremonies I had observed in North Africa and Haiti. I have always believed that physical healing relies greatly on mental outlook, and this ceremony reinforced my belief. It's really a case of mind over matter.

While I was in Turkey I hoped to visit the president, so Admiral Bristol arranged for me to travel by train into the interior province of Anatolia, where Kemal Pasha had established the new capital city. On the way there, I stopped in Bursa and visited the market, where I saw great piles of silk cocoons and observed the peasant women filling the fronts of their blouses with silk worms. When I asked them why, they explained they carried them this way to keep the silk worms warm during the cold Turkish winter.

In Bursa I tried the famous Turkish baths for the first time. First, I was directed to a small private booth, where I undressed and locked up my clothes. Then, wearing only a white sheet–like covering, I entered the great steam room. All around the wall were stone benches. In the middle of the room, a fire roared under a huge pile of rocks several feet high. Half–naked men threw buckets of cold water over the rocks, filling the room with clouds of hot steam so dense that I couldn't see the occupant on the next bench. When I could not stand the heat any longer, I went into another room, where I had a brisk massage and then entered a tub of cold water.

This experience refreshed me for the long train ride to Eskisehir, where a division of the Turkish Army was quartered. I stayed there for a day and visited the first Meerschaum mine I had ever seen. Meerschaum, or prehistoric compressed sea foam, is taken out of a deep mine looking and feeling like laundry soap. It hardens up quickly, after being exposed to the air and is then carved into the shapes required for pipes, pipe liners, and cigarette holders. Items made from this rare substance are then exported to all parts of the world.

Ankara, the new capital of Turkey, was the terminus of the railway. There were no hotels yet built, so I found a large caravansary in which to spend the night. This was an arrangement where loaded wagons were driven into a courtyard and the horses were stabled below. The drivers slept on the floor in rooms above the courtyard, open to balconies that looked down on it.

Provisions were limited, and I had to be inventive with my lodging. I found the frame of an old iron bed with no spring or mattress, gathered some boards, and bought a fairly large rug—red background with multicolored designs—from one of the wagons. The man who sold me the rug told me that the women of his family, who lived in Anatolia near the Persian border, had spent six months weaving it by hand. (That was fifty-seven years ago, and as I write this in my studio in Haiti, my two favorite dogs are asleep on it.)

I spread the rug over the boards and slept well the first night. The next morning I walked through the street looking for a restaurant, but there was none. I bought several large pretzels from a street vendor. Then I picked up a clean shingle from where a house was being built and asked a man in a shop to dip the shingle in a tub of honey. With the honey dripping from the shingle, I sat down on the step of the house under construction and dipped the pretzels in the honey. This unusual breakfast was finished off with two cups of thick Turkish coffee I bought from a tiny coffee booth nearby.

Later that day, I arrived at the residence of the

president and presented my credentials. I was graciously received by Kemal Pasha. Since there were no hotels, he insisted I stay with him. As much as I loved my new rug, I was glad to sleep in a bed. I remained there several days.

During my stay, I received a telegram from Admiral Bristol telling me that Mr. Wiley, the managing editor of *The New York Times*, was in Constantinople and would like to interview Kemal Pasha. I talked with Kemal, explaining that Mr. Wiley represented the most important newspaper in the United States. Although Kemal was reluctant to give interviews to the press, he agreed to allow Mr. Wiley to come.

Kemal was very kind to me, posed for several pictures—one with a group of puppies that were only a day or so old—and told me many interesting things about his life. It was just then that he was passing laws abolishing the veil and giving Turkish women equal rights with men. Shortly after my visit, the caliphate, or spiritual leader of Islam, was renounced, and Turkey became a secular society.

After I returned to the United States, I gave a lecture about my trip to Turkey at the New York Museum of Natural History.[49] I illustrated my talk with photographs that I had taken in Constantinople and Ankara. During my talk, I explained that Turkey and its people had been unfairly represented in the United States, and I felt that this stemmed from religious bias. I found the Turks to be an upright, kindly people who were more faithful to their religious tenets than most.

After presenting my illustrated lecture about Turkey, I discussed an interest in the founding of a Turkish–American society in New York. As other countries, such as Japan through the Japan Society, were represented in America, I felt strongly that Turkey should be allowed to share in these advantages.

---

49   "Lecturer Defends Turk's Reputation," in *New York Evening Post*, 25 March 1924.

MUSTAPHA KEMAL PASHA

TURKEY—*The Newest* REPUBLIC

TURKEY has ever been a land of supreme interest. In the days of the sick man of Europe it was always a topic for daily news; now that it has almost lost its hold on Europe and become one of the strong men of the Near East, it is more than ever a land to be studied and watched. It is a country of much beauty and picturesqueness; it is a land of political and artistic rebirth. Everyone wants to know what is taking place there, and Mr. Ashton, like many others, shared this curiosity. He went there and brought back an account that does him credit.

He tells a true and unbiased story of conditions in Turkey today under the rule of Mustapha Kemal Pasha and the Grand National Assembly. It was only quite recently that Mr. Ashton visited Kemal Pasha at Angora. Mr. Ashton was with him and talked with him. He got a first-hand idea of what is going on in this new Republic. He learned their national aims, their ambitions and their hope in a future relation with America.

He learned their life and their customs, and his artistic and life-like motion pictures illustrate every phase of Turkish life, in Constantinople, amid the ruins of ill-fated Smyrna, in Broussa, the first Turkish capital, and in the heart of Anatolia. Angora, the newest capital, thousands of years old, but resembling a boom mining town, is pictured realistically. Many Turkish notables, including Kemal Pasha himself, posed for Mr. Ashton's camera.

In this talk one finds a combination of the picturesque and the political, of the old and the new. Men with fezzes walk side by side with the new Turk, who has given up the wearing of the tarboosh. Unveiled women, rejoicing in their new freedom, are found in the same pictures with harem women who still live in the past. Minarets pierce the sky and modern business penetrates the new life in the streets. It is an old nation trying to become accustomed to the feel of new blood coursing through its veins. It is not yet wholly awakened to the rejuvenation, but it is a picture well worth studying and one that will not let the attention flag.

* * *

"I want to thank you once again for the most delightful entertainment you gave us. The pictures are wonderful and of great educational value. Your talk is just right; it is light and amusing, and very instructive. The audience were all delighted."—Edward R. Hewitt, 47 Gramercy Park, New York.

❖ ❖ ❖

Under the Exclusive Management of

JAMES B. POND, *The Pond Bureau*, 25 West 43d Street, New York

To whom all inquiries regarding terms and dates should be addressed

This article recounts Horace Ashton's time in Turkey with President Kemal Ataturk.

* * *

If I do say so myself, I was looking particularly dapper in the 1920s, resplendent with a waxed handlebar mustache. Attractively confident and somewhat of a celebrity, I had been described as "intelligent, witty and a delightful cicerone" by the newspapers. My notoriety—and I like to think my charming personality—attracted the interest of the ladies.

The very pretty Helen Pitt–Smith, a New York interior decorator, attracted my attention from the moment I met her, when she and a friend came up to speak to me after one of my lectures. Her friend was all female flutter, but Helen seemed fascinated by my experiences with the troglodyte cave–dwellers and was curious about the harem women.

Helen, who had grown up in Yonkers and was the niece of Frank Ford, had rarely driven to the countryside for a picnic, let alone traveled the world, but I loved her enthusiasm. She was eager to spend her life with me, eager to accompany me on my adventures, and I was hopelessly smitten. I proposed and invited her to spend our honeymoon in the troglodyte caves.

They say love is blind, and perhaps it is. Helen's conventional New York society friends told her they liked her tall, gray–eyed Virginian, but they questioned the wisdom of marrying a man who had spent the past twenty years traveling the world in search of adventure. They didn't think she was suited to the life I led. But Helen was in love and bubbling over with excitement about her upcoming honeymoon among the troglodytes of the African desert. Her friends were sure she'd never be able to stand it, and our marriage would be over practically before it began.

We married in 1923. While on our honeymoon in Africa, Helen was a good sport, tolerating the desert heat and primitive living conditions, riding on camels eight hours a day, and charming our hosts. Although I had been well received on my first visit, the sheik had informed me that several tribe members were concerned about the presence of a single male, worried that I was there to steal their women. This time, by bringing my mate, I hoped to gain access to take photographs that would have been forbidden in the past, since a white man had never been able to photograph Muslim women or view them unveiled.

When we first approached the troglodyte village, all eyes were on Helen. The tall, bearded sheik greeted me and asked, "Is that one of your wives?"

"She's the only one I have," I answered.

"I should like to buy her," the sheik returned.

When I explained that Helen wasn't for sale, the sheik invited her to visit the harem, which was exactly what she'd hoped for. The women crowded around Helen and kissed her hands, examined her clothes, and even took down her hair. "They have at least one trait in common with the modern flapper—they are fast workers," Helen told me later with a grin. "If a cave girl isn't settled in life by the time she's fourteen, she's a hopeless old maid. But an American woman would go crazy in a week if she had to live as they do. The only time they get out of that cave is Friday nights, when they go to the cemetery."

The newspapers featured Helen's unique version of our African adventure. The following excerpts appeared in a feature article by Caroline Gordon, titled "My Thrilling Honeymoon Among the Troglodytes," that was picked up and run as a feature by several papers, complete with its headline written in the type of script one might see on the front cover of a superhero comic book.[50]

> "I stepped through the guarded door and stood where no civilized woman ever had been before—in the troglodyte Harem. Then suddenly I heard something that made my blood curdle—a woman's scream. I thought the woman was being murdered and was numb with terror . . ."

> This is what pretty Helen Pitt-Smith Ashton told about the most exciting experience of her honeymoon journey through the wilds of Northern Africa with her husband, Horace Ashton, the explorer. Inexperienced in desert travel, totally unfamiliar with primitive people, she nevertheless succeeded in an undertaking which the

50   Carolyn Gordon, "My Thrilling Honeymoon Among the Troglodytes," in *Newspaper Feature Service*, 1925.

Pharaohs of Egypt abandoned in despair five thousand years ago and which the emperors of Rome attempted unsuccessfully—that of penetrating the underground harems of the cave dwellers of the Dark Continent.

The screams Helen heard came from a low, vault–shaped room. In the center of the floor was a raised platform covered with rugs and pillows that served as the bed, where a man and woman were struggling. The woman fought like a jungle animal— scratching and biting and screaming—until finally the man reached for a great knotted club and, while he held the woman firmly by the hair with one hand, brought it squarely on top of her head with the other. I explained to my terrified new wife that the man and woman were bride and groom, and this was a local marriage custom, similar to the one I had learned about earlier.

The cavewomen of the Sahara were the most beautiful women I had ever seen among the primitive peoples, and I was anxious to photograph them. At first the women were horror–stricken by the idea. But after living among them for months and communicating by sign and our small troglodyte vocabulary, Helen finally persuaded them, and the chief granted permission for me to enter the harem with my camera.

They were the hardest subjects I ever photographed, bar none. The girls were veiled at the age of twelve when they married, so the idea of raising their veils, even when sanctioned by the men of their family, frightened them. Sometimes after they raised their veils, I felt like urging them to put them down in a hurry, because although the troglodyte women are extremely beautiful in their early youth, the dry climate dulls the luster of their skin and hair and ages them quickly.

CAVE MEN OF THE DESERT

A VISIT to the Troglodytes of the Sahara—thirty thousand people who live in holes in the ground—gave Horace Ashton the material and data for this most interesting lecture. Twice he has journeyed into the rugged, inhospitable Ksour Mountains of South Tunisia for the purpose of studying at first-hand these little-known tribes of the Berbers, who are the direct descendants of the Mercenaries who fought with the Caesars in the overthrow of fair Carthage. In this lecture we are told and shown that in twenty-two hundred years or more they have stood still, defying not only all enemy invaders, but, in their curious underground dwellings, even the passage of time. They live and dress precisely as they did before the Christian era. Here survive quaint native customs, the origin of which are hopelessly lost in antiquity. Some of these customs are so odd that their description almost defies belief. To quote from "The Boston Sunday Herald": "Every bride must be knocked out with a club before she's really married. Tooth and nail, hand and foot, she throws herself upon the bridegroom as though to blot out his very existence. Manfully he fights back until she is at length overpowered, then comes the crowning climax of the wedding. He takes her firmly by the hair, holds her at arm's length, and grasps the 'marriage stick' in the other hand. Then, to put it brutally but truthfully, he knocks her out, picks her up, throws her over his shoulder and carries her off to their new home."

For its human interest, this is one of Horace Ashton's most popular talks. It shows him to be an unusually keen observer of human nature and possessed of more than ordinary tact and diplomacy in overcoming the barriers of language and fanaticism which have so long isolated these Cave Men of the Desert, for he was allowed to enter the sanctity of their harems and photograph, unveiled, their women, who have never before been seen by the eye of another man than their husbands. He says that it is his sense of humor which gets him through, and after hearing this talk you will agree with him.

Magazine article tells of Horace Ashton's life among the troglodytes of North Africa.

Upon returning from our honeymoon, we moved into a home in Yonkers, but we spent little time there. One occasion when we were home found me at Roosevelt Field on Long Island after a picture-making flight. I watched another plane land and taxi up to the hangar with interest, because not many planes landed there. A very dapper pilot, wearing shiny leather boots, fawn–colored riding breeches, and a French blue tunic with silver wings embroidered on his breast, alighted. As I greeted the pilot, who sported a waxed mustache like the one I wore, he lifted down an Airedale dog wearing goggles. This was the predecessor of his famous "copilot," the lion cub Gilmore, who later logged 25,000 miles with this equally famous racing pilot, Colonel Roscoe Turner.

As there were no taxicabs at the field, I offered Roscoe and his flying dog a ride and ended up bringing them home to meet Helen and to stay with us. The following day, I drove Roscoe into the city, and perhaps out of gratitude or compassion for my love of animals, he gave me his little Airedale, who had stolen my heart. I named the dog Roscoe, but I never saw the man again. In the 1930s I avidly followed pilot Roscoe Turner's thrilling career as he set speed records, flying with his lion mascot, Gilmore. Later, at the age of seventy–two, Turner broke the sound barrier with a T–38 jet.

Determined to assist me with my lecture tours by taking notes during our travels, Helen studied French and shorthand. She accompanied me to Paris, which she loved, and then to India, where we visited a maharajah I'd befriended on an earlier trip. Before we left for India, Helen was quoted in a Yonkers newspaper: "I have no idea what visiting a maharajah will be like, but I know it will be great fun!"

Despite her "can do" attitude, Helen and I were very different people. She enjoyed city life, dining in fine restaurants, and attending society parties dressed in her latest flapper finery. I enjoyed exploring the world and had once said, "You see, I don't like cities, and I'm not awfully fond of civilized people. In cities we go too fast to think, so we have no wisdom. On the plains, in the deserts, and in the mountains, you will find people who will amaze you with their wisdom."

Chapter 29

Trapped

Butch
April 5, 2001
5:40 p.m.

Death, I think, bringing myself back to the present. *It could be my death.*

For the past fifteen minutes I have been silently praying for help. The car is cool now, and my meditation has calmed me. I feel my strength returning but am careful to show no outward sign of it as I continue to feign weakness.

The killer beside me is drumming with one hand on the seat to the beat of the music on the radio, while cradling the Uzi with the other. Suddenly, the music is interrupted by an alert: "A prominent American businessman, Marc Ashton, has been kidnapped. Be on the lookout for a beige 2001 Toyota Land Cruiser, license number XYZ."

The two thugs in the car with me freeze and then frantically begin discussing what to do without the leader there to tell them. About the same time, I hear the unmistakable whirr of helicopter blades, an unusual sound in this remote place. The sound circles slowly overhead and then seems to die away as the helicopter leaves; then it returns again.

The dripping-wet swimmers charge back to the car in a state of panic. Everyone knows that only the president of Haiti has access to helicopters. Flown by American mercenaries, they often accompany him on his outings. Apparently it hasn't occurred to my kidnappers that anyone but Myriam would try to find me. I hope this attention will convince them they've made a mistake, and it would be better to release me and go on their way.

The leader jumps into the front seat, grabs my cell phone and my walkie-talkie, and rips the batteries out of them. "They're tracking us from the radio signals!" he shouts to the others and then begins to issue orders.

Everyone is back in the car, and all guns are on me. During the melee, I calmly keep praying, focusing on the sound of the helicopter blades, willing them closer. *Perhaps the authorities will find me. Maybe the pilot will look down at this exact spot.*

My kidnappers grow deadly serious again. The driver maneuvers the Toyota under some thicker brush to better hide it from above. That done, the killer pulls a roll of duct tape and a cloth hat out of the bag he used to conceal the Uzi. They place duct tape over my eyes and mouth, and roughly pull the hat down on my head to cover my hair. They came prepared!

The whirr of the helicopter fades away, and so does my hope for immediate rescue.

With my eyes and mouth taped, I concentrate on breathing through my nostrils, on taking in enough air to fill my lungs. My difficult breathing is no longer an act, but I continue to feign weakness while I focus on my captors' voices in the blackness.

The helicopter has unnerved them completely; even the leader is unsure what to do next. Myriam, other family members, and friends have no doubt initiated a search for me, and the helicopter was most probably partaking. Whether we were being tracked, as the kidnappers suspect, I don't know. I do know their plan to kidnap me for easy ransom is not going well.

* * *

April 5, 2001
About 6:30 p.m.

My eyes and mouth are still covered with duct tape. It feels hot and itchy, tight against my skin. I try to guess how much time has passed. Another hour?

Pretending to be nearly unconsciousness, I follow the Creole conversation and analyze the situation. During my ordeal so far, the leader has been negotiating with both Myriam and me regarding the ransom, but it doesn't appear we are getting any closer to making final arrangements. I am now afraid that the criminals' reaction to having all their plans backfire might be to simply kill me.

When the car doors open and I feel the cooler air on my bare arms and face, I know that night has fallen. Under the cover of darkness the leader sends the driver and the novice to get another car while he and the killer stay behind to guard me.

Slumped in the backseat, occasionally letting a soft moan escape from under my taped mouth, I listen intently to their hasty discussion of new plans. With my vision cut off, my hearing seems more acute and my mind sharper. *Or is it my prayers that give me clarity?*

As they wait for the others to return, the two discuss moving me to a new location and what "safe houses" are nearby. Their plans become more and more disjointed, and they even indulge in a fanciful, typically *facteur H* discussion of how to spend the million and a half ransom money.

I double over and gasp for air, feigning a heart attack. I act as if I'm choking, having a seizure . . .

The leader scrambles to rip the tape from my mouth and prop me upright. Unsure of what is happening to me or what they should do, he starts the Land Cruiser, and we speed away. Even though they had managed to remove the license plates somewhere along the way, they feel it is risky to move the car into the open.

I pray someone will recognize the beige Toyota of "kidnapped businessman Marc Ashton." I also recall other seemingly impossible situations I've faced and how I've overcome them. I must think of a way to get out of this situation.

* * *

Years ago, after Myriam and I lost the lease on the Kyona Beach resort, we were both somewhat disappointed and discouraged. Even though it had been hard work in the kitchen and the bar, we'd loved the upbeat atmosphere and the time spent on the weekends at the beach with so many friends. Much of the fun had gone out of our lives.

One of the lowest periods of our lives began to intensify as we struggled to make ends meet, and Myriam was pregnant with our second child. Our daughter Daska had been born three years earlier, and after that Myriam suffered a miscarriage due to waterskiing. Now problems arose with this pregnancy, too, causing her to stay in bed.

I needed to find a way to supplement our financial situation and help Myriam feel better. Eventually I came up with a plan about how we might repeat our Kyona Beach success and make it even better.

One evening I returned from the countryside and burst into the bedroom with great enthusiasm, eager to share my news with Myriam. "I have a surprise present for you. I bought us a new beach property!"

What I thought would cheer her up only upset her. "What? You bought property without my approval? How did you pay for it?" She nearly gave birth on the spot.

To her surprise I explained that I had sold our car and combined that money with our savings to buy a property. It cost

$4,000. I could barely contain my excitement and hardly wait to show her the property.

A few weeks later, when Myriam was able to get out of bed, I took her to see it. She broke down in tears as she stared at nothing but rocks and cactus.

I tried to calm her. "Use your imagination, Myriam. Think of the possibilities. Over six hundred feet of beachfront! Can't you just see our fabulous waterfront resort here? You know what we're capable of when we put our minds to it. We can do this."

But she couldn't agree. Not that day.

"How could you throw our hard-earned money away? It's nothing but rocks beside a railroad track. How could you buy this piece of junk? And for so much money!"

I wasn't about to give up on our dream—or to be more honest, *my* dream. But then I've always been the dreamer, or as I like to think of it, the visionary of our team. Myriam soon came around, as she consistently had.

But then we were faced with other dilemmas: how to develop the property and build the resort. We didn't have any money left, and bank financing was unavailable for projects like this, so we brought in partners to help with financing and construction.

Within eighteen months we transformed "nothing but rocks and cactus" into a lush, tropical paradise we named MaiKai Beach Resort. We created the perfect location for me to receive my duck-hunting and scuba-diving groups, which I had created in the meantime as a new endeavor through our travel agency. With Myriam in the kitchen and me in the bar, working hard—and having fun—we built our beach resort business all over again. This time, we had ownership and control in it.

Within weeks of opening, the crowd from Kyona Beach heard about our new endeavor and followed us to MaiKai. It became the new, popular "in" place to go.

If I could take rocks and cactus and turn them into a thriving resort, I can surely devise a way to escape my current situation. Though she's not present, I know Myriam is with me.

* * *

Captive in my car, my thoughts return, unbidden, to the comfort of my father and his life. *Why do I keep thinking about him during the worst day of my life? Is there a lesson in his stories I am supposed to see that will help me now?*

Dad was a true gentleman who often helped others out of difficult situations. If someone asked for help, he was at their service, doing whatever he could to assist them. During his lifetime, he rescued several individuals, often placing himself in jeopardy, yet he never let these experiences dampen his spirit or keep him from another encounter. He was a kind man who had compassion for others and lived his beliefs, always trying to do the right thing.

He immersed himself in the Haitian culture and became a part of it, speaking only the universal language of spiritual beings. Like a true diplomat, he had a way of getting along with everyone and sharing his experiences with them.

My father trusted completely in the good of others, and I see now that he must have taught me this. Perhaps I have a tendency to trust people too much. My wife and daughters obviously thought so when they frequently referred to me as "Ali Baba." (In the Arabian tale *Ali Baba and the Forty Thieves*, the protagonist was a great do-gooder who surrounded himself with a bunch of thieves who were stealing him blind.)

My daughter often says, "Daddy can never find anything wrong with anybody."

But it was my father who taught me there is a reason behind every wrong, and so, like Ali Baba, I look for it and forgive. Despite my private resentment of him, I always made excuses for my father. I trusted in his goodness. Even today, whatever the situation, I try to put myself in the other person's place, as he taught me to.

Maybe if I can think like my kidnappers and anticipate their next moves, I'll have a chance to save myself.

I pray for my father's help, and I am awed that in some small way I may be getting it. But at the same time, I wish with all my heart that he didn't know of the terror in his beloved Haiti or that his son's life was now being threatened by it.

I am trapped, yet I recall the time my father was trapped. He managed to find his way out of a dark cavern without a light. I will find my way out of this nightmare too, with my father's guidance. He is my beacon.

CHAPTER **30**

Above and Inside the Earth, 1925

Horace

The spring of 1925 found me on a large sugar plantation in the Oriente Province of Cuba, making a documentary film about a new cane—harvesting machine. Listening to the evening news on the radio, I learned of the proposed test voyage of the great Zeppelin ZR—2 that the United States had purchased from Germany and renamed the *Los Angeles*. Early the next morning, while standing in a sugar cane field, I had another one of my brainstorms.

I ran back to the plantation office and cabled Rear Admiral Moffat, chief of naval operations, offering to record the airship's maiden voyage on film. Admiral Moffat knew me as a lecturer and liked my work. Since he wanted publicity for his pet hobby—lighter—than—air navigation— he jumped on my idea. The next day, orders arrived for me to report to the United States Naval Station at Guantanamo to be flown to Lakehurst, New Jersey, where I was to report to Captain Steele, commanding officer of the *Los Angeles*. An article in *The New York Times* later announced:

> Horace Ashton had the distinction of being appointed by the Secretary of the Navy as Special Observer for Naval Intelligence to accompany the airship *Los Angeles* on her flight to Puerto Rico and the Virgin Islands. He was therefore the first civilian passenger ever taken on this great Zeppelin and made the longest overseas trip ever attempted by a helium-filled airship.

I was extremely fortunate and honored to participate in this historic airship journey, which departed April 28, 1925. I later wrote a lengthy feature article describing my experience, which was published in *The New York Times Magazine*[51] and another article for *The Literary Digest*.[52]

On the morning the great airship was scheduled to leave, a stiff northeast wind blew, and a cold gray mist settled over Lakehurst. I stared in amazement at the enormous structure, looming in unbelievable dimension, which housed the *Los Angeles* and the *Shenandoah*. (I later learned that its interior was the largest single room in the world and when empty it could develop its own microweather system—clouds could form, and rain fell indoors!)[53]

The *Los Angeles* carried 4,500 gallons of fuel, enough to take us 4,000 miles under normal conditions, but a forty-miles-per-hour headwind made it extremely risky to attempt an inaugural 1,750-mile-long jump from New Jersey to Puerto Rico. The great hangar doors remained closed as everyone anxiously awaited the morning weather map, which was to be radioed from Washington. It arrived about eleven o'clock and showed conditions decidedly unfavorable for a start. All we could do was remain ready . . . and wait.

Finally, about half past seven that evening, the "stand by" order was given. Just after dark, I watched the huge hangar doors roll back and the great silver ship, borne forward by more than three hundred men, emerge silently and almost ghostlike into the night. The rays of electric torches and occasional clusters of floodlights on the hangar, reflected from the silver coat of the ship, added to the weirdness of the spectacle.

---

51   Horace D. Ashton, "Overseas in the Los Angeles," in *The New York Times,* magazine section, 31 May 1925.

52   *The Literary Digest*, 4 July 1925.

53   "Describes His Trip on Dirigible," *The Coatesville Record*, Coatesville, Pennsylvania, 1 February 1926.

Once the 656-foot ship was clear of the hangar, the great doors once more rolled back into place, and the land crew started on their long walk with the ship, more than half a mile, to the mooring mast. The *Los Angeles*, safely hooked up to the swivel-cone mooring on the 160-foot mast, stood out against the sky like a giant weather vane.

Early the next morning, I rode a little elevator up to the top of the mast and then climbed a vertical ladder to the main platform, where I waited with the others for boarding orders. "One man aboard!" came the order, and an officer scrambled up the stepladder and onto the small gangway which, when closed up, formed part of the nose of the ship.

As each man climbed aboard, he had to go immediately to his "landing station," a prescribed position that he must assume whenever taking off from the mast or making a landing. To compensate for his weight, water ballast must be dropped. Calculations had to be exact. Even a very slight gust of wind or an infinitesimal loss of buoyancy in the gas would cause the tail to crash to the ground.

My turn came in a few minutes. "Mr. Ashton, aboard!" I lost no time entering and made my way quickly down the narrow inclined passageway to the keel, located just above the control car, as instructed. Here I disposed of my baggage and went immediately aft along the cat's walk, passing with difficulty the several men who were already at their stations and had to lean far over to let me pass. About four-fifths of the way back a tiny hatch with a small folding ladder led down ten feet into the rear motor gondola, or "Number One Car," and here I found my position for making pictures of the takeoff.

From my vantage point the entire bottom of the ship, the four other gondolas, and the rear of the control car were visible. Racks for my motion picture camera, constructed of duralumin, an alloy known for strength and light weight, had been built onto the windowsills of several of the motor gondolas.

I was dressed in a flying suit, goggles, and helmet, because climbing up and down the folding ladders from the main body of the ship to get back and forth between these positions would require my exposure to the rushing wind.

Anticipation mounting, I waited in a somewhat cramped position in the gondola as water ballast was released from several parts of the ship, and in answer to the horn-like toot of the ship's telephone, men were moved back and forth along the keel. We were about to attempt the longest journey ever made by a helium-filled airship.

At last we arose slowly from the mast with motors still. As soon as we were clear and our nose pointed slightly upward, all motors were cut in at full speed. With a roar and a mighty push of 2,000 horsepower, the great dirigible, hesitating for a moment, gradually began to forge ahead and upward at a steep angle. I filmed the mast and watched the landing field sink away astern as we passed up and over the pines and the lakes of New Jersey, heading out toward the Atlantic.

The start was quite bumpy, owing to the gusty nature of the wind and the difference in air temperature over the sand field and the surrounding pines, but I managed to shoot the takeoff footage I wanted. In a few minutes I was filming Barnegat Beach, stretched across our path far below, and the line of snowy breakers that marked our last land until we should sight the coast of Puerto Rico, 1,750 miles away. As we moved farther over the ocean, I spotted a rumrunner (this was during Prohibition) speeding off to escape the huge dirigible shadow passing over its head, leaving a crisp white wake on the dark blue sea.

When we were well underway at an altitude of about 2,000 feet, I was free to leave the gondola and move about the ship. Holding on tightly against the terrific wind pressure, I climbed the tiny ladder and entered the bottom of the ship. I made my way forward along the keel to the companionway in the rear of the control car and then along the corridor, between the ship's galley and the head, to the door into the main car. Somewhat like a glorified Pullman sleeper, the main car contained roomy curtained passenger compartments with windows and upholstered seats that made up into ample beds.

I removed my flight suit and made myself comfortable. Looking out the window, all I could see was the shadow of the ship moving swiftly over the surface of the white-capped sea below and the occasional thick cloud that passed between us and the sun, blotting out our shadow.

The thrill of the takeoff seemed to have given everyone ravenous appetites. After a pleasant lunch of ham, cheese, and bologna sandwiches; spaghetti; coffee; and a variety of fresh fruit, I looked out the window again.

The sun shone as we flew above the blue water of the Gulf Stream, and the striking contrast of the dark shadows of cumulus clouds on the glistening sea was enough to bring an artist to tears. I spotted two large whales, one at least one hundred feet long, and water spraying high in the air from the splashes of their mighty tails.

The next afternoon, after thirty-one and a half hours, we sighted land. Just off the coast of Puerto Rico, we circled above the mast ship *Patokah*, which served the same function at sea as the mast on land in New Jersey. The difference was that the warm tropical air caused the airship's helium to expand, significantly increasing the craft's buoyancy; we had to circle around and wait for the helium to cool as the night air approached. Unlike hydrogen gas, helium was such an expensive, carefully conserved commodity that venting it was unthinkable.

After many attempts, heading into the wind with all motors driving their maximum, we were finally within five hundred feet of the water, but by that time it was so dark that our cable dangling in the water was hard to see. Finally the cable was caught, and the connection made. We then began the slow process of hauling the giant airship down with a winch. For balance, all hands, including mine, had to move up and down the keel. The smoke rising from the oil engines of the boat below and the unaccustomed tropical heat of Puerto Rico made it extremely close inside the airship.

This time, there was no elevator, and we descended one hundred feet in the dark by ladder to the deck below. After spending the night on the mast ship, the next morning dawned bright and clear. I was eager to go ashore. Swarms of Puerto Ricans came out in small local boats to welcome their strange giant visitor.

The following day, back on the airship, our roaring motors again took us aloft. As we passed along the north shore of Puerto Rico, I filmed the aerial view of the gorgeous island fringed with coconut palms, the interior as far as the eye could see under systematic cultivation. Perfect roads stretched like white ribbons across a green velvet carpet for miles. Crowds gathered along the shoreline to watch our progress, and all schools had released their pupils to stand in the yards and wave to us as we passed over. As we flew over San Juan, we were greeted by the blowing of every whistle in town—steamers, locomotives, factories, and even automobile horns.

Late afternoon found us over St. Thomas in the Virgin Islands. We encountered several bumps caused by air currents from the mountains, but this time we managed to moor to our mast ship with considerably less difficulty. However, wind gusts created such a problem as we lay at the mast that we couldn't disembark. All the next day, the *Los Angeles* was swinging so badly that the tail of the airship touched the water twice, and all extra boats had to be pressed into service just to keep the *Patokah* from under the airship.

Eventually, it calmed down, and we took off for the return flight to Lakehurst, New Jersey. Almost immediately our radio operator established communication with Arlington and Brooklyn Navy Yard.

Out of sight of land, I bowed to the power of nature expressed in the ocean's vastness. A magnificent flame—and—crimson sunset ushered in an unmatched night view of the clear tropical sea with its glittering phosphorescence under the light of a full moon. It was so clear that at times, even from 2,000 feet above, I could plainly see the coral bottom thirty or forty feet underwater. A passing shower gave me my first view of a circular lunar rainbow— not all the colors of the spectrum in consecutive bands like a traditional daytime rainbow but a truly beautiful and unforgettable sight.

With all that beauty spread out below, it was difficult to go to sleep, but I was determined to be up early to film the sunrise. I dozed throughout the night, rising often to look out the window. Five o'clock the next morning, I sat in a gondola with my camera ready to capture the spectacle. A huge disk of fire thrust itself eagerly from the horizon, surrounded by the softest lavender and rose light, and painted the underside of the ship with its golden rays. I could just make out the Florida coastline ahead through the morning haze.

In half an hour, we were circling over Miami—the city and its suburbs spread like a huge map for twenty miles in all directions, and the long white strip of Florida beach was visible for more than forty miles north and south. At this altitude I could not help thinking what an aid to the real—estate salesmen such a ship might be in the future. Crowds in the streets waved and honked their horns as I ate breakfast above the coral—hued Flamingo Hotel. A seaplane came up to greet us as we headed northward along the beach.

A south wind rose, and soon we were making more than eighty miles an hour. As we circled Palm Beach, we passed over the charred ruins of the recently burned Breakers Hotel (now rebuilt in all its former glory), and I saw the gaunt chimneys still standing. Continuing northward, we reached Charleston, South Carolina, at sunset, in that quiet hour just before dark, when even the air is still.

In a backwoods clearing below lay a tiny cabin, and in the yard I spotted a mule, three cows, and some chickens and turkeys. A thin curl of smoke climbed up toward us from the chimney, and I could visualize the family group inside the cabin—Mama busy at the cookstove; the old man tilted back in a chair, smoking his pipe, while several children waited impatiently for their meal.

Meanwhile the mule in the yard began to switch his tail and shake his head at the great roaring monster above him. Suddenly, he bolted for the cabin, butted his head against the door, and dashed inside, followed by a cow. Almost at the same instant, the entire family with a couple of dogs burst out the back door, awestruck. And there we left them.

I slept that night as we continued toward Lakehurst, and the next thing I heard was Commander Klein calling, "Landing stations." At the end of this remarkable journey, I wrote, "It was one of the most thrilling, and for its novelty, the most enjoyable I have ever had." Afterward I presented illustrated lectures about this fantastic voyage, which were covered by several local newspapers.

The Philadelphia Enquirer wrote, "The newsreels are supplemented with a most interesting photographic record of the recent cruise of the United States Navy dirigible *Los Angeles* to Porto Rico [Puerto Rico]. The entire trip is explained by the man [Horace Ashton] who made the pictures themselves from one of the gondolas."[54]

The Evening Public Ledger added, "The surrounding program is very interesting. A film entitled, *Through the Air to Porto Rico Aboard the Giant Airship Los Angeles* is being shown here for the first time. Horace Ashton, the cameraman, appears in person and talks entertainingly about the trip."[55]

---

54   *The Philadelphia Enquirer*, Philadelphia, Pennsylvania, 19 May 1925.

55   *The Evening Public Ledger*, Philadelphia, Pennsylvania, 19 May 1925.

The New York Times
Magazine Section

(Copyright, 1925, by The New York Times Company.)

NEW YORK, SUNDAY, MAY 31, 1925   TWENTY-FOUR PAGES

Section 4

OVERSEAS IN THE LOS ANGELES

Only Civilian Passenger Describes the 4,000-Mile Flight to Porto Rico and Return —Marvelous Beauty of Sea, Land and Sky as Seen From Car of Dirigible

HORACE ASHTON had the distinction of being appointed by the Secretary of the Navy as Special Observer for Naval Intelligence to accompany the airship "Los Angeles" on her flight to Porto Rico and the Virgin Islands. He was therefore the first civilian passenger ever taken on a trip on this great Zeppelin and made the four thousand mile voyage through the air, which was the longest overseas trip ever attempted by a helium-filled airship. On the trip he made four thousand feet of startlingly beautiful motion-picture films which show clearly every phase of the thrilling voyage. In the lecture he tells you every detail of life aboard, of the intricacies of the rigging and the operation of the great ship. You live with him over again all of the thrills which come to one on his first experience in the great Leviathan of the air. He tells of the difficulties of aerial navigation in a lighter-than-air ship as compared to aeroplanes and of the startling effects of sudden climatic changes on the sensitive helium gas and tells in lively detail all the excitement incident to the stay at Mayaguez, Porto Rico, when the heat melted the cement of the water ballast bags. Everyone in America is intensely interested in the Navy's pioneer work with helium gas and Horace Ashton's lecture answers every question that could possibly arise in the average mind concerning the airship. The return flight along the Florida coast gave them an opportunity to circle above every coast city from Miami to Norfolk, and in the films all of these cities are clearly shown. Some of the most beautiful sky effects ever photographed—thunderstorms, showers, sunsets, moonlight, sunrises, etc., are shown during the lecture, for the entire voyage was made through the clouds. The Navy has been strongly criticised by newspapers and individuals who have not taken the trouble to get the facts, for their experimental work with helium gas and lighter-than-air ships. Horace Ashton answers these critics with a clear and comprehensive and an exceedingly entertaining presentation of the truth of the whole matter.

The New York Times Magazine describes Horace Ashton's journey
in an airship.

* * *

After floating above the earth in a lighter-than-air ship, I never imagined I'd be wedged inside the bowels of the earth, but that is exactly where my next adventure took me. I hadn't been home long when I received a call asking me to represent the Explorers Club in a joint expedition with the American Museum of Natural History. The trip's purpose was to find the endpoint of the well-known Endless Caverns in the Shenandoah Valley near Newmarket, Virginia.

Following my air voyage, a little trip underground in my native Virginia offered just the sort of variety I craved, so I accepted and joined the party. My wife declined to accompany me to Virginia and instead remained in New York. Regarding our marriage, the writing, as they say, may have been on the wall at this point, but I was anxious to explore the walls of caverns and didn't pay much attention to Helen's reluctance.

The expedition consisted of Dr. Chester A. Reed, geologist of the American Museum of Natural History; E. J. Foyles, Dr. Reed's assistant; Henry Collins Walsh, founder of the Explorers Club; Miss Bettie Larimore, a reporter for *The Boston Post*; Merl LaVoy; Garrick Mallery; Gordon Brown; and me. We were all equipped with coarse coveralls, rubber hip boots, electric lamps, and several lengths of stout rope for our expedition into this underground labyrinth, accidentally discovered by two boys chasing a rabbit in 1875.

The caves had been open to the public since 1920, and large parties visited daily to view nature's unbridled beauty. Visitors could wander for more than a mile along the caverns' marvelous passageways, with their succession of chambers. The ceilings and floors were draped with crystal stalactites and stalagmites, the work of water dripping slowly through the limestone mountains for millions of years. Prehistoric underground rivers that had long since evaporated formed some of the passages.

Early the next morning, we were all up and ready, having agreed the night before to attempt to find the end of Endless Caverns by tracing the unknown course of an underground river running through them. I suggested that an empty bottle containing a note be placed as far up, and another as far down, the river as we could go. The note, signed by all members of the party, read, "This bottle is placed at the farthest point penetrated by members of the expedition of the American Museum of Natural History and the Explorers Club of New York, May 1925. If anyone finds it and can carry it still farther, please report to the American Museum of Natural History."

Inside the caves, we found the long chamber known as King Solomon's Temple and then used a stout rope to descend ninety feet straight down to the river below. The water was shallow and the ceiling so low that it was necessary at first to crawl upstream on hands and knees. Sometimes the ceiling was as low as eighteen inches, and the only way we could progress at all was to lie face−up, flat in the water, and squirm along on our backs. Occasionally, we came out into fairly large chambers where we could stand up and stretch.

Foyles and I mapped the river's course as we went along. We discovered that cavern exploration is slow work, since we'd only covered about two hundred yards in our first hour and a half. As we trekked forward, the ceiling abruptly descended until we would have had to go underwater to proceed. We turned back and discovered a small side passage just above our heads, but a short distance beyond, our journey was blocked by huge stalactites clinging to the ceiling and stalagmites rising from the floor.

We retraced our steps and then worked our way downstream through another outlet, along the way sketching animal tracks (raccoon and groundhog) and collecting specimens of microscopic life for the museum. The passage ended at a fifteen−foot silent waterfall, down which we might have gone if we had brought our ropes with us, but they were still attached to the upper levels for our return. Placing the first bottle here, we made the long journey back and climbed the ninety−foot rope, hand−over−hand, emerging exhausted into the main passage.

Having spent seven and a half hours underground

on our first day in the caverns, we were so stiff and sore the next morning that we decided to wait until evening to continue our exploration. After a light dinner, we entered the caverns, a little more than a mile beyond the tourists' entrance. Here, we started to crawl. The stalagmites that covered the floor made crawling very painful, and some of the openings between the rocks were extremely narrow. After a while we skirted the edge of a deep chasm, where most of the party had to resort to a hand rope. I led, and as I crawled along a narrow ledge, my hand disappeared over the edge of another precipice into darkness that our feeble light could not penetrate. I stopped and dropped a rock. After several seconds, I heard a faint splash as it hit the water. This assured me that we were following the course of the river upstream on one of its higher, more ancient levels. We kept on.

After we had been inside about four hours, crawling along the ledge, we came upon a huge chamber. The ceiling was so high our lights could not illuminate it, and the floor was the bed of the river far below, where water rushed in total darkness. Three of us decided to explore the underground river further, so we descended a long rope and left the others in the huge chamber above to send for help in case we did not return.

This descent into the unknown—more than a mile farther than any other person had ever been—was thrilling, to say the least. At the bottom we separated—two went upstream, and I went downstream. I traveled as far as possible, reaching another point several hundred yards beyond the point of descent, where the ceiling closed in so much that it met the water. Not being sure how far underwater I would have to go before I could come up for air, I turned back to discover that the others had traveled a like distance upstream, where they had left the second bottle and then had returned to meet me.

As we used only ordinary pocket flashlights for illumination, we soon discovered they had become much the worse for wear. Because of the fading light, we decided to stay close together. Shadows barely played on the cavern walls now, and it was difficult to see the person in front, let alone where I was going. Somehow I fell further behind and made a wrong turn in the near darkness.

I did not realize I was lost until it was too late for the sound of my voice to reach the others. Nobody answered my call. At first, I thought it wise to remain where I was and await a rescue party. Then, certain I was heading in the right direction, I decided to press on. In a little while, the ceiling closed in on me until I was compelled to crawl. The floor slanted down toward my right, and I had to brace myself to keep from sliding down into the black void. I continued for perhaps an hour, struggling through this steeply sloping crevasse until it finally leveled off into a long broad shelf, almost obstructed by small, needlelike stalactites and stalagmites. With my rapidly dimming flashlight, I searched for an opening through which I could crawl, but all I could do was forge ahead, shearing off the sharp formations with my hands and knees. Then the ceiling lowered again, forcing me to lie flat on my stomach and wriggle along as best I could.

Suddenly my flashlight died, and I was plunged into inky blackness. There I lay, alone in the bowels of the earth in the darkest of darkness and the most silent silence imaginable. For the first time in my life, I actually experienced the sensations of total blindness and deafness and realized what the loss of sight and hearing might mean.

I shouted as loudly as I could, again and again, into the endless eclipse. Only the hollow echo of my own call came back to my waiting ears. My mind imagined strange sights and sounds that weren't there, and my body was raw with cuts. I grew more and more disoriented as I made several futile attempts to turn back. Black may be black, but it surely is even blacker when you get right down inside the earth where there has never been any natural light.

Finally, I lay still for what seemed a long time while

I practiced a mental process I had acquired to rid myself of all fear and panic. At the same time, by relaxing my body and mind, I regained some of the strength I had lost by the fatiguing efforts of my crawl.

Somewhat rested, I was determined to make a final effort to escape. Feeling my way in front of me with my hands, I wriggled forward. The ceiling was not more than eighteen or twenty inches from the uneven floor, but I persevered by feeling my way on all sides. Inch by painful inch, I broke through the ever-stronger formations. The sound tinkled on the floor like broken glass, and I felt genuinely sorry for the damage I was doing to those jewels that nature had been building for ages.

As the ceiling lifted slightly, my progress grew a little easier. Encouraged, I picked up speed and was almost able to get up on my knees and really crawl when the ceiling closed in on me once more. I had to sprawl and wriggle along as before.

After a short rest period, I reached out to feel the way ahead and discovered a sharp precipice! I lay still and breathed deeply, my hand on the edge of the precipice. Strangely, I felt no panic, but thoughts tumbled over one another in my mind. Was this a crevice, and how wide was the rift? How deep was it, and where would it lead? Would I have to turn and make my way back in the utter darkness?

After a few minutes, I worked my way nearer the edge, reached over, and felt around, hoping to discover something about this new barrier. Suddenly I touched a board.

Petrified wood? It couldn't be. It had splinters.

As I felt along this board, my hand stopped on a round metallic object at the end. In the middle of the object was a key. I turned it, and bright lights illuminated my rock prison, so startling that I was momentarily blinded.

I began to laugh. I'm not sure whether it was relief or the incongruity of being lost in the bowels of the earth, away from civilization, and suddenly coming upon—of all things—an electric switch!

Now that I was back in the lighted section, I knew my way and hurried to the entrance. There I met the rest of my party, about to set out on a search for me, and together we went on a new and important search—for food.

As dawn broke through the window of a delightful old Newmarket farmhouse kitchen, bacon, eggs, and grits never smelled so good. But before I took a morsel, I silently thanked my guardian angel for my rescue.

For those of you bored by the mad rush of our so-called civilized life, I can highly recommend several hours of the kind of silence found in caves. My account of the cavern exploration, titled "Lost Inside the Earth," from which I have paraphrased here, was included in the book *Through Hell and High Water* published in 1941 by Robert M. McBride and Company for the Explorers Club.

One of my colleagues on the trip was Bettie Larimore, a reporter for *The Boston Post*. At the end of the exhausting trip she remarked, "If anyone ever finds those bottles and carries them on, they deserve more than an empty bottle."

I have included excerpts from her detailed account, headlined "Travels Miles Under Ground and Wades Through Lake Where No White Man Has Ever Been," published in the *Boston Post*.

Finally we reached a place where we had to take to the water or swim. Ashton, the leader, leaped boldly in and found the water not too deep. He rounded a corner, and came to a leap. Here the water was up to his waist, but he found a sight to reward him. When we rounded the corner, we beheld Ashton kneeling before a shining white altar high above the lake. He had placed his candle on a convenient stalagmite atop the altar, and the effect was most sepulchral, many miles under the earth . . .

Ashton had led the way going back, although he was unaccustomed to the past. We had crossed further than the first chasm, when we missed him. We were not worried, for he is an experienced climber, and we thought he was just ahead of us . . . All the time we were crawling along the edge of that crevasse, I had the unhappy feeling that Ashton had taken the wrong turning, had tried to pass and failed. I feared to look into the bottom of the pit. For we had called again and again to Ashton and there was no answer.

Although we hurried on as fast as we could, and called repeatedly, we never caught up to Ashton. Soon we had crawled through the last crack, and stood in the illuminated section. And there stood Ashton![56]

12

NEW YORK EVENING POST, ... JULY 22, 1926

This Enchanted Isle

Explorer's Trick Photo of Roosevelt Jumped Its Value $4500 for Honesty

THE mere fact that, at one particular moment in his slightly adventurous life, he had nothing to do made an explorer out of Horace D. Ashton. That's why his career doesn't quite fit in with the usual "He got the job" sort of success effusions. None of our best "go-getters" would recommend even five minutes of idleness as a start for any one.

It all took place in Washington. Ashton as a youngster had gone in for photography. He was among the first to make photographs for newspapers when the half-tone came along and edged out the old-fashioned woodcut. And usually the job of photographing all the celebrities that from time make their way to Washington kept him more than ordinarily busy.

On this particular day, however, there was nothing to be done. And the exceedingly young Ashton didn't care much for doing that. So, in the studio, he began idly to mess around with the pictures lying about him.

IN THE process he happened to notice that the position of the head of a young ... hurdles at Chevy Chase was exactly the same as that of President Roosevelt, in another picture, bowing to a crowd from a carriage. It struck him that it might be amusing to paste the picture of T. R.'s head on the flying ... He did so and showed it to the boss.

"Where'd you get that?" was the startled inquiry.

And Ashton, brought up in the town named for the man who never—well, hardly ever—told a lie, explained. Whereupon the boss, more interested than ever, got some sandpaper and the two smoothed the composite picture down so well that the most naked eye in the world wouldn't have been able to guess it was a fake.

Then they submitted it to a magazine editor. He was so completely taken in that he offered $5000 for it. Theodore Roosevelt ... hurdles was something worth seeing. But once again the Washington influence prevailed and they told him the truth.

"Why don't you get some real ones?" was his comeback.

AND, on thinking it over, Ashton thought that was something in the way of ideas. He took himself to the White House, finally got in to see the President, submitted the photograph, was greeted with sheer astonishment, and after again telling the by this time bitter truth got the President to agree to go to Chevy Chase and do some hurdle jumping. The real pictures sold for $5000, which goes to prove, one might infer, that honesty is worth $4500.

All of which leads up to the fact that shortly thereafter the Russian-Japanese war broke out. The magazine editor who had bought the pictures telegraphed to Washington asking Ashton to visit him in New York. The result was an offer to send him to the front. Ashton accepted. But, because he had to make way for Richard Harding Davis, he didn't see much there.

HOWEVER, the trip had served to fill him with the desire to see strange places and do rather daring things. He had a look at Palestine and Egypt. He did a bit of prowling about Venezuela when that hectic spot was filled with soldiers of adventure and revolutionaries. He piloted across the American continent the first passenger-carrying automobile to make the trip. And that was something of a trip. It is a little too recent to be history, but it will be some day.

Then he settled down in New York for some scientific picture work. He made movies of the mosquito's daily grind. He did portraits of cockroaches and mice and other strange creatures.

AFTER the war, however, his most interesting work began. He had become enamored of the theory that the Celtic people had originated in Asia and trekked to Ireland and Scotland by way of Arabia, Africa and Spain, leaving behind them on the march the Tuaregs, the Troglodytes, the Berbers and the Basques. So he went off to have a look at Africa.

Perhaps the most interesting colony he visited was that of the cave-dwelling Troglodytes. Near the frontier of Tripoli he found them, 300,000 persons living in holes in the ground. On his first trip in 1919-20 he made considerable progress in cultivating them. When he went back in 1923-24, he took his wife. He had found that the tribesmen suspected him because he was unattached. They guard their wives and daughters carefully and thought he had come to steal them.

BUT Mrs. Ashton's presence allayed suspicion. She is an unusual person, a woman of great charm, and her influence aided materially. The two were able to build up such confidence that they actually entered Troglodyte homes—the strange wells they sink in the desert sand and from which they burrow the tunnels in which they live.

Ashton has had other experiences as well. He visited Haiti when the marines were in control there, fought with the marines, or rather with the native constabulary they have organized, and he took pictures of a real Voodoo dance, which he describes as the most horror-inspiring thing he's ever seen. He also has explored the endless caverns of the Shenandoah Valley and hopes to return this summer and find the ends of them. And he expects soon to go on with his Celtic investigations.

"The most fascinating discoveries in that field," he says, "are those which have to do with the arts of those African peoples as compared with those of the Scotch and Irish. Their languages are entirely different. They are alike in physical characteristics to a certain extent. But the greatest likeness is to be found in their music and in their jewelry."

So Mr. Ashton, whose career began when he pasted pictures together, will go on trying to solder strange far-off peoples together. It's a good trick if he does it. And a thrilling, exciting, fascinating life of adventure, even if he doesn't.

MANN HATTON.

New York newspaper article describes Horace Ashton's early career.

---

56   Bettie Larimore, "Travels Miles Under Ground and Wades Through Lake Where No White Man Has Ever Been," in *The Boston Post*, Boston, Massachusetts, 1926. (This publication folded in 1956 after more than one hundred years.)

CHAPTER 31

Filmmaking and Flight, 1926–1927

Horace

In addition to being an explorer and lecturer throughout the 1920s, I played an active role in the motion picture industry, primarily as a cinematographer, working for most of the big Hollywood studios and on many of the popular pictures of the day. Among other things, I shot sandstorm sequences in the Sahara not once but three different times, horse–show sequences in Florida for a Gloria Swanson film, and rodeo sequences in Nevada for a western. I made numerous documentaries, including one of the barren lands of northern Canada, as part of an exploration for the New York Museum of Natural History.

I was part of the cinematography team for the acclaimed films *Wings* (released in 1927) and *Lilac Time* (1928) and later served as chief cinematographer for *Silent Enemy* (1930), an epic of the American Indian. *Wings* and *Lilac Time* were great wartime epics, and I did most of the aerial cinematography for both films.

Kelly Field, Texas, was our base for the films' aerial sequences. During the filming of *Wings*, we crashed twice. The first time, the pilot was killed, and remarkably, I walked away unhurt. In the second crash, the pilot was not injured, but I broke my nose yet again. As usual, I did what was necessary to fix my nose and later was told by intimate friends that my beauty had not been spoiled.

In making *Lilac Time*, we crashed while filming an

aerial dogfight, and sadly, another pilot was killed. My poor nose was flattened again, but I felt much more fortunate than my colleague.

Amazingly, I survived a total of seven plane crashes while shooting aerial photographs, escaping all with no more injuries than a broken nose or burned feet. I never in my life doubted the presence of my guardian angel, but these incidents further confirmed it.

* * *

I could probably have made a living in Hollywood, but traveling was still always on my mind, for I was not one to be content in any one place for too long. As a member of the Royal Geographic Society, the Explorers Club, the American Geographical Society, and the American Academy of Sciences, I was driven to continue my explorations and study the world's inhabitants, not stay home and sit in an armchair in front of a fire—or even work in an office or stand in front of a lecture hall, discussing past exploits.

But when it came to choosing a wife, had I made a mistake? It seemed that Helen was not the adventurous traveler I'd hoped her to be. By this time she was no longer thrilled by the novelty of being married to an explorer, and unfortunately, my marriage seemed to be heading in the wrong direction.

In the fall of 1926, which is spring south of the equator, I was anxious to return to South America. I arrived in Lima, Peru, to discover that flying ace Lieutenant Jimmy Doolittle, on furlough from the army, was due to land shortly. I was eager to renew our acquaintance. Doolittle arrived with another pilot, named McMillen, who had flown me on many of my early picture–making flights. They had come to South America as representatives of the Curtiss Company to sell planes to the Peruvian, Bolivian, and Chilean governments.

Since I knew the brother–in–law of the president of Bolivia, we had no difficulty in obtaining an audience. The president invited the heads of the army to join us. They were interested in purchasing the planes only if they could take off from Lake Titicaca with pontoons.

While awaiting the arrival of the pontoons, I learned of a man named Wallin who owned a gold mine on the Brazilian side of the Andes. Having traveled for a week by mule through hostile Indian country, he was interested in finding a faster way to travel to his mine. Doolittle and I assured him that a plane would certainly shorten this journey.

Through his twelve–year–old son who knew Morse code, Wallin sent a message to the mine's engineer, requesting that the miners clear a strip long enough to land an airplane. Within a week, the answer came back that a strip had been cleared. Doolittle, Wallin, and I decided to attempt to reach the mine by air.

Wallin told us the mine was located at an altitude of less than a thousand feet on a horseshoe bend of a small river, where workers panned enormous quantities of alluvial gold. After calculating our present altitude, we realized the mine was almost 13,000 feet below us! We were relieved to have an expert pilot like Jimmy Doolittle making the initial pass.

Our plane was a small Curtiss with two open cockpits. Doolittle sat up front, and Wallin and I wedged ourselves in the rear along with a twenty–gallon can of gasoline. At that altitude, the plane required a long trip down the runway with the extra weight.

Just as we ran out of runway, the wheels left the ground. Off to the northeast towered the snow–capped peaks of the Andes, some 20,000 feet high. Jimmy had found a pass on his map that he headed for. But when we got there, we went straight into a cloud. Through the filmy atmosphere, I could see blue glaciers and rocky precipices not more than a mile away. Making it through that pass was a miracle.

When we burst out of the cloud, the clear air at about

15,000 feet opened over a sea of milk below. It was icy cold, and my almost—frozen feet chattered against the cockpit floor as we flew. I spied a hole in the clouds about the size of my thumbnail and could make out the horseshoe curve of the small river below. Leaning forward, I tapped Jimmy on the shoulder and pointed down. He nosed the plane over, and we dived through the clouds. When we leveled off, Wallin, who had never flown before, was vomiting over the side of the plane; I had a nosebleed.

As we got closer, we saw that the so—called "cleared" strip contained the stumps of all the cut—down trees! There was no place to land. We circled around, dropping packages of mail, and medicine to the men below.

The difference in altitude was extreme. We'd taken off from the 14,000—foot—high airfield at La Paz and climbed another 2,000 feet without oxygen and then descended almost 15,000 feet to circle around the mine. Now, when we tried to climb, we had problems because the water from condensation that had been collecting on the plane weighed us down. Jimmy pointed to a large pump beside me and signaled me to pump hard. I pumped as hard as I could for three or four minutes until I thought my arm would drop off. As the water dripped off its wings, the plane slowly began to gain altitude, and we climbed until we found the pass through the mountains again. By this time, the clouds had blown away.

When we landed and lifted poor Mr. Wallin out of the cockpit, he couldn't speak. He'd been sick twice in flight, so we took him into the hangar and waited until he could walk. I felt sure that there was no possibility of a sale there, but I heard later that Wallin had not only bought two planes but learned to fly one himself.

After our experience with Mr. Wallin, the pontoons we'd ordered for the Bolivian government arrived, but our experiment failed. The planes lacked large enough wingspans to take off from Lake Titicaca with the extra weight.

I bid Jimmy and the others good-bye and headed south to Chile, where the government had hired me to make a series of documentary films showing their two major industries: mining and wine. In doing so, I discovered that Chilean wines are as fine as any in the world. In fact, I saw tankers taking great casks to France, where they were bottled and sold as French wines. They must have been very potent as well, for I heard a funny story in Chile about my friend Jimmy Doolittle.

Apparently he had been honored at a banquet in Santiago where the wine flowed plentifully, and he'd given an enthusiastic speech about what makes a flyer, ending with "A flyer is not made; he is born. Why, I could fly this table if it had a good motor." Leaping on the table, he said, "Hell, I don't need a motor," and he soared over the balcony rail and crashed on the marble floor below. Having broken both his thigh bones, he was hospitalized for weeks with his legs in casts.

Unlike Doolittle, I enjoyed my time in the south of Chile and did not make headlines. I photographed beautiful Lakes Llanquihue and Todos Los Santos in sight of active volcanoes. Between the two lakes stands Osorno, one of the most magnificent mountains in the world, matching Mount Fujiyama in Japan in its symmetrical snow-capped dignity. The scenery in the south of Chile is as breathtaking as anything in Switzerland, and the area later became famous for its marvelous ski runs.

In Valparaiso I witnessed the aftereffects of what had to have been a spectacular earthquake. Alerted to an imminent tidal wave, I grabbed my motion picture camera and ran to the bluff overlooking the harbor. In a few minutes, a forty-foot-high wave from the Pacific Ocean swept onto the shore, dragging all ten ships in the harbor from their anchorages. Two turned over, and a 10,000-ton cargo ship was lifted over the top of the Customs House and dumped in the main street. People died, and the property damage was enormous. The harbor was a boiling mess of wreckage, foaming water, and human and animal bodies.

Given the seriousness of the disaster, I tried not to openly gloat over my luck at being there at exactly the right time to capture the most amazing footage. My momentary elation was squashed by the Chilean government, for whom I was making a documentary. They seized the film and destroyed the negative, explaining its release would be bad for tourism.

I left Valparaiso and traveled even further south for my next assignment, having been engaged by the Chilean Navy to attempt to air map the Strait of Magellan. The narrow and tortuous channel connecting the Atlantic and Pacific Oceans at the southern tip of South America was infamous for some of the world's worst weather. Most geographers at the time considered mapping it an impossible task, but I accepted the assignment because, for some unknown reason, I was sure of my success.

We used two large, six-engine Dornier-Wahl seaplanes and a Fairchild camera to undertake this daunting task. For the first time in the recorded history of that region, we had nine clear days to do our job. On the morning of the tenth day, just as we'd completed our assignment, the fog rolled in.

When I returned to Santiago, I found a cable from the New York Museum of Natural History. It asked me to return at once to lead an important Arctic expedition to learn more about the Eskimo culture. I was delighted, although the logistics of getting there in time concerned me. I knew that traveling from near the southern tip of South America to the Arctic Circle, the direct opposite end of the earth, would be a difficult feat. I believed that my path would reveal itself, and this is what happened.

The Chilean Navy helped with the first step by flying me to Callao, Peru, where a friend flew me to Ecuador in his small cotton-crop duster. From there I flew to Panama, where the United States Navy flew me to Guantanamo, Cuba, and on to Lakehurst, New Jersey, where I boarded a car for New York.

I was eager to explore the Arctic after hearing so many tales from my friends at the Explorers Club. I didn't realize it then, but my jungle and desert days were behind me, for I would spend most of the next two and a half years involved in Arctic expeditions.

Chapter 32

Adventures in the Arctic and Antarctic, 1926–1929

Horace

My adjustment to Arctic temperatures began in New York with a chilly reception at home and a preliminary discussion of divorce, but I packed quickly and then grabbed a taxi for Grand Central Station. There I boarded the first of several trains to travel north to Le Pas, Manitoba, the end of the line and our departure point for Canada's Northwest Territories and Baffin Island, where I would lead the Burden Expedition by dogsled. The long-term purpose of this expedition was a comparative study of the Eskimo tribes from Greenland to Siberia for the American Anthropological Society and other scientific studies for the museum.

I didn't think about this at the time, but in remembering my frantic journey all the way from South America to the Arctic region, I wonder if I might have set some kind of travel record. It really was an amazing feat to have traveled practically from one tip of the earth to the other in a time before international air travel.

The contrast in climate, from the heat and humidity of South America's jungles to the bone-chilling cold in the far north, was extreme. Oddly enough, I found cultural similarities at opposite ends of the earth. The inhabitants of both regions lived simple lives, depending upon hunting and fishing for their food, and all relied on their surrounding terrain for shelter and sustenance. In the Arctic, I lived among the natives and witnessed their attempts to survive amid great hardship. I had seen the same survival instincts in the South American natives who lived in the high altitudes of the snowcapped Andes Mountains.

Horace Ashton survives the frozen North.

While living among the Eskimos, my expedition of four traveled by dogsled and by canoe. The Eskimos searched for the migrating caribou that sustained their native people. As I documented the barren land on film for the Museum of Natural History, we passed many small lakes. Those I remember best were Reindeer Lake, Lake Wollaston, and Lake Nueltin, above the Arctic Circle.

One day, surveying the area with my field glasses, I spotted what appeared to be a dog sitting on a small island in the middle of a lake. I paddled out to the island for a better look and found a large, fine-looking dog, sitting there with over thirty long porcupine quills through his nose and mouth. He was miserable. He couldn't eat and was slowly starving to death. I gently placed him in my canoe and returned to camp.

That night I started to extract some of the quills. He appeared to appreciate what I was doing and would let me put my hand and pliers in his mouth. Over the next few days, I gradually removed the quills and then began spoon-feeding him until he regained his strength and could eat on his own. I named him Scout. I was very fond of dogs and happy to help this one. Being very intelligent and already trained as a sled dog, Scout became one of my leaders and would soon repay my kindness by saving my life.

A few weeks later, as the expedition continued to search for the migrating caribou while I filmed our journey, my six dogs and I crossed a lake in a milky snowstorm, pulling my heavily loaded sled. All the other dog teams were out of sight, and we were traversing new, thin ice. Suddenly, I heard a sound that made my visible breath stop cold—the unmistakable crack of ice.

As we sped across the lake, I saw the water slowly begin to rise. Realizing we weren't going to make it with my weight on the sled and knowing that I'd go through the ice if I stood, I rolled off and kept on rolling. I called to my lead dog for help. Since Scout was loose, he turned and led the other dogs around so that the rear of the sled was within my reach. I grabbed it, yelled "Mush!" and they galloped off, dragging me to safety. If I had jumped off that sled—the most natural thing for a frightened person to do—I would have gone through the ice and not been found until millions of years hence, when the Arctic warmed up again and the ice melted.

I believe in signs. Finding the starving dog at the beginning of my journey symbolized what was to follow. As I lived and worked among the Eskimos, I saw no caribou, migrating or otherwise. For some reason, this particular year they did not follow the trails south that had been their path for many years. The Eskimos, who depended on these animals for food and warmth, suffered greatly.

The Arctic's harsh climate brought out strengths I didn't know I had because of the challenges it presented. At one point our provisions ran low, and I was sent south to a trapper's hut where our party had cached some flour and bacon for our return trip. The hut was about two days' journey from our camp, so I hitched up a dog team and headed south for the food.

I took only two thin slices of raw bacon and a few crackers for me, and a few frozen fish for the dogs. I had been traveling about six hours when a blinding snowstorm hit, so I quickly made a small lean-to and took shelter. The storm lasted a full day, and my dogs and I stayed put. When I continued my journey and reached the cache, it was empty. Not a trace of anything we had stored on our way north was left.

I made the return journey during the next two days with six starving dogs that were near death. I felt awful for them, but there was nothing I could do except get off the sled so they wouldn't have to pull my weight. All I had was a bit of raw bacon that I placed in my mouth and sucked on as I ran across the snow with the dogs. Ignoring the gnarling pain in my stomach, the numbness in my toes, the icicles in my beard, and the frost attempting to glue my eyelashes shut, I focused on all of us making it back alive.

There was a much bigger problem in the Arctic that year—far more important than studying a culture, making films of the Canadian North for the museum, or worrying about my own hunger and the numbness in my toes. Having survived my brush with starvation, I had the option of returning to "civilization," but the Eskimos were not going to be so lucky. After months of searching in vain, we had found no caribou. I realized that unless I got word to the outside world, the Eskimos were going to starve to death. But I had to do so before the trails became covered by snow and ice, so I left the main expedition and set out on the long trip back to Le Pas. Several articles about my trying journey appeared in area papers, such as the excerpts below:[57]

Scientists Find Eskimos Starving, Unable to Find Migrating Caribou

Word was received yesterday that an expedition sponsored by William Douglas Burden, a trustee of the American Museum of Natural History, and sent out under the auspices of the museum to investigate the condition of Eskimos living in Barren Land, in the Northwest Territory of Canada, had found the natives in danger of starvation because they had been unable to locate the annual caribou migration upon which they depend for sustenance.

Horace D. Ashton, head of the expedition, reported the party, which left its base at The Pas on August 14 in four freight canoes, had reached Barren Land in 62 degrees north latitude on October 1 and had found the 200 surviving Eskimos in a precarious condition.

"Forty of the Eskimos had died from starvation a few winters ago, and the survivors were faced with the same fate," Mr. Ashton said. "The most remarkable feature of the return trip was that not a single wild animal was seen, despite the efforts of several experienced hunters to track them."[58]

---

57   "Missed Caribou Migration: Now Without Food," in *Winnipeg Tribune*, Winnipeg, Manitoba, Canada, 27 December 1928.

58   "Scientists Find Eskimos Starving, Unable to Find Migrating Caribou," in *Canadian Press*, 27 December 1928.

NEW YORK EVENING JOURNAL * * America's

ASHTON DESCRIBES THRILLING

Evening Newspaper * * SATURDAY, APRIL 13, 1929   H-B 15

ADVENTURES IN FROZEN NORTH

ENJOYED FARE OF ESKIMO EXISTENCE

Six months old babies smoke pipes filled with plug tobacco.... men gamble away their wives at cards ...whole families live in one room ...they eat nothing but meat and they eat it raw....they chop off frozen chunks of caribou beef and chew it ice cold in sixty degrees below zero...,

Fantasy? Nothing of the sort! It's a commonplace at the Explorer's Club which has just opened at No. 544 Cathedral parkway. And what has here been related comes from the lips of Horace Ashton, F. R. G. A., globe trotter extraordinary, debonair, suave and carefully attired. Ashton is the latest explorer to return home, and he immediately took a room in the new club in Harlem. Celebrated explorers trooped through the building, examining its every cranny much as they might a curious, wild exhibit far from civilisation. Ashton, who modestly disclaimed any recognition as an explorer, admitted that he had just come back from a trip to the Northwest territory, most inaccessible spot on the entire North American continent.

Different Eskimos

"The Eskimos that lived there are different from any I've ever seen," Ashton said. "The spot is about 160 miles north of Hudson Bay and it's south of the magnetic pole."

"These Eskimos I lived with are a nomadic people with practically no earthly possessions and apparently no desire for them," explained Ashton, who does not look the part of the adventurous man he is. Rather, Ashton seems a complete city product, more at home in the luxurious lounge room of the new club than sleeping in a swamp at forty degrees below zero in the frozen North.

"We had to travel by canoe for forty-seven days and we made ninety-seven portages," Ashton said. "We travelled about 1,400 miles over absolute waste land to reach these Eskimos They live in small skin tents in Summer and in Winter, their igloo walls are made of snow, with a skin roof.

Raw Meat Eaten

"They live on raw meat mostly. They leave the dead animals on the ground, and when they want food, simply chop it off. Caribou moss, a vegetable which might appear inedible in civilization, is their only vegetable delicacy.

"The Eskimos of the Northwest Territory are polygamous, as well as nomadic. A man is allowed to have as many wives as he can support. He can give his wife away any time he wishes, and a man generally wins a woman by bluffing her family or taking her away by force or, maybe, buying her.

"Many men win wives at gambling games. Children are supported by the husband.

"These Eskimos are constantly coughing. I believe they have acquired this bronchial cough from over-smoking. The babies in arms puff at pipes containing plug tobacco, and if they can't get that, they use dried tea leaves that have been brewed five or six times. Sometimes they use dry cranberry leaves for tobacco. The kiddies seem to thrive on it.

Hunt with Spears

"They kill their animals with rifles, or spears. Frequently they camp on a crossing—where deer or caribou cross bodies of water—and when the flock of animals comes along they get into their canoes. They paddle out to the swimming animals and spear them in the hindquarters, paralyzing them. After they have thus incapacitated about forty or fifty they tow them into shore and kill them.

"The animals are not dressed, as we dress beef, but are allowed to lay and freeze and are eaten as the whim of the Eskimo dictates, sometimes cooked, but generally without any cooking.

"The Eskimos are hospitable. They treated me genially and we used sign language to communicate with each other mostly. These Eskimos we visited are shorter in stature than the Alaskan Eskimos and darker."

One of the most curious of Eskimo customs is that among the women. Ashton explained that Eskimo women wear brass bands on their foreheads. If the band is high on the forehead, close to the line of hair, it indicates that the wearer is unmarried. If it's in the middle of the forehead, the girl is married, and if low on the forehead, over the eyebrows, the sign is that the girl is looking for a husband.

Eskimo women have a headdress of their own design. They use sticks about eight inches long to make curls and then wrap the curls in gaudy material, giving the appear of miniature barber poles which hang before the ears. The favorite married women of a family wears a beaded collar. The attire of men

and women, made of skins, is generally similar.

Ashton's latest trip took him to Katzebue Sond, in what is known as The Buckland, Alaska. He spent six weeks among the Eskimos there, travelling with dog teams over vast waste spaces.

Thrives on Food

"What did you eat when you were among the Eskimos?" Ashton was asked.

"I ate what the Eskimos ate," he laughed, "and I didn't mind it so much. I couldn't eat that stuff here, but I was hungrier up there. When I left, I was kind of flabby, and suffered from neuritis, but even though I had to sleep many days out in the swamp without covering, in forty degrees below zero, the enforced exercise cured me, and I got stronger than ever."

During the long trips over frozen waste lands, Ashton had to carry about two tons of camp equipment which included food. He explained that the equipment must be complete, because in one of his overland journeys of 1,400 miles, only five human beings were seen, and these could not have helped him and his native guides.

Ashton is not merely an Arctic explorer—no, sir! Just before he went on his northern trips, he had been to the Straits of Magellan, at the southern end of the Western hemisphere, and there had contracted rheumatic troubles now, happily, gone. He loves to travel, and says he likes to come home to Harlem.

On Again, Off Again

"I like it better when I'm coming back, after a trip. Then I like to go off to sea again," he explained, enigmatically.

"And say—" he turned to his friend, Captain Harold Noice. "Here's a real explorer. When the newspapers print interviews, they get some fellow like myself, who hasn't ever been any place, and they overlook a fellow like Captain Noice, who has really been places and seen things."

Captain Noice, another celebrated traveller, shrunk into a corner and puffed nervously at his pipe.

"I'll say something, some time," Captain Noice promised, "but really, I can't remember anything now."

Newspaper article describes Horace Ashton's exploration of the Arctic.

I was greatly rewarded to learn that my efforts had helped to save these people. Aid was soon sent to the Eskimos, and most of them survived another winter. The following year, the caribou migrated as usual, and the delicate balance between that harsh land and its native culture was restored.

On future trips I visited some of my Eskimo friends again, and of course, I kept Scout and my favorite dogsled team. As I explored the physically and emotionally challenging northern region over the next few years, my travels included much of the Canadian territories, Alaska, and even Siberia. During my Arctic explorations I would travel 8,000 miles by dog team, running half that distance and sleeping in sleeping bags on the ice in an average temperature of sixty–five degrees below zero Fahrenheit.

* * *

During the production of the epic Paramount film *Silent Enemy*, arrangements were made through Reveillon and Hudson Bay Company that while traveling in the Northwest Territories we would be assisted by their local agents in our efforts to film the fabulous migration of the caribou. Sure enough, one of Reveillon's men was waiting for us when the train pulled in at the station in Le Pas, and all our equipment was unloaded. The agent had already arranged for twelve husky Cree Indian porters and a cook to accompany our expedition, so it took us only a couple of days to get underway.

We traveled up the one–hundredth meridian, from river to river and lake to lake, with four large Canadian freight canoes, one of which was fitted with a Johnson outboard motor. We made over one hundred portages with all our equipment, following what was locally called the "Lobstick Trail." This trail, which had been followed by the Ojibwa for centuries, consisted of a series of tall fir trees near lakeshores or river landings that had been trimmed so that one prominent branch was left plainly visible near the top, pointing in the direction of the portage.

Later, four men remained in our expedition, one of them—thankfully—being the cook. Christmas overtook us when we were encamped in the most northerly of Reveillon's tiny stations, a one-room affair with a storeroom in the rear. The main room was about fifteen-by-twenty feet with a long counter at one end, a pot-bellied stove in the center, and four bunks stacked at the other end. The temperature on Christmas Day was sixty-five degrees below zero Fahrenheit, but even in that remote location, we held a holiday open house. Our guests included two priests who had traveled over one hundred miles each with their dogs from opposite directions; a Canadian territorial policeman; and the noted Norwegian explorer, Helge Ingstad, who had come two hundred miles to be with us.

The party lasted for three days and nights. Seven men in a small room can go a little crazy, and there were a few incidents. One night, the cook, an ex-policeman from Quebec, brandished a kitchen knife and declared he was going to cut the heart out of the first man he could reach. He was quickly disarmed and thrown out the door into the snow. Realizing he would be frozen solid in minutes, I dashed out the door without putting on my mukluks and hauled him in. He was in bad shape, but the cold almost sobered him up. I held the pail for him the rest of the night, while the rest of the party played poker.

I learned later that our cook, while serving as a policeman in Le Pas, had been fired for breaking a law. Apparently the captain had sent our man with a dog team and an Indian guide about forty miles out, where a gruesome frozen hand had been discovered sticking out of the ice in a small lake. With great effort our cook had chopped the corpse out of the ice and then discovered the stiff awkward shape would not fit on the sled and pass easily through the underbrush on the return journey. To solve the problem, he sawed off the frozen limbs and lashed the neat bundle to the sled, only to learn the hard way that it was against the law to alter a corpse before the coroner could see it. The Arctic is the ultimate challenge that can bring out some remarkable characteristics in a man.

The far North took its toll on my body and my emotions. It also taught me to appreciate simple pleasures, and I learned new skills. There was a period when I was snowed in and unable to travel for a couple of weeks. While confined in the igloo, I made an excellent knife out of an old file used for sharpening axes. I carved a design of my loyal dog team around its ivory handle, and one of the Eskimos made me a good sheath of walrus hide to attach to my belt outside my parka.

When the weather cleared, I ventured out. Returning later to the igloo, I bedded down the dogs in a snowstorm, took off my parka, and crawled through the crooked entrance. Inside, the Eskimos offered me a piece of raw meat. It was the custom to place it between the teeth and cut it off beyond the nose, but I could not find my knife. I suddenly felt upset.

My host, Homoguluk, called a young medicine man and sent him outside. The medicine man jumped up and down in one spot and made frightful sounds, which the Eskimos called "making medicine." After twenty minutes of dancing, he came to me with his hand out. I was told to give him something that I had been carrying. I fished out a small box of matches. Then he took hold of my hand, pulling me. I put on my parka and mukluks and followed him outside.

The thick snow had become trackless, and I had difficulty locating the small mounds under which my dogs lay. Suddenly, the medicine man stopped, shoved his hand elbow deep into the snow, and pulled out my knife from the mound!

* * *

For most of my life I'd had dogs as pets and often took them along on my journeys, so it was no wonder that my Arctic exploration would involve training and nurturing a fine dogsled team. Over the course of my time in the Arctic, I would train eleven dog teams and sixty-five dogs, some of which were full—blooded timber wolves. In working with Alaskan huskies in particular, I was often reminded of their striking intelligence and highly developed intuition. A very strong bond developed between me and the lead dog I had rescued. Scout would save my life a second time.

In 1928, I traveled to Elephant Point, Alaska, and landed on the snow in a plane equipped with skis. As the plane approached the landing site, I could see people moving about below. After it landed, I stepped out, and the people scattered in all directions.

I was dressed as an Eskimo and had a full beard. When I tossed back the hood of my parka, my long blondish hair blew in the wind. A small crowd gathered around, but no one approached. They just stood and stared. I couldn't imagine why these Eskimos looked so awestruck.

Finally, someone ordered several of them forward. They crept up slowly, grabbed my gear, helped me unload the dogs and sled, and then dashed off to the bunkhouse. I settled in while the locals kept their distance, still eyeing me warily. Later, at dinner, the waitress asked, "What'll you have, Jesus?"

I looked at her aghast.

"Haven't you heard? When your plane approached in the sky, one of the workers looked up and exclaimed, 'Jesus Christ!' Then a little Eskimo boy ran off to tell everyone that Jesus Christ had come, so when you stepped out with that long hair and beard, they were certain you were Jesus. You see, they've been educated by the Russian priests, and they are all very religious," she explained, pouring my coffee. "Better shave off that beard if you plan on stayin' 'round here."

Not only had I walked in Jesus's footsteps in Palestine and slept in his monastery cell in Tibet, but it was amazing to me that I was actually mistaken for Jesus on two occasions in my life. The second time would occur some years later in Haiti.

In Alaska I shaved off my beard and carried on with

my explorations. A few weeks later, I was still in Elephant Point, shooting footage for a motion picture. I was warming my hands on a steaming cup of hot chocolate at a Lomen Company reindeer station, when I heard about a seventeen-year-old girl in Candle, about sixty miles away, dying of pneumonia. There was no doctor available. Having a talent for doctoring and more than a little experience during the course of my travels, I remembered a miraculous cure for pneumonia, called "hot and cold," that I'd seen a Maori woman perform in New Zealand.

I immediately packed my sled, readied the dog team, and set off for Candle, speeding across the snow and ice. I took along a bottle of rum for "central heating" on the way. After traveling for several hours in fifty-degrees-below-zero weather, I had consumed over half the bottle. Feeling sleepy, I rolled off the sled. You would think those dogs would have been glad to be relieved of my weight and taken off at a gallop, leaving me there to freeze. Instead, they stopped when they felt my weight leave the sled. Scout came back and put his cold nose on my face, awakening me.

Sober and awake, I arrived in Candle to find the young girl unconscious, her mother and sister frantic with worry. I had them soak bath towels in boiling water, and we lay the girl on top of one of the hot towels and then heaped snow on her chest for five minutes. Turning her over, we reversed the process. In half an hour, she was sitting up and complaining only of the blisters on her skin from the hot towels.

* * *

Three years later, I gave my best dog team, with lead dog Scout, to Admiral Byrd for his exploration of Antarctica. When I attended the showing of the film he'd made during his visit to Little America in the Antarctic, I was enraged by the final scene.

Admiral Byrd and two others had flown onto the south polar ice cap with a small sled and my dog team. They had taken the dogs along in case something went wrong with the plane, knowing they could attempt a return by dogsled. When the plane tried to take off on the return journey, it could not climb with all that weight at such a high altitude. Admiral Byrd left the sled and dogs behind.

As the plane gained altitude, one of the men filmed the dogs sitting on the ice, looking up as the plane departed. Those noble dogs were left behind with nothing to eat, and no possible escape. There in front, appearing to be aware of his fate, stood Scout. That was one of the rare times in my life when emotion got the better of me. I couldn't keep my tears back.

Nor was it my nature to resort to violence, but at that moment I jumped up and punched Admiral Byrd in the face. "You dirty SOB!" I shouted. "Why didn't you at least shoot them? You know they would only have each other to eat, one by one before the last would eventually suffer an agonizing and painful death!"

CHAPTER 33

Helpless

Butch
April 5, 2001
About 6:45 p.m.

The car stops and my captors order me out. *Is this the end of the line?*

I am breathing more easily without the tape over my mouth, but my eyes are still taped. Stronger and more alert than they know, I estimate we have just traveled about five miles in the direction of Lilavois, another remote place in the countryside. I have been involved in several business activities in the area over the years and am quite familiar with the area.

The last thing I am going to do is get out of this car voluntarily and stand blindfolded before two men with guns. Besides, I feigned a seizure earlier, and I need to play up that strategy while I hope and wait for help or an opportunity to escape. I pretend to be too weak to stand, incapable of walking on my own.

They tape my mouth again to keep me from calling out for help and then pull me out of the car. I drop to the ground. I feel raindrops on my face and smell humidity in the air and the muskiness of damp earth. With one man on each side of me, they lift me up. Supporting my buckling legs, they lift me over a stone wall that is wet and slippery. I am at least thirty pounds heavier than either of my kidnappers, and I make sure they work hard to lift my limp, heavy body over the wall. Then they drag me through tangled vegetation. Winded, they finally haul me up a step and inside a building.

Their voices echo, and the air smells like mildew. When I hear a match strike and smell sulfur, I fight the urge to scream and force myself to think logically. We are probably inside a dark, unfinished, uninhabited house out in the "boondocks," and someone just lit an old scrap of candle. They lower me to a seated position on a piece of splintering plywood, my back propped against a cold cinder-block wall. My eyes and mouth are still taped, but they have not bound my hands or feet. *Facteur H?*

Good! My strategy is working. They must think I'm in such poor health that I'm too weak to be a danger to them.

A few minutes later, I feign another heart attack, which causes the leader to sprint back to the car to retrieve my drinking water. By making major facial contortions during the episode, I manage to create an opening at the bottom of the duct tape over my eyes, just enough to allow me to get an occasional glimpse of my surroundings in the dim, flickering candlelight.

I confirm that we are in an abandoned unfinished house, and I am quite confident that I know where we are. The killer sits beside me, drumming his fingers insistently on the Uzi, as if frenzied music plays in his head. His behavior convinces me that my heart attack idea is a far better plan than attempting to run right now. On the other hand, I need to be careful not to overplay the act and become too much of a problem for them.

Earlier, I overheard them discuss the possibility of dousing me with gasoline and setting me afire, so there will be no evidence, if it appears they aren't going to be able to keep me alive. This practice, known as *Pere Lebrun*, has become all too horrifyingly frequent in Haiti nowadays.

When the leader returns with the water and takes the tape off my mouth so that I can drink, I pretend to recover slightly.

They seem somewhat reassured and turn their attention to coming up with a safer location in which to hide their hostage. Since the other two men did not return before I was moved from where they'd left us, the leader and the killer hastily make new plans again. Knowing it is unwise to keep driving around in my Toyota Land Cruiser, which is being searched for and repeatedly described on all radio stations, the leader now decides he will get a different car.

Tonnerre! I am left alone in a remote abandoned house with a mentally unstable assassin, who is high on something and holds an Uzi! Could the situation get any worse?

With only one captor to deal with now—albeit a crazed killer, salivating at the chance to finish me off, I pray fervently for another opportunity to escape and put myself into a meditative state, as my father taught me. I'd had little time or inclination to practice meditation with him during his lifetime, but now I turn to it with more conviction.

Please help me be strong and help me get back to my wife and daughters alive. Don't let me die at the hands of these salopries.[59] *Come on now, Dad. I'm asking for your advice. I need one of your brainstorms here!*

After what seems about ten minutes, a positive, calm feeling creeps over me. A thought steals into my mind: *I will have to create my own opportunity.*

With my eyes and my mouth taped, I have nothing but time to think about my situation—and hope my potential executioner will fall asleep. I have always created five-year plans for me and my family. I was just into the second year of my current five-year plan when I was kidnapped.

Myriam and I had accomplished most of our previous plans, pretty much as we'd envisioned. Although Villarosa had been a burden when we were first married, and we had trouble making

---

59   Scum.

ends meet, we found a viable solution by renting it to the German Embassy for three years. After our Kyona Beach Resort became successful and the German Embassy's lease expired, we moved back into our beloved, beautiful Villarosa with our growing family. Our second daughter, Militsa, was born during those years.

With our larger family, Myriam and I needed more space and privacy. We constructed our own home—a three-bedroom, three-bath apartment below the main house in an open-area basement with views of the bay. Our little family lived in this comfortable dwelling with a private entrance, and my parents lived in the main house above us. Villarosa became the paradise we envisioned.

We reopened the bed-and-breakfast at Villarosa that my mother had started years earlier and regularly had houseguests. We never advertised. Our paying guests were mostly friends of my mother's or my father's, who came from the United States or Europe to spend the winter months with us. Those friends referred other friends, and our four extra bedrooms were full most of the time. It was a joyous period at Villarosa, filled with people and life. We spent some of our happiest moments during those years.

I remember when we first opened the bed-and-breakfast after my father retired in the 1950s. A number of prominent people visited over the years. Teddy Roosevelt, grandson of President Theodore Roosevelt, and his wife, Anne, who traveled together on hunting safaris throughout the world, had heard about us through mutual friends. They visited in the late 1960s, and I made arrangements to take them and some of their friends duck hunting. One of the couples was Kip and Caroline DuPont.

I really hit it off with the DuPonts, of the DuPont de Nemours chemical fortune from Delaware. We developed a strong rapport. They had invested in a resort property called Third Turtle Inn on Providenciales in the Turks and Caicos Islands. A beautiful spot, the Third Turtle Inn boasted perfect beaches but nothing else. Everything had to be imported, even the drinking water. The DuPonts established a little airline and regularly flew to Haiti from the Turks and Caicos to pick up supplies that I had arranged for them.

I knew of a unique, historic hotel property with full facilities for sale on the north coast of Haiti in the town of Cap Haitien and proposed a business partnership. This base of operations would cut their flying time in half and make it easier for them to develop the Third Turtle Inn.

Haiti had been the wealthiest French colony during Napoleon's time. Cap Haitien had been its capital when Haiti won independence from France in 1804. Now, centuries later, the charming old hotel in Cap Haitien, *L'Hostellerie du Roi Christophe*, was steeped in history and character—a wonderful attraction for tourists. It had been the property of King Christophe of Haiti, who built the Citadelle La Ferriere, a UNESCO World Heritage Site.

Myriam and I still owned the travel agency in Port-au-Prince that we had purchased in 1965. Our new plan was to direct people to our hotel in Cap Haitien, eventually developing a package with three days in Cap Haitien and three days in Turks and Caicos at the DuPont's resort.

I was coordinating this package when I attended my first American Society of Travel Agents convention in Puerto Rico. After the travel agents kept asking me how to get clients to Cap Haitien, since the drive from Port-au-Prince was eight hours over horrible roads, I naturally decided we needed our own airline.

I persuaded the government to issue a license, convincing them that we'd lure attractive tourist dollars to our small island. With the help of a friend of the DuPonts and his contacts with an existing airline in Turks and Caicos, we started our own airline. This airline eventually became the national airline of Haiti, Haiti Air Inter.

By my late thirties I had achieved a degree of success on my own and finally saw myself as a survivor capable of "making it." I had more confidence in myself and my abilities than many of my friends who had inherited their fortunes or businesses. Myriam and I had the travel agency, the beach property, the hotel in Cap Haitien, and now a small airline. Life was going well.

But that didn't stop me. I'd become hooked on business and the rush that each success brings. I began to explore more opportunities.

While I searched for new endeavors, I still was also heavily involved in various agro-industrial projects. I primarily grew labor-intensive produce to export to well-known companies such as Campbell's (Campbell Soup Company) and others in the United States and Europe during the winter months.

In the midst of all this, I purchased a second assembly operation with eight hundred additional employees. We assembled everything from the bags for Crown Liquor to radios for BMWs, to power supplies for Motorola. Haiti had an abundance of inexpensive, hardworking, eager-to-work labor available.

Discussing ideas with friends, I found several investors who wanted to put together a major citrus operation. We began a pilot project on 150 acres in the Artibonite Valley. We would ship all the produce we could to Europe and the United States. With the climate and conditions in Haiti perfect for growing citrus, we planned to turn Plantation Dauphin, a former 33,000-acre sisal plantation where I had worked for Myriam's uncle in the sixties, into a thriving citrus grove. Because of international trade advantages and the abundance of low-cost labor, the business had tremendous potential. Our 150-acre lime grove became the proving grounds for a 10,000-acre citrus project.

I had different groups of partners and financing arrangements in my various endeavors, and with those came different problems. The volatile political climate in Haiti often exacerbated those problems.

For instance, the World Bank offered twenty million dollars funding for the citrus plantation—on the condition that we match that amount from the private sector. I worked tirelessly to raise the money and was far advanced, after having leased the land from the government and ensured that our pilot project was successful and growing. The export market was strong and flourishing, and we were shipping two to three million pounds of limes a year. Everything seemed to be in place—and then Baby Doc's government collapsed. After Baby Doc's departure, a group of feuding peasants came along and cut down all the trees in this thriving citrus grove to make charcoal.

Fortunately, a friend and I had purchased the exclusive Toyota dealership in 1984, and we quickly built it into a successful business. It, too, was completely destroyed in 1987 after Baby Doc's departure. Undeterred, we rebuilt it, and it thrived again. It still does to this day.

In 1989 I sold the travel agency, as Haiti continued to deteriorate and tourism declined and became practically nonexistent.

By 1998, with the continually deteriorating political situation and the surge in violent crime, pollution, and overpopulation— and nothing being done to address these issues—Haiti's outlook grew bleak. I knew our lives would have to change. Myriam and I began to plan our retirement in Florida, where we already had a foothold.

But now, while we are in the process of selling Villarosa and scaling down as part of our plan, I am the victim of a violent crime that we had hoped to head off. We have worked side by side so hard for so many years.

I can't help but think, *I was so close to accomplishing my lifelong objectives, but now I'm so far from reaching them. In a split second, everything changed. What will Myriam do if I'm killed? What will Daska and Militsa do? They all believe in me and my fearless ability to accomplish the near-impossible. They need me.*

Having survived Duvalier's jail; all the numerous revolutions and potentially fatal situations in Haiti; the Vietnam War era; financial ups and downs; major heart surgery four years earlier; and being so close to accomplishing my exit/retirement plan, will I die at the hands of such wild-eyed, low-life dregs of society? Has my luck run out? Are my plans dissolved?

No way! I decide I have too much to lose and convince myself I am up to the challenge. My survival instincts kick in big time. I am familiar and comfortable with guns from my training in the United States Army and my days as a professional duck hunter. I begin planning. I will disarm the one watching me, kill him, and find my way home.

I roll my shoulders and relax my body, leaning back as comfortably as I can against the hard, cold cement, wanting the killer to think I am weak, resting, and no threat to him. From the slits under the tape I can keep an eye on him. For now he remains seated beside me but obviously in his own world. I can't help but think of overtaking him once he falls asleep. I could grab his Uzi, take him hostage, and work my way back to civilization.

* * *

As I sit on the rough plywood, my mind jumps from one subject to another, occasionally recalling some great memories. I think about Myriam and our daughters, the people I hold dear and to whom I desperately want to return. And I begin to think of the other woman in my life whom I loved: my mother. I loved my parents, but I adored my mother. I remember how much fun she was to be with, and I remember how kind she was to my young wife when we were first married. My mother became Myriam's best friend and mentor. She introduced Myriam to the Haitian social scene by frequently inviting her to the numerous parties and lunches.

One night at an American Embassy ball, my mother proudly introduced her daughter-in-law to the United States ambassador and suggested he open the ball by dancing with her. My brave, timid wife suddenly found herself waltzing with the ambassador in front of three to four hundred members of Haiti's high society, most of them strangers to her.

But Mother was as comfortable at home educating and entertaining her grandchildren as she was attending society events. Having had three sons, she'd always wanted a daughter and loved spending time with our two girls. Daska and Militsa (both Yugoslavian names from my mother's family) dearly loved "Baba," as they called their grandmother.

Myriam credits my mother with teaching her how to face the world more gracefully and how to be a lady in difficult times. Mother showed Myriam how to entertain well and how to appreciate what we had without comparing to others.

There was nearly a twenty year age difference between my parents. My father had adored my mother from the first moment he set eyes on her, and that only seemed to deepen over time. Even at eighty years old, a softness came over his face and love misted his eyes when he looked at my mother. He always took care of his appearance and tried to look his best for her. He was most attentive to her, honored her, and nothing she ever said or did was wrong in his eyes. Every day he told her that he loved her—every single day!

My father claimed age was all in our minds; that we were capable of feeling as young as we thought we were. There seemed to be no limit to how young he felt and no limit to his physical abilities. In his sixties he took up spearfishing and became one of the best. Even in his early eighties, my father asked me to drop him off in the mountains. About nine hours later I'd pick him up in the woodlands below, after he'd hiked about fifteen miles searching for and collecting wild orchids. With the agility of a much younger man, he climbed trees to collect his coveted orchids and carried them in a knapsack on his back.

I remember an article about my father, written at the time of his art exhibition in Mexico City that described him as a "bright, quick-minded octogenarian." Knowing he was a pilot, the interviewer asked if he planned to fly his own plane to get there, and my father replied, "Why, I haven't flown a plane since I was twenty-eight!"

CHAPTER 34

European Travels and Dignitaries, 1928–1929

Horace

My insatiable curiosity as a filmmaker led me to take my camera out to meet the forces of nature head–on. These forces had touched me spiritually, emotionally, and physically, and my experiences had reaffirmed my respect for nature. I'd felt the power of nature's extremes: the frigid Arctic, the sweltering Sahara, the mountains and precipices of Tibet, the rainforests of the Amazon, and the tropical splendor of Haiti. I'd witnessed nature's fury: sandstorms in North Africa, volcanoes in Italy and Martinique, and earthquakes in Jamaica and San Francisco.

Of all the exploring I had done, my recent trips to the Arctic had taken the greatest toll on me. In late 1928, after more than two decades of travel, I went to Paris, my second home city, to rest. But I didn't rest long before I got another of my brainstorms.

It occurred to me that my experience producing hundreds of documentary films qualified me to try to make one of which I had often dreamed: *A Day in the Life of the Pope*. Knowing how much protocol would be involved, I wiped all doubts from my mind and pictured only what I would say to His Holiness when I was received. Then I drove to Rome.

There I approached my good friend, whose nephew, Count Pecci–Blunt, had married the Pope's niece. Count Pecci–Blunt was most courteous and encouraging. He introduced me to his friend, Count Moroni, the official portrait painter of the Vatican, who might be able to obtain an audience with the pope for me. Moroni's studio was a study in scarlet. He explained that during a year he would use gallons of red paint for the robes of all the cardinals. He was working on two full-length, life-sized portraits, and his whole studio glowed with that beautiful crimson color. When I started to explain what I wanted and why, he replied that Count Pecci-Blunt had already told him. Count Moroni had already spoken to His Holiness, and I would be granted a private audience the following morning.

At the appointed hour, I presented myself to the Vatican, and I was ushered into the private study of Pope Pius XI. He received me very kindly, and we chatted a while before I presented my plan. "Your Holiness, I am honored to see you again. When I was a journalist in Chicago, I met you when you attended the Ecumenical Congress as a cardinal."

The pope politely replied, "I remember your face. Tell me what you have been doing since we met in Chicago. Count Moroni told me that you are an explorer and have traveled extensively."

This gave me the opportunity to tell His Holiness of my experiences making documentary films and my desire to make one titled *A Day in the Life of the Pope*. I continued, "Your Holiness, three principle cities in the United States—Baltimore, Philadelphia, and Boston—are predominantly Catholic. There are thousands of American Catholics who would be most happy to see such a film. I am a professional lecturer, and my intention is not to show the film first in motion picture theaters but to present it several times along with a lecture in each of those cities. Naturally I would submit the text of my lecture to you for approval."

Pope Pius XI appeared to be very interested. "My dear Mr. Ashton, I am not free to make such an important decision alone. Your request must be approved by the

College of Cardinals." The pope pushed a button and asked his secretary to summon six of the cardinals present in the Vatican, while I waited. I was grateful, having already taken up nearly an hour of his time.

When the cardinals arrived, Pope Pius XI presented me and asked me to explain my plan again, while an interpreter repeated it in Italian for the cardinals who didn't understand English very well. Afterward, they all talked for about twenty minutes in Italian, which I didn't understand. My heart sank when I saw several of them give the thumbs-down sign.

His Holiness thanked them, and they left the room. He turned to me and said, "I'm truly sorry, Mr. Ashton, but I was advised that it might be considered undignified if I allowed such an intimate exposition of my personal life in the Vatican."

I thanked him sincerely for the time he had given me and withdrew. Not long after my audience with the pope, I heard that a film documentary called *Time Marches On* had been made about the pope. For most of my life I had a knack for being in the right place at the right time, but this was one occasion when my timing was off.

Back in my hotel room in Rome, I would not allow my disappointment to deter me. Since I had no plans on the horizon, I decided to contact the Italian Tourist Organization and propose three films on northern, central, and southern Italy for lectures in the United States and elsewhere. I approached the director of the Italian Tourist Organization with my plan, which involved a considerable sum of money. He informed me that I'd have to present my plan to Mussolini, and he made an appointment with Il Duce.

A few days later the director of tourism ushered me into Il Duce's presence. We passed between two guards at the door and entered a large room about fifty feet long. Mussolini was seated behind a desk on a platform about a foot above the floor at the far end of the room. This arrangement reminded me of my old school days, when the teacher always dominated the room in this manner.

We walked the whole length of the room, giving Il Duce plenty of time to look me over. He rose when the director presented me, and I was astonished to see that Mussolini was not a tall man. Now I understood the reason for the platform.

Mussolini allowed me to present my plan and explain all of its details. He said that he had given my idea a great deal of thought since talking with the director the previous day. "Mr. Ashton, you have an excellent idea. The only difficulty is the sum involved. It will take time to arrange that kind of financing. The director of tourism will keep in touch with you through the Italian consulate in Paris."

I thanked him and left. Months passed, and I returned home to New York in 1929. I never heard from the director of tourism again.

* * *

Never one to sit idle, I soon had another brainstorm. Interestingly, while at my house in New York with my dog Roscoe sleeping at my feet on my treasured Turkish rug and surrounded by other mementos from my travels around the world, I found myself thinking of France. For many years I had traveled extensively throughout France by train. As I'd looked out the window and spied the country's smooth, inviting roads that passed through alluring towns in a countryside reeking with history, I promised myself that one day I would bring my car and explore them. There was no time like the present.

In 1929 I formed a plan to lead the first automobile caravan through Europe, similar to the one I'd led across America eighteen years earlier. New horizons were opening up for motorists, and we would travel in our own cars that were shipped across the Atlantic. Paris would be the departure point for our grand journey.

I was excited. In front of my door in New York, I loaded my baggage and Roscoe into my car and then drove to Pier 57 of the French Line, where the porters put my things in my cabin and my dog in the kennel on the *Ile de France*. I watched my brand-new shining black Buick and some of the other cars being hoisted high in the air to be loaded, uncrated, into the ship's hold as excess baggage.

When the *Ile de France* docked in Le Havre, the cars were hoisted onto the pier, where French license plates were attached. I debarked, along with forty-six other Americans bound for the caravan, and we met the representative of the Automobile Club of France. He provided us with a neat aluminum case that contained a number of documents: drivers' licenses for the drivers; registration certificates for the cars in France; a book of coupons for passing the numerous European customs' offices; and an International Certificate of Touring.

The next morning, I led the caravan to Paris with Roscoe perched on the passenger seat wagging his tail. We drove the first fifty-two kilometers in a northeasterly direction, passing through the pretty little towns of St. Romain and Bolbec to Yvetot. We then turned southeast into the Seine Valley, through beautiful, rolling, emerald-green farm country to Rouen.

It was July, and our trip was blessed with good weather. As we drove through Normandy, we observed quaint farmhouses, peaceful sloping fields, and long rows of fat, contented cows tethered near patches of red clover. Snowy mountains of cumulous clouds floated in the turquoise sky above as the route south from Rouen to Paris followed the lovely Seine River, taking us through the towns of Vernon and Nantes. Sometimes the road ran on top of hills, from where we could see miles of blue ribbon winding like a serpent through the valley below, and at other times we viewed the river more intimately from along its tree-bordered banks, listening to the whistles of boat traffic.[60]

In each village my Buick seemed to attract a lot of

---

60   Horace D. Ashton, F.R.G.S., "Car Goes Abroad as Open Baggage," in *The New York Herald*, Paris, France, July 1929.

attention, as did the novelty of the caravan. American cars were generally much larger than French automobiles, and all new cars were always admired. Driving leisurely from Le Havre, it took us a little over four hours to make the journey to Paris. We entered the City of Light via Avenue de la Grande Armée, and both sides were lined with the booths and decorations of a great street carnival. We passed around the Arc de Triomphe and down the Champs-Elysées to our hotel, where I made final arrangements for the extensive road trip of which I had long dreamed.

The ramble through France was everything I'd hoped for and more; for me, it was the fulfillment of a number of dreams. I drove through Brittany with its medieval chateaux, its straw-thatched cottages made of stone, its black-dressed, lace-bonneted women with smiling eyes, and its men in blue smocks wearing little round velvet hats with long streamers and wooden shoes on their feet. I visited Mont St. Michel, that curious, picturesque group of buildings surrounded by a wall and topped off by a lofty cathedral spire that appeared to be afloat in the dim evening light, like a painting on a blue gauze curtain. I spent the night close to the sea in St. Malo, where a profusion of red, pink, and white roses bloomed against the gray stone walls of the thatched cottages and the intensity of their perfume drowned out the smells of seaweed and salt mist.

Sunday morning dawned bright as I drove south to Concarneau through the music of pealing church bells. On the way I passed numerous two-wheeled carts on which peasant girls—dressed alike in black velvet with tight-fitting bodices and full skirts, white lace collars, and the daintiest of white lace caps—were seated three abreast, heading to church. Not unlike other Christian communities I had seen, there were twice as many women as men among the church-goers.

The most striking feature of motoring through France, which made it most enjoyable, was the absence of traffic upon the roads. There were hundreds of miles of marvelous roads through beautiful country and no motorcycle cops! No speed limits. None was needed, for where one is free to do as one pleases, he seldom abuses the privilege.

Gasoline was rather expensive in France, and the average price at filling stations was about forty cents per gallon. Oil also was proportionately high. On my only night run I discovered, almost to my undoing, that there was not a soul stirring in the villages after ten o'clock at night. On my return trip, when I was still a hundred miles from Paris and had about a gallon of gasoline left in my tank, I had nearly given up hope of going much farther. Just then, the headlights of an approaching car loomed out of the darkness, and ahead of me, the driver drew up in front of what turned out to be a dark garage. He unlocked the door and turned on the lights, just as I arrived. I bought a tank full of gasoline and went on my way. All the rest of the way to Paris, I did not see another car.

After traveling 725 miles, I pulled up in front of the Savoy Hotel in the Rue de Rivoli to end the dream fulfillment portion of my odyssey. I would continue the caravan through Europe and take another automobile trip through Western Mauritania, Africa, with archeologist and fellow Explorers Club member Byron de Prorok, who'd uncovered the tiles I'd seen in my vision of ancient Carthage in Tunisia. But my intimate journey through the beauty of the French countryside, especially Brittany, would forever remain close to my heart.[61]

---

61   Horace Ashton, F.R.G.S., "Brittany Charms Motoring Visitor," in *The New York Herald*, Paris, France, 21 July 1929.

READY FOR AN-
OTHER TRIP — Byron
de Prorok and Horace
Ashton, archaeologists and
members of the Explorers
Club of New York, inspect
their new automobiles in
Paris. They will soon make
a trip through Western
Mauritania, Africa.
Photo Wide World.

Byron de Prorok and Horace Ashton prepare to explore Africa by automobile.

* * *

In the summer of 1929, I had only just returned to Paris
from my auto caravan, when I ran into a friend, Dr. Daniel
Hally-Smith, who had been invited to go hunting with King
Alexander of Yugoslavia. The king planned to hunt the
illusive chamois that dwelt among western Yugoslavia's
highest peaks in the Julian Alps. This was a case of my
timing being perfect. If I was allowed to accompany the
hunting party, I could obtain a rare motion picture record
of one of the most difficult big-game hunts in the world.

ALL NATIONS HUNT — The chamois baggers here shown are Prince Paul and King Alexander of Yugoslavia, Prince Nicholas of Greece, Dr. Hally-Smith of Paris and Prince Obolenski of Russia. *Horace Ashton Photo.*

KING TAKES AIM — When King Alexander of Yugoslavia goes hunting, no attendant is asked to fire the shot. Scene, Julian Alps. *Horace Ashton Photo.*

European royalty hunt in the Julian Alps.

Dr. Hally–Smith contacted the king, who apparently knew of my reputation as a photographer and explorer, and I was invited to join them. I would record the big–game hunt on film, in addition to taking pictures of the dignitaries and the breathtaking alpine scenery.[62] In great haste, Daniel and I traveled from Paris to Bled, Slovenia, the summer capital of Yugoslavia, situated just south of the Austrian border.

On the first day of the hunt, we departed Bled at an extremely early hour, drove about thirty kilometers to Mojstrana, and then turned south into the beautiful valley of Krma in the direction of Mount Triglav. In the bottom of the valley we turned north again, traversed three meadows of small farms, and stopped the car at a farmhouse beside a queer fence–like hayrack to await the arrival of the royal car. Seeing the caravan with equipment and provisions, most of it to be carried on the backs of men, and the scope of the preparations, I anticipated an unforgettable experience.

In a short time, King Alexander's machine rolled up, and the young monarch, just forty–four years old, stepped out to greet us. With him were his cousin, Prince Paul of Siberia; Prince Nicholas of Greece, who was Prince Paul's father–in–law; and Prince Obolensky of Russia.

Accompanied by the large supply caravan, we marched along a wide forest trail for four hours, and by midmorning, we reached a hunting lodge surrounded by high, rocky peaks. The view was magnificent, but no time was lost looking at it. Leaving the caravan and supplies at the lodge, the hunting party immediately started out on a further climb of an hour or more.

We scanned the hillside with our glasses for the first signs of the fleet and elusive little animals, whose abode is among the clouds. At last, far up on the mountainside adjacent to me, a small stone tumbled down. I strained my eyes but could see nothing moving. My guide pointed, but I was not used to spotting chamois. Again a stone came tumbling down.

This time I caught a glimpse of two chamois, far up

---

62   Horace Ashton, "Hunting the Chamois With King Alexander," in *The New York Times*, New York City, New York, 12 January 1930.

the rocks, coming straight down toward me. With as little movement as possible, I quickly readied my camera. In a few moments I was making my first pictures of chamois in the wild, using a telephoto lens. On they came, closer and closer, until they were within hearing distance of the camera. Then they turned tail and abruptly fled.

The director of the royal hunt, Plemelj, would organize nine different hunts in these mountains, moving all the men and supplies through this beautiful valley, resplendent with the largest and oldest willows and oaks in the world. I was amazed at the elaborate production of each hunt. Each member of the hunting party had a guide; numerous porters carried equipment as the "beaters" drove the chamois into the valleys.

The shouting of the beaters grew louder and louder, their cries echoing back and forth on the mountainsides, and at last they would come into view. I could not believe my eyes. How could men climb down these almost vertical cliffs? On they came, almost straight down without the aid of ropes, shouting as they came.

The second hunt was a more intimate one. Only King Alexander, Dr. Daniel Hally–Smith, and I went, accompanied by the usual complement of beaters, guides, and porters. Starting just after daylight, the drive was on. Never had I dreamed of such a sight. More than thirty chamois came down the mountain, almost together, heading straight for the king. Does and fawns were never shot, and because they were so close together, the king did not fire. He let the chamois procession pass by while I photographed them to my heart's content. When they turned and began to climb the hill again, the king selected a good buck and fired, felling the animal in one shot. I captured the whole scene on film—the king making a clean kill at two hundred yards and a telephoto view of the animal falling down the mountainside.

Alternating days of hunting and fishing in these mountains lasted for a month. Daniel and I were preparing to return to Paris when the king announced another chamois hunt in Bosnia. He urged us to join him the following week and travel with him on his special train to Jablanca. The king was a splendid fellow, and we were both keen for another hunt. Meanwhile, we spent a week having fun in Yugoslavia's summer resort city.

During all my travels in the four corners of the world over the past two decades, it would be a single moment in Bled, Slovenia, that would have the greatest significance in my life.

CHAPTER 35

Yugoslavia Brings a New Bride, 1929–1935

Horace

It was the trend among fashionable Yugoslavians in the late 1920s to "take the mountain air" for their health by spending summers in Bled, Slovenia. Daniel and I checked into the elegant Grand Hotel Toplice on picturesque Lake Bled.

Every afternoon the hotel held a tea dance, and in nice weather they set it up on the lakeside terrace. I waxed my handlebar moustache and dressed to look my best for the afternoon affair. I dressed in pressed trousers, a striped vest, starched white shirt, and maroon tie and then joined Daniel on the terrace. We found a table and ordered our tea. After placing our order, I sat back and puffed on my pipe, enjoying the view. Behind the hotel, perched high above, sat Bled Castle, and out on an island in the center of the emerald-green mountain lake sat a little white church, all amid peaks of the Julian Alps.

The sun shone, the mountain air smelled fresh and clean, and well-dressed people were gathering on the terrace. In the warmth of the afternoon, many of the men had opted to wear stylish vests in various colors rather than suit coats, as Daniel and I had done. Some of the women were dressed in Old-World elegance, while others wore the latest flapper fashions from Paris and London. All around me people laughed and chatted, flirting in a socially acceptable, lighthearted way, and as the string quartet launched into their first Strauss waltz, several couples lined up to dance.

Suddenly, heads turned as a tall, slim, blonde young lady walked onto the terrace with an elderly "grand dame," whom people seemed to know—no doubt her chaperone. I straightened up and forgot my pipe as I too admired the striking young lady, who wore a straight-cut, yellow chiffon confection with beading around the slightly scooped neckline and a floating hem. But it was more than her statuesque beauty or the whimsical headband circling her blonde bob that riveted my gaze.

The life inside her visibly glowed. She possessed a regal presence and distinctive sense of style and a "knowing" quality that may have intimidated some people but only drew me to her. She was as confident as I was.

It was an amazing thing to realize, and I was fascinated. There was only one lady in this room for me, and I had to know her. However, noted explorer or not, I knew that in this society I couldn't just walk up and ask her to dance without an introduction to her chaperone first.

As luck would have it, the good Dr. Hally-Smith knew Milica Bela Popovic, the young blonde's titled maternal grandmother. Daniel gave me a proper introduction, making sure to stress the fact that I had just accompanied the king on a royal hunt. After seemingly endless minutes of polite conversation, I asked Lady Popovic for permission to dance with her granddaughter, Gordana Dimovic.

The old lady smiled as if she knew a secret. I led Gordana onto the dance floor for a Strauss waltz, where I had to do an inordinate amount of bowing and clicking of heels, but I would have done anything to spend time with this fascinating lady. Her height complemented mine, and she was light on her feet as a dancer; her dress flared like a filmy sunbeam when I turned her. I imagined we must have looked like the perfect couple on the dance floor. But my instant attraction to Gordana went much deeper than how we looked and fit together. Her smile warmed my soul, and her small hand in mine felt like it had always belonged there.

When I escorted Gordana to her table after the dance, I

found Daniel seated there, conversing with the old lady. As I slid a chair out for Gordana, I noticed that her grandmother met her gaze briefly, smiled, and then invited me to join them. I spent the rest of the afternoon enchanted by the sound of Gordana's delightful laugh and innate intelligence reflected in her soulful blue eyes as I recounted my adventures.

I danced with Lady Popovic and twice more with her granddaughter. Gordana spoke fluent English, and we talked almost nonstop. I learned her father was a playwright and a doctor, and she was the eldest of five, having three younger sisters and a brother. A twelfth-century castle in nearby Gradac, Slovenia, was the annual gathering place for the extended family. Gordana longed to see more of the world, but her parents rarely took her on vacations abroad. Apparently the castle was the focus of her mother's life, and every year, when her father offered to take her mother on a fabulous vacation, she chose to use the money instead to restore the castle.

Lady Popovic—whose title was a little vague and came by way of a relative's marriage to the Italian King Emanuel III, a short man who wanted a tall wife to increase the stature of his heirs—seemed to approve of me. When she pointedly mentioned that she usually brought her two eldest granddaughters to the tea dance most afternoons, I knew with certainty that every afternoon would find me at the dance until I had to leave Bled.

The next afternoon, I invited Gordana to go for a rowboat ride on the lake so I could take her picture. She refused and explained that boat riding with a man just wasn't done. Undaunted by her rejection, I rented two rowboats, since the social rules did not prohibit her from going out in a boat alone. I followed and snapped some lovely pictures.

I had learned to trust my intuition, and I knew from our first meeting that Gordana was the only woman for me. Everything about her seemed so right. She had a terrific sense of humor, and no matter how unpleasant things appeared to be, she would make a joke of the situation. I thought that together we would make a perfect team.

With her grandmother seated at a table on the terrace nearby, we conversed gaily back and forth between our two boats, flirting in that socially acceptable way. Near the end of the afternoon, I brought my rowboat alongside hers so I wouldn't be overheard by others. "I'll return to Yugoslavia in one year. If you are still free, I'll ask you to marry me," I promised.

She laughed, a musical sound that made everything right with my world. "Oh, that's just what an American would say."

She did not believe me—and for good reason; she knew I was already married. As much as I wished to be free to follow my heart, I would need a year to finalize my divorce from Helen before I could properly propose to Gordana. I had no right to ask her to wait for me. Outgoing and confident, she could have the world at her feet and any man in it. I was older and had little to offer financially, but I believed with all my heart that we belonged together, and I hoped to convince her of that.

When I joined King Alexander and Daniel in Bosnia for the hunt, my mind was far from chamois. Every night thereafter, when we retired to the lodge, I wrote letters to the love of my life. The one thing I wanted most from my trip to Yugoslavia was the one thing for which I had no right to ask—Gordana to marry me.

* * *

After the hunt, I returned to Paris and boarded a ship for New York. There I took care of my affairs and began the divorce process, which would take a year. I yearned to be with Gordana, but I would not see her again until I was a free man, able to offer her what she deserved. Meanwhile, there was nothing to keep me in New York, especially since the woman I loved lived in Europe. Looking for a new opportunity and a new residence, I contacted Paramount Pictures in Paris.

After a decade as a lecturer, I was finding the touring schedule tiring. Each night after my lecture I'd check out of the hotel and take the night train to the next city. The following day I'd give press interviews, perhaps appear at a Rotary lunch or dine with the head of the organization presenting my lecture, and then go to the auditorium, give my lecture, and repeat the same grind day after day. During my career as a lecturer, my greatest satisfaction came from lecturing in schools, where I was often astonished at how intelligent and insightful the students' questions were.

I packed up all my belongings and moved to Paris, where I went to work for Paramount. Sadly, my traveling companion, Roscoe the flying dog, was killed one day by a truck as he ran down the street barking at an airplane overhead. I missed having a dog, and despite many old friends in Paris and thoughts of my new love, I was lonely. I adopted a little Scottish terrier named Andy.

Every day, I wrote a letter to Gordana, often using Paramount stationary. I told her of my travels, of my hopes and dreams, my thoughts on spiritual matters and what I had learned. I told her of my life in Paris and my friends and my work. Gradually, while still being a gentleman, I told her more and more of how I felt about her. In one year, I sent Gordana over three hundred letters. She wrote me back—more formally and not as often, but she wrote. The more I learned of her, the more convinced I was that we were meant to be together.

As soon as my divorce was final in 1930, I kept my promise and returned to Yugoslavia, where I proposed to Gordana on bended knee. She said yes and then added with a grin, "I have to marry you just to stop from getting so much mail."

When she told her grandmother about my proposal, Lady Popovic replied, "My darling, even if you have to scrub floors, this man will always treat you like a queen."[63]

We took the Orient Express to Paris, where we were

---

63   John Allen Franciscus, "Mr. and Mrs. Horace Ashton: A Pioneering Haitian Love Story," in *The Last Frontier*, June 1987.

married in style. After a short honeymoon at a Paris hotel, we traveled to Gradac, Slovenia, and spent the rest of the summer with Gordana's family at the castle. I got along well with the adults, and I played imaginative games with the children, who all loved my little terrier.

In Yugoslavia, however, dogs were kept strictly outdoors. Gordana's parents and grandmother disapproved of my bringing Andy into the house. They thought it uncouth and very "American." They seemed to love me anyway and tolerated the "odd American tastes" of the rogue explorer who had joined their family. At times they teased me about it, especially when I repeatedly went into the kitchen and told the cook not to boil the vegetables for so long. Watery, tasteless vegetables were the custom, and undercooked vegetables were positively uncivilized.

As usual, Gordana's mother, also named Milica, spent the summer involved in castle restoration. As I enjoyed decorating and gardening and knew how to build things, I pitched in with the work. My bride and I had our first disagreement when we set out to decorate one of the rooms together (there were eighty furnished rooms in the castle). I wanted to use a violet and green combination, but Gordana thought those colors could never be used together. "Look at nature; look at the plum tree," I told her, eventually winning her over.

I thought it was odd that I saw no fireplaces in all those rooms in the castle. It was a twelfth-century castle in the mountains, and I felt strongly that it must have had fireplaces at one time. Although Gordana and her mother didn't feel this was important, they humored me as I persistently searched all the walls. Sure enough, to their great surprise and delight, I uncovered a beautiful marble fireplace and restored it.

I hadn't saved any money or cared about financial planning in my life. Having a wife had never changed this particular character trait. The money I'd earned had always gone into my next expedition or adventure. I didn't have enough money to move back to Paris and start a new life with my Yugoslavian bride, but I was reluctant to leave her and seek my next opportunity.

The custom in Yugoslavia was not to give wedding presents to newlyweds but to present them with a monetary gift. In the fall, Gordana's father asked if I would renovate a house he owned in a small village in Serbia. This job lasted about six months, and with good–natured input from Gordana, I came up with some good ideas and single–handedly renovated the house. My father–in–law was pleased. He paid for our move to Paris and presented us with a small endowment to get started.

Gordana was excited about living in Paris and traveling with me. We packed up her belongings and, of course, my terrier, Andy. I got another job at Paramount, and Gordana learned to appreciate Andy's residing in our Paris apartment and not having her vegetables cooked too much.

* * *

In the 1920s I had been treated as a guest of the French government. During that period I became acquainted with some prominent citizens of Paris, such as Madame Boaz de Juvanelle, the head of the Bienvenue Francaise and the wife of a well–known French statesman. She took me into the homes of many of the old French families and to several chateaux in the Loire Valley. I met many interesting characters in Paris between the wars, including writer Ernest Hemingway; sculptor Jo Davidson; Emir Faisal, who later became King of Iraq; King Farouk of Egypt; the Aga Khan; Ganna Walska; Baron Henri de Rothschild; the maharajas of Kapurthala and Patiala; Mistinguett; Cécile Sorel; and Maurice Dekobra.

When Gordana and I returned to Paris to live, many of the people I'd met during the 1920s were still there, which made our social life very pleasant. We also met the young Princess Huang Ti Te, a ward of the French government, the daughter of the exiled king of Amman, and two charming Indian students, who were studying at the Sorbonne.

As newlyweds, we enjoyed Parisian life and attended many delightful social engagements. One evening, we were invited to be the guests of an elderly friend at the Ambassador Restaurant in the Champs-Elysées. There would be a gala banquet and the ladies' costumes would be judged.

A few weeks earlier, Gordana had looked at the invitation, aghast. "Oh no, I haven't anything suitable to wear. We must decline, Horace."

Instead, I took her shopping, and we bought some mauve organdy fabric. Although I had no previous experience as a fashion designer, I laid it out on the floor of our apartment and cut out my own design. Gordana sewed it into a beautiful evening dress. At the dinner, several people admired her outfit and said that if she had entered the contest, she would almost certainly have won a prize. I'd designed the mauve dress with love, and it set off her natural charm to perfection.

On another evening, we attended a more casual gathering with some friends. There I discussed my theory that I had lived during the time of the Punic Wars and perhaps had accompanied Hannibal in his attempt to conquer Rome. I told them that Hannibal had actually built a road along the French and Italian Rivieras and sent his army into Italy by that route, to my recollection.

My friends eyed me suspiciously, but they humored me and suggested that I pursue my reincarnation theory. Shortly after this discussion, I became reacquainted with the pilot with whom I'd crash-landed in the Sahara and been rescued by Berbers. He was now a French Army colonel.

Over lunch I told him, "I believe I lived during the Second Punic War, and I question the tale that Hannibal marched on Rome via the Alps. It seems unlikely that he would take those lumbering beasts up the treacherous mountains when he could just as easily have marched in from the coast."

"Horace, let's test your theory," he suggested, being a man of action like me. "Go get your camera, and let's take a short flight in my plane."

I readily agreed, and soon we were off. Flying above the French and Italian Rivieras with my friend, I photographed the clearly visible ruins of the route I theorized and somehow remembered from that past life. It could not be seen from sea level because it was now, nearly 2,000 years later, submerged in about twenty feet of water.

The pictures proved my theory and convinced me that I had indeed lived during the time of ancient Carthage in a past life. I put the question to rest and accepted a belief in reincarnation, the same belief taught by the abbot in China at the beginning of my spiritual quest. Over the years, I continued to have other memory flashes from times past, but none were as vivid and convincing as these.

* * *

From 1931 to 1935, I worked in Paris at Paramount Studios at Joinville. I was almost daily in the company of Sacha Guitry, Yvonne Printemps, Maurice Chevalier, Josephine Baker, and many leading actors from all parts of Europe. At the studio we made French, German, Spanish, Italian, Swedish, Danish, and Dutch versions of some of the most successful Hollywood productions. I did a number of jobs at Paramount, everything from acting, directing, and cinematography to dealing with the stars.

At that time those countries did not have many artists who had appeared in films, and we were forced to recruit our casts from the theater. As a result, there were many amusing complications. I was assigned to receive all these foreign companies and see that they had suitable hotel accommodations and that the leading female stars were properly costumed for the parts. Initially, that part of my job was simple, but when the actors became acquainted with one another and visited about, the storm broke. They'd burst into my office and demand an explanation as to why Madam X had better rooms than they. Because of the different standards of beauty in their home countries, some of the stars were quite heavy, and they would ask why Miss T looked so much better in the same costume. That's where I began my graduate training as a diplomat, handling those temperamental prima donnas.

An amusing incident occurred about a year after we moved to Paris, which could have caused a serious problem for my bride. I was an actor in the Gaumont production of Tristan Bernard's comedy *L'Anglais Tel qu'on le Parle*, with the French comedian Traumel. The studio was out beyond Joinville, and Gordana and I lived in Passy. One morning when I arrived at the studio and was already made up as the British banker, I discovered that I had left my waistcoat at home. I telephoned Gordana to bring it by taxicab as soon as possible, which she did. She had never been in a motion picture studio, and when she arrived, they showed her where the dressing rooms were located.

I had not warned Gordana of life backstage, and she arrived at my dressing room door to find two women in my room. Neither wore any clothing above their waists. In modern parlance, they were topless. One was seated in a rocking chair, knitting something for her baby, and the other, wearing only a cache—sexe, was seated on a high stool telling her risqué stories.

My wife stopped in the doorway, surveyed the scene, and crisply said, "*Bonjour.*"

"*Bonjour*," the actresses responded in unison.

Then Gordana handed me my waistcoat, gave me a kiss, and left. What a shock that must have been for a new wife! I'm glad to say she was broadminded about it, so I didn't have too hard a time smoothing things over when I got home.

Another example of bad timing occurred when I ran into my old friend Jimmy, the Duke de Alba of Spain, in Paris in 1931. I proposed a travel documentary for Spain, similar to the one I had proposed to Mussolini for Italy, except this documentary would include a colorful bullfight scene. Jimmy thought the film was a great idea. When he returned to Madrid the following week, he talked it over with his cousin, King Alfonso XIII.

The king remembered me and liked my idea. Ten days later, I received a cable from Jimmy saying that he was coming back to Paris with a contract. As far as he could see, everything was satisfactory.

Two days after the cable arrived, I learned that King Alfonso had been deposed. It seemed that this particular brainstorm was not meant to be. When the gate closed once again to show me this was not the way I was supposed to go, I finally paid attention and gave up trying to go through this particular fence. Instead, I spent most of the early 1930s in Paris with the love of my life.

* * *

In January 1933, my wife and I boarded a ship in Le Havre, where we departed for Haiti via New York. I had a motion picture assignment in Haiti, and I wished Gordana to see my beloved tropical island, the place I had visited in 1906, 1912, and 1915, and where I had lived for a year in 1919. Enchanted by the scenic beauty and colorful culture of Haiti, she came to understand why I loved it so.

Upon our arrival in New York, we were photographed disembarking and then interviewed by a staff writer for the society page of *The New York World Telegraph*. Our romance was the focus of the article. In it my lovely wife told an amusing story about an evening in 1930, just before we were married, when a fire broke out next door to her home near Lake Bled. Her grandmother, our chaperone, ran out to see what was happening. "The first moment we were alone," Gordana said, "was the moment of the fire. We went hand in hand to look at the fire. And this was the first time we talked alone. We talked of two fires, the fire in the house and the fire in the hearts . . . *voila*!"[64]

The article also mentioned my hunting trip in Yugoslavia with King Alexander and quoted me, referring to Gordana. "This is what I found, and so I've stopped hunting . . . A distant relative of the king, she is . . . we don't say much about it," I joked.

---

64   Marguerite Young, "Horace Ashton and Gordana Dimovic, Playwright's Daughter, Tell of Romance," in *The New York World Telegraph*, New York City, New York, 18 January 1933.

NEW YORK

Globe-Trotter Back Home, Won Bride on Royal Hunt

18 January 1953

Associated Press Photo.

Mr. and Mrs. Horace Ashton on their arrival.

Horace Ashton, Photographer, Tells of Romance with Gordana Dimovich, Playwright's Daughter, While on Trip with King Alexander, of Jugoslavia—Couple Arrive on Paris.

By MARGUERITE YOUNG,
World-Telegram Staff Writer.

Horace Ashton, globe-trotting American photographer, member of the New York Explorers' Club and the New York Academy of Sciences and a Fellow of the Royal Geographical Society, is back in New York after three years' absence with tall tales to tell of hunting with a king . . . and with a beautiful blonde wife, relative of the potenate.

"This is what I found," said Ashton, "and so I've stopped hunting."

Speaks English.

He indicated his wife, who sat beside him on the promenade deck of the French liner Paris. Ashton, a loose-knit, sturdy man, left it to the slender young beauty, who speaks English fluently, to fill in gaps left in his story of their romance.

Ashton has travelled twenty-eight years. In 1929 he went to Europe for a visit.

Then, he said, King Alexander of Jugoslavia invited him to go hunting.

It was then he met Gordana Dimovich, daughter of a Jugoslav playwright. "A distant relative of the King, she is," he said. "We don't say much about it." They were all

at Lake Bled, formerly Veldes, Austria, the summer capital.

He Went Back.

"You know," said Ashton, "after a day's hunting, we'd dress up every night and go to dinner. You couldn't help meeting the pretty girls."

"We met one morning," supplied Mrs. Ashton, "and after talking for two hours, he said he would come back within a year, and, if I were free, ask me to marry him. I laughed and said, 'Only an American could say such a thing.' Then every day he was writing to me, one letter or two, and he did come back."

"King Alexander?" Ashton continued. "A splendid fellow. Just 44. His wife, you know, is the second daughter of Queen Marie of Roumania. He hunts two months of every year in a private valley in the mountains near Lake Bled.

**Gordana and Horace Ashton
return to New York.**

During our five years in Paris, we enjoyed a delightful lifestyle while I continued to act, direct, and produce films. The arrival of our first child on September 9, 1933, named John Burdette Ashton after my father, brought us great joy.

Burdette was born in Zagreb, Yugoslavia, because Gordana wanted to be with her family when the blessed event occurred. Throughout her life, no matter where we lived, she remained close to her family and communicated regularly by letter. In the summers we often traveled to Slovenia to visit them at the castle in Gradac, and we went back to the tea dance at the hotel on Lake Bled, where I had first set eyes on the love of my life.

We had Burdette baptized about five different times to conform to all of our religious beliefs. My wife had a Greek Orthodox upbringing; my early years were filled with Episcopal and Christian Science influences. Then, of course, I had studied the world's religions, and my spiritual beliefs had been influenced by many of them. Later, during our years in Haiti, Burdette chose to participate in the Vodou religion with me and was baptized again in a Vodou ceremony.

* * *

In 1935, we moved to Zagreb, Yugoslavia for a short period, where I became the literary editor of *The Yugoslav Times*, an English–language weekly newspaper. As a spiritual being, I wrote about Orthodox Easter, saying, "In these days, when devotion to the church and its ritual is not so pronounced in the Western world, it does one good to see that religious customs are still observed in all their beautiful simplicity here in this charming country."[65]

By the end of 1935, the political situation in Europe had worsened, and I decided it was time to return to my native Virginia, where the Ashton family's roots were firmly planted. Our lengthy honeymoon in European society ended, and I spirited Gordana and our young son away to the United States to live a very humble life.

---

65   Horace Ashton, "Easter in Yugoslavia," in *The Yugoslav Times*, Zagreb, Yugoslavia, 21 April 1935.

CHAPTER 36

Exhausted

Butch
April 5, 2001
7:09 p.m.

I have now been held captive for a little more than five hours. My life means absolutely nothing to this killer if he can't exchange it for the ransom. I need to be careful not to cause him any trouble because I suspect he is looking for an excuse to pull the trigger. There is nothing I can do in this moment but turn inward, except this time I can't quiet my mind and find the stillness.

As I face almost certain death, thoughts race through my mind like the passing streak of headlights on a dark, rainy highway. I think of all the unfinished business I have yet to take care of. I think of how I take so much for granted in my life and vow that if I get out of this alive, I never will again. I think of the fragility of life and the wonderful life I've had up to now. I think of how much I love my family and how regretful I am for causing their terror . . . and their grief.

Exhausted, my thoughts slow down. To the best of my unpracticed ability I suspend my skepticism and give in to my father's belief in an afterlife. I summon his spirit with every ounce of power I have inside, praying that he will fulfill his promise to be my guardian angel.

Again, I begin to feel that same positive, calm feeling,

but this time it's a palpable energy that gives me strength and determination. My survival instincts—reinforced as a result of my military training in the United States Army some thirty-eight years earlier—start to kick in. Confidence in my ability to outwit my captors grows. My direction is clear. This is not how I want my life to end!

I would rather risk being shot during another escape attempt than be outright executed by these thugs. I will seize the moment. The only control I have left is not allowing them to choose the time and possibly horrific method of my death. If a chance to escape, however slim, presents itself, I will fight until I draw my last breath.

Energy ripples through my body and mind, but I am careful not to let it show. Although the meditation and my newfound determination have revived me, I continue to let the killer think I am on the verge of unconsciousness. I hope he dozes off or otherwise drops his guard. Right now, before anyone else returns, it is one-on-one. I steel my resolve and get ready.

Before my window of opportunity opens a crack, the leader returns with another car. My captors decide to move me to a different safe haven. Complications! Now I must find a way to kill them both.

I continue to play the best hand I have—weakness. Again the two men have to prop me up, help me walk, and lift my nearly dead weight over the wall. When they put me in the passenger seat of a small blue car, I have to shift my leg quickly to avoid the door being slammed on it. I don't think they notice. The killer climbs into the backseat, pressing the ever-present Uzi submachine gun against the back of my head.

The leader jumps in the driver's seat and then peels away at high speed as gravel flies up from under the tires.

My captors haven't noticed the tiny slits under the tape on my eyes. I am never more appreciative of the digital illuminated clocks found in most cars today. The dashboard clock blinks 8:11 p.m. It's now been more than six hours since I was taken.

We drive about five miles at breakneck speed. Careening over the road, they stop at another safe house, this time in what I believe to be Varreux. Again, they have to carry me inside. But this house is inhabited, and a lengthy, heated discussion with the occupants ensues. In the end, the leader's argument proves unsuccessful, so we go on to another house.

The pressure is on. We drive to another house and then another. Their well-thought-out plans are not materializing, making the kidnappers more and more frantic.

I count six different safe houses, and each one is reluctant to take me. People are concerned by the attention my kidnapping is getting on all the local radio and television stations. Nobody wants to be implicated in the crime. Each time we leave one house, the angry driver, increasingly frustrated, drives faster to the next. Letting my head bounce around in the car or loll back when I am being carried, I use the opportunity to peek surreptitiously from the spaces under the tape. I know exactly where I am now.

The last three houses are in a ghetto called Cite Solidarité. At the fourth house the wiry driver carries me piggyback across a stream too deep to drive the car through.

Hanging over his back, with only the Uzi-bearing killer following us, I let my arms flop lifelessly while I try to locate the pistol I know he has stuffed somewhere under his shirt. If I find the pistol, my plan is to grab the driver in a choke hold and use him as a shield while I shoot my other captor. Then I'll hold my human shield as a hostage.

Unfortunately—or in hindsight, fortunately—I scrap the plan when I can't find the pistol. The chance of survival of a *blanc* in the ghetto in the dead of night—a *blanc* who has just killed a Haitian or two—is slim to none. Had I found that pistol, I most probably would have been chopped into pieces long before I had a chance to explain.

Did you hide the pistol, Dad?

* * *

I wonder if my kidnappers know who my father was in Haiti, or if they know what powers they are dealing with. Am I starting to believe in his powers—or my own?

Whether it was power or not, I don't know. But when my father was alive, he always had an uncanny way of making things turn out all right. However, the one thing he tried to fix and never succeeded with was the political situation in Haiti. For his efforts, though, he was decorated with the highest honor available to a civilian, a medal I still treasure with pride.

He told me it broke his heart to see his adopted country torn apart by so much trouble after having already suffered more than a hundred years of civil strife, but he was always hopeful.

I would hate to be the one to dash his hopes and tell him that history likely will view Haiti's future as even darker. Now there are gangs of armed thugs roaming the streets in Port-au-Prince. They no longer stick to the hills, as in my father's day. They kill people in their homes and grab them from their driveways, as they did me. These gangs are poor, uneducated, hungry, and angry. They'll do anything for money.

I know, Dad, if I think positively, today's version of the Cacos you battled in the mountains won't murder me. I can hear you telling me now, gesturing with your pipe for emphasis: "Mind over matter, son. Mind over matter!"

* * *

My father talked about this constantly and practiced it daily. I remember when he and his friend Duclos built my first boat for me. Dad was always puffing his pipe, but it frequently went out and had to be relit. Rather than use the Zippo lighter he always carried, he reached out with his bare hands and grabbed a piece of hot charcoal from the fire on which the tar for caulking the boat was bubbling. From his years as a Vodou initiate, he knew it wouldn't hurt him to grab the charcoal and light his pipe, so he did it. He never burned his fingers.

His ability to put mind over matter worked for him, but when I tried it, at the age of ten or eleven, I was not as fortunate. I picked up a hot piece of charcoal in imitation of my father and immediately screamed. The flesh on my little fingers turned black and started to blister.

Dad laughed gently. He said it was part of my learning process. If I wanted to pick up hot charcoal, I'd have to become a Vodou initiate, what they called a *kanzo*, who understood how the brain controls messages in the body and can make cold hot and hot cold and control it through faith. I wouldn't have believed it possible if I hadn't personally seen my father do it so many times.

I never understood faith, but I know Dad had more than most. Years later, when he was in his eighties, he performed surgery on himself. He had been disassembling one of his orchid houses to make room for the construction of a studio for his new interest—painting the beauty of Haiti. A four-by-eight-foot wooden beam, twelve feet long, dropped from approximately twelve feet overhead, hitting him in the back. It created a very large and nasty hematoma, or blood clot. Our butler called me at work to tell me my father needed immediate medical attention.

I called our family physician and personal friend, Dr. Madsen, an experienced and successful surgeon, who had operated alongside Dr. Michael DeBakey, the famous heart surgeon from Texas.

I rushed home to find Dr. Madsen already there, examining the injury as my dad lay face down on his bed. Dr. Madsen wanted my father taken to the hospital immediately.

Dad was obviously in tremendous pain, but he'd overheard the doctor's instructions, and his reaction was typical. He tactfully told Dr. Madsen that he didn't need his help; he was fully capable of taking care of himself. The doctor pulled me out of hearing range and explained that if my father wasn't hospitalized immediately, his chances of survival were slim. He needed surgery to drain the injury.

After the doctor left, I tried to convince Dad to let me take him to the hospital, but it was no use. After arguing with him for several minutes, I tried to enlist my mother's and wife's help to convince him to go to the hospital.

While I was upstairs, my father ordered our butler, Justin, who had been with us for more than ten years, to bring him his shaving mirror, his straight razor, and a large pan. He instructed Justin how to disinfect the razor's blade with the flame of his Zippo lighter and then showed him how to hold the mirror and the pan in the positions he indicated.

Keeping his eye on the mirror, my father used his razor to cut the hematoma open and drain the blood. All this occurred in a matter of minutes, with no anesthesia and no assistance except for the butler holding the mirror and the pan.

When I realized what he'd done, I quickly called Dr. Madsen. He was absolutely flabbergasted and warned me that the self-proclaimed medic probably would not make it through the night.

It was the longest night of my life—until tonight. I sat all night by his bedside, finally going to bed just before daybreak, assured that he was sleeping peacefully. Around seven in the morning I got up to see how he was, and his bed was empty. Alarmed, I searched the house calling for him. I eventually found him back on the job site, working as though nothing had ever happened.

* * *

8:44 p.m.

Listening to the conversations at each stop, I now realize there are many more people involved in my kidnapping than the four who actually abducted me. Every time I am moved from one location to another, my primary worry is that the killer will finally snap in frustration and shoot me on the spot. I also worry that the inexperienced speed-demon driver will cause a fatal accident, or that we will be involved in a shoot-out at a police blockade. Because I am on blood thinners, I will bleed to death.

As I am being driven and carried, there is not much opportunity for quiet, but I keep up a constant silent prayer. By now my mind is open, and I readily admit that I need a guardian angel, *want* a guardian angel. My thoughts keep returning to my father and the lessons he tried to teach me, the lessons I had, until this life-altering experience, mostly ignored. *Dad, if you really have those extraordinary powers, just give me an opportunity and I'll show you what I can do!*

Remembering the great Horace Ashton's unshakable faith and confidence, I hear him saying, "You can do it, son!" Taking energy from his words, I grab onto a feeling of absolute certainty that my opportunity will soon come, a feeling that inexplicably grows stronger as the warmth and comfort of it swells in my chest.

In gratitude, I promise myself and my father that if I make it out of this mess alive, I will write a book and tell the story of his extraordinary life.

CHAPTER 37

Government Service, 1935–1946

Horace

Having returned to Virginia in 1935, I went to work at the Works Progress Administration Office in Washington as a speech writer for Harry Hopkins, President Franklin D. Roosevelt's secretary of commerce. In my spare time I gave lectures about my travels to local audiences. For nearly thirty years I had taken journeys to interesting places off the beaten track, and I still felt compelled to share with my fellow Americans what I had learned about the world outside the United States.

In particular I wanted to bring more awareness to Haiti. My film and descriptive lecture on that politically struggling, but beautiful and spirited, country was said by critics to be a most comprehensive and enlightening story of the tiny black republic to the south, which has for so long been a thorn in the side of the world.

While I was busy creating speeches and making presentations, Gordana tended to young Burdette and me, creating a warm, loving atmosphere in our Virginia home. It was a joy to return home from work, and I never wanted to be away from my beautiful wife for a minute longer than I had to be. Every day I told her how much I loved and appreciated her.

Early in 1939, Gordana became pregnant with our second child. On October 17 of that year, our second son, Marc, entered the world. I immediately nicknamed him "Butch." He was baptized in the Episcopal church in Virginia, as I and many Ashtons before me had been. I felt truly blessed.

During the 1930s, I underwent a transformation from global explorer to happily married man with two wonderful sons. I felt my life was complete, and I couldn't imagine how it could possibly get any better. But more blessings were about to come my way.

One year after Butch's birth, the United States needed a cultural attaché in Haiti. Due to my extensive knowledge of the island and the Vodou religion, I received the appointment. Now I would return to my spiritual home surrounded by my loved ones. For me, the circle was complete, and it was a perfect world.

When we arrived in Haiti in 1940, Gordana and I were welcomed by government officials and the diplomatic corps. There were few foreign residents in Haiti in those days, only a handful of Americans, and it was a small world. I was seen as something of a local character—a gray-eyed, very white man with a striking-looking European wife. We attended many social engagements, entertained regularly, and developed a circle of friends.

A social butterfly at heart, Gordana took to diplomatic life easily. After all, she was related to royalty, however distantly, and it showed. She made the perfect diplomat's wife and enjoyed her role as hostess. Dinner at the Ashton house around a large dining room table that seated a dozen guests was always like a party, no matter what was served. Life was grand, and we had a good time.

Our homes in Haiti were all very fine—elegantly decorated with European furnishings while at the same time cozy. Between Gordana and me, we had a flare for decorating, and over the years we enjoyed putting our own touches on our homes, even the ones provided by the State Department. As a diplomatic family, we were well taken care of and had many luxuries, including servants, which is the norm in Haiti. Gordana dressed well and got her hair done every day. The delightful woman I loved never lost her sense of humor or her beauty; she remained young in spirit always.

During my six years as cultural attaché, I was able to do some good and effect change in my adopted country. In the 1940s Haiti had no paved roads outside of Port-au-Prince, few knew about the country, and tourism didn't exist. I formed the Haitian–American Institute as a place for Haitians and Americans to meet and learn from each other via cultural exchange.

An American artist and English teacher at the government school in Port-au-Prince, Dewitt Peters, and a group of young Haitian intellectuals approached me enthusiastically with the idea of starting an art center. I arranged a meeting with Haiti's then-president Elie Lescot, who endorsed the idea, and the Centre d'Art was born. From this beginning came the explosion of Haitian art, the distinctive style that would later be appreciated worldwide by collectors. Along with Dewitt Peters and Bishop Voegeli, I chose the artists who painted the now famous scenes in the Episcopal cathedral.

Believing that education was the key to unlocking the straitjacket of poverty in Haiti, I worked on a program whereby hundreds of promising students were sent to the United States to learn and bring back their knowledge. I brought in weaving experts to improve local weaving methods, and Haitian cotton became a household word. Ceramic teachers were brought in, which gave birth to another new industry.

In 1946, Harry S. Truman became president of the United States. It was customary for a new administration to appoint its own diplomatic corps, and Truman followed that precedent. As I was already sixty-three years old and nearing mandatory retirement age, I retired and elected to stay in Haiti. The island was an inexpensive place to live that afforded my family a very comfortable life with good service. The free, do-it-yourself attitudes found in this country suited me, and I had many friends here. My spiritual connection with Vodou, the Haitian people, and the island's abundant natural surroundings provided me a kind of peace that I'd found nowhere else in the world.

In 1947 I was awarded the grade of officer in the Haitian National Order and decorated with the National Order of Honor and Merit, the highest decoration attainable for a civilian in Haiti. President Estimé presented it to me "for distinguished services to the Republic beyond the line of duty."

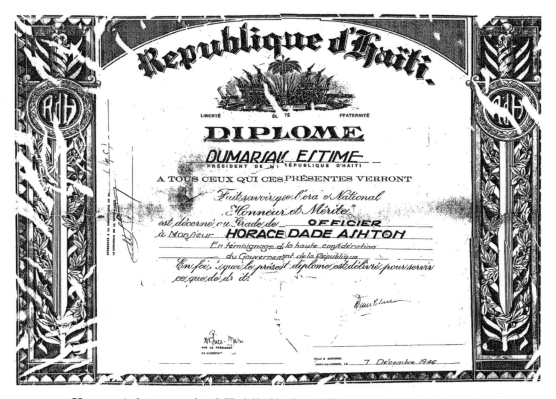

Horace Ashton received Haiti's National Honor and Merit Award.

* * *

The study of religion has always played a major part in my life, and although I was baptized in the Episcopal church, I pursued my interest in Vodou after settling in Haiti. But when I first arrived in Port—au— Prince, I learned I had been mistaken for Jesus a second time (the first was in

Alaska years earlier). Naturally I was flattered by this, but I never could understand why it happened.

As I'd always loved to sail and I now lived on an island, it was only fitting that I should build a sailboat. I inquired around to find a local man to build a small boat for me and was taken to a prominent Vodou houngan named Toussaint, who had formerly been a boat builder. He found Duclos, also a houngan, to build my boat. The work progressed satisfactorily, and one day I sat chatting with Toussaint when he suddenly said, "Wait."

I kept quiet, and soon I heard the houngan, who was working on the boat not far away, singing in Creole. We waited until Duclos finished his traditional chanting–type song and then Toussaint asked, "Were you here about twenty years ago?"

"Yes," I answered. "I lived here for a year then."

Interpreting the chant for me, Toussaint told me its story. It seemed Duclos had been a fisherman. One stormy afternoon he was returning from a fishing trip in his small sailboat when a squall blew up, tore off his sail, and swamped the boat. Something must have hit him because he sank to the bottom of the sea in about twenty feet of water. He opened his eyes and saw Jesus, with long blond hair and beard, walking on the water wearing a white robe and sandals. Jesus reached down his hand, and Duclos rose to the surface of the water. Then Jesus walked with him on the water for an hour or so, before depositing Duclos at his mother's doorstep. "And now Duclos swears it was you who saved him," said Toussaint.

I tried to convince Duclos that I was just an ordinary man like anyone else, but he never wavered from his belief that I had walked on water and saved his life. He treated me in a most embarrassing manner. He wouldn't take a cent of pay from me for boat building or anything else and made no important move without me, until his death. Nonetheless, over the years we became close friends. Later, Duclos often told the story of how I'd saved his life, as I quietly sat by, neither denying it nor acknowledging it. I came to accept this treatment from Duclos, as he was a houngan, and it was the backbone of our strong relationship.

After Duclos finished building the boat, he insisted that I allow him to baptize it with a Vodou service. The baptism was quite impressive. He named the boat *Immamou*, another name for the spirit of the sea, Agoue, who is the Haitian Neptune. After making a *vever*, a cabalistic design, for the spirit Immamou on the deck in front of the mast, Duclos broke an egg on it. Then he and his assistant tied bunches of green leaves to the forestay, which prevented me from using the jib and thus shortened the boat's maiden voyage considerably.

As we got underway, he broke another egg over the stern into the water and then withdrew the tiller from the rudder with a flourish, as an officer would draw his sword from its scabbard. Bowing, Duclos solemnly presented the tiller to me, thus designating me the new captain of the *Immamou*. I scrambled to insert it back into the rudder before the boat lost headway. We returned to the dock shortly after our departure.

* * *

I don't think I truly appreciated what it was to be a father until after my retirement. Now I had more time to spend with my sons, to share my love of nature with them, to teach them what I knew about the world, and to influence the men they would become. I taught them to sail and dive, and we shared special times together.

Shortly after my retirement, Gordana became pregnant once more. Stuart Todd Ashton was born on September 18, 1947, in Washington, D.C., where Gordana and I traveled to have our baby. I had married my soul mate, and we shared a wonderful life together in a tropical paradise. Now we were blessed with three fine sons.

I had no retirement income other than Social Security, but I was still highly regarded, both in diplomatic circles and in the community. Opportunities came my way. For a time I managed and maintained United States Embassy properties and later took charge of all incoming materials for Brown and Root in the building of the hydroelectric Peligre Dam. I continued to be involved with local projects, such as the art center.

Haiti was a recreational wonderland, especially for ocean sports. My family and I spent most weekends on my sailboat for many years. I loved the fresh sea air, exploring the underwater world, and sharing the spectacular nightly sunsets with them.

Because I was in the water so often, I was often asked, "Aren't you afraid of barracuda and sharks?" I always answered, "Not at all." Then I explained that Haitian waters teem with minnows and small fish so thick that at times I encountered shoals of them that made the water opaque. When swimming, I had to push them aside with my hands to pass through. Because of this abundant food supply, there was no chance of encountering a shark or barracuda hungry enough to attack a man.

I do have to laugh when I think of the first time I saw a barracuda with my friends, and I picture again the sight we must have made—three grown men circling a helpless fish with our spears drawn, ready to do battle. We soon realized that barracuda, like many other fish, were only curious of these funny–looking human creatures without gills that had appeared in their domain.

One time, Gordana and three–year–old Todd were swimming behind me over one of the reefs at Pelican Shoals. The water covering the reef is only four feet deep. After swimming through a patch of slightly milky water that had been disturbed by the wind, I encountered a five–foot great barracuda lying directly across my path as though it were asleep. I raised my head and waved my wife and son toward me. The three of us huddled together for several minutes, floating only about three feet from the barracuda. We watched it, and it watched us. Then it took off like a shot.

Another time I anchored my sailboat on the reef in shallow water and decided to spearfish alone. As I cruised along underwater around the edge of the reef, I spotted a huge angelfish not far below me. The fish was about fifteen inches long and fifteen inches tall with two-inch black-and-white vertical stripes. I went after it, but the fish kept just out of range, turning on its side to look up at me. In my enthusiasm for the fish, I didn't notice that the sea bottom was sloping and I was descending.

Suddenly I saw a twenty-foot-long shadow reflected on the ocean floor. Assuming it was my boat, I was afraid it had gone adrift. As I turned and swam toward the surface, I realized the shadow was not my boat but the largest shark I'd ever seen in these waters. Since I was only wearing a snorkel, I couldn't stay this far down, but I did not want to attract the shark's attention with my movements. I swam quietly, near the surface but underwater, to a large coral head very near him and sat on a piece of brain coral, keeping my snorkel out of the water so I could breathe. I watched the shark. There was nothing else I could do. If it decided that I looked appetizing, I had no chance.

As I sat there breathing through my snorkel, I noticed the shark had unusually big eyes and that the great mouth curving around under him was easily large enough to swallow a man. (I didn't mention that to him, though.) After the shark observed me for several minutes, it slowly swam away. That was the only time I did not feel comfortable in my beloved ocean, but I didn't let the experience stop me from sharing the recreational wonderland with my family and friends.

In fact, it was a family day on the water that caused us to meet a man who became a dear lifelong friend. One morning, we loaded up a picnic basket, our dog, and other equipment to go sailing. We drove to Petit Arcachon, about seven miles from Port-au-Prince, where I had leased a small waterfront plot. There my friend Duclos and I had built a pavilion and a fifty-foot pier that extended from the shore, across the shallow water, and out to where I kept the boat in six-foot-deep water. That day, when I walked out on the pier, I noticed something odd in the water not far from shore. I grabbed my binoculars and focused on the object, which turned out to be a raft. Upon the raft sat a pretty woman, all alone. I watched her for a while, and after a few minutes I saw a man's head bob out of the water. The man stayed on the surface for a moment and then submerged once more.

My curiosity got the best of me, so I walked to a point along the shore near the raft and signaled the couple. A few minutes later, a large blond man emerged from the surf wearing a facemask and snorkel, towing the raft with the woman on it. He introduced her as a woman he'd met on the plane from Italy to Haiti. My family entertained the couple with a picnic lunch, and from that day forward, Gustav Dalla Valle and I became close friends.

During World War II, Gustav had been in the Italian Navy, engaged in underwater demolition. He was an expert diver, and we soon dubbed him "Tarzan of the Sea." I learned a great deal about undersea life from him, and for several years we spent about five or six hours every Saturday, Sunday, and holiday in and under the water. Using only snorkels, we would free-dive sometimes up to thirty feet while holding our breath and hunt many fine fish and lobsters with our spearguns. Although, I must admit, there were times when the speargun would get lodged in coral, or a fish, once speared, would swim away with it, resulting in a dangerous rescue mission. On different occasions both of us suffered the painful effects of staying underwater for too long.

Gustav was an emotional man, and he amused us often with his noisy demonstrations of enthusiasm. One day at La Gonave, the large island about thirty miles out in Port-au-Prince Bay, he and I descended from a boat. He went one way and I another. Floating outstretched and pulling myself carefully across the large reef by my hands—because the water above the jagged staghorn coral was only about twelve inches deep—I suddenly came to the edge, where I spied two red snappers about fifteen feet below. Since Gustav was too far away to call, I determined to go after them myself. Just then one of them put his head in a hole in the coral, with two-thirds of his body sticking out. I left my spear gun in the coral above and dove. I grabbed the snapper with my bare hands, inserted one hand in his gills, clamped him against my naked chest, and arose. I didn't see Gustav, so I anchored the fish to a sharp coral antler with a piece of wire. Then I peered over the edge, dove, and caught the second fish in the same manner.

I was a bit scratched up from the coral, but it didn't matter. I had two large snappers and was happy. When, having had no luck himself, Tarzan of the Sea returned and saw the beautiful fish I'd caught, he let out a yell so loud that I thought his lungs would burst. Jumping up and down in the boat like a two-year-old, Gustav grabbed his speargun and pitched it into the water. He didn't speak to me again for several days.

One Sunday morning when we were fooling around on Sand Cay, we saw that the French training ship *Jeanne d'Arc* was in port. About an hour later, while snorkeling and spearfishing around the edge of the reef where the depth was nearly one hundred feet, I saw what looked like several men walking on the bottom in the dim light below. I couldn't believe my eyes! That was before I'd ever seen or heard of an aqualung.

A few minutes later, six men came scrambling up the side of the reef. They were members of the *Jeanne d'Arc's* crew, trying out the new aqualungs. We visited with them for about an hour on our boat, and they returned to the water, descending the side of the reef to the bottom for the walk back to their ship. They did not swim but wore weighted shoes so they could walk on the bottom. I turned to Gustav after they'd gone and said, "It takes all kinds of people to make a world."

Soon afterward, we obtained aqualungs, and they became more common. But my first sight of them was a real surprise.

The two of us eventually organized the Skin Diving Club of Haiti and built and operated the first glass–bottomed excursion boat to Sand Cay, a most spectacular reef. We would take tourists out over the reefs to see the sea urchins and fish, and then one of us would dive under the boat. Haiti's reefs were so plentiful that I often had to brush off the curious small fish that crowded the glass of my mask, trying to look at my eyes. My friends and I would break open a sea urchin and place small pieces between our lips. The fish would arrive in swarms and nibble the delicacy from our mouths. The tourists loved the show.

One of my greatest joys was snorkeling over the reefs and observing the colorful sea creatures in their own habitat. I was at home underwater, floating with the current over gently undulating purple sea fans, punctuated by the occasional shock of flame–red or lime–green coral as schools of neon–blue tangs flitted their way through my undersea garden. I loved to watch the huge spotted sea rays darting through the water, or gaze into the wise, round eyes of a shy sea turtle, all the while listening to the crunching sound of multicolored parrot fish munching on the coral. The way the sun reflected on flounders lying on the bottom, emitting beautiful rays, was magical. Flounders take on the color of the sand, and to find them you must stare at the bottom for a while until you see a slight movement. The flounder's small dark spots become beautiful, colorful circles that gradually grow larger and larger until they disappear, like the circular waves on still water after you drop a stone into it.

I happened to live in Haiti when William Beebe came to gather material for his book *Beneath Tropic Seas*. He said that these reefs were the richest he'd ever seen for variety and color of their myriad inhabitants.

* * *

As I mentioned, my life's pattern was to spend money when I had it. Otherwise, I wasn't too concerned about financial matters. My attitude about money occasionally annoyed my wife, but I gave her many things that money couldn't buy. I cherished Gordana, worshipped her, and never took her love for granted. The two of us often spent long hours in the evenings just talking. We could always talk about everything.

I was a good builder and gardener, talented with my hands, and handy around the house. I was full of imagination and big ideas, but perhaps I did not always know how to cooperate with daily life. Gordana understood this about me, and she'd joined me on our adventure together with eyes wide open. She was a strong woman who adapted easily to life's curves, and her sense of humor and upbeat personality got her through many hardships. She knew she wasn't going to change me.

An equal partner in our husband–and–wife team, Gordana was resourceful and talented in her own ways. With our income dwindling after my retirement, she turned our home into a guesthouse, similar to a bed–and–breakfast. It was not a traditional business because our paying guests were mostly friends who came over from the United States to spend the winter months with us. Gordana never had to advertise. News of our guesthouse spread by word of mouth, and we were always full to capacity. Our large home was often full of guests, interesting people with whom I enjoyed conversing. At this stage in my life, although I was very active and often took my guests hiking, diving, and sailing, I enjoyed the comfort and informality of being able to sit with my pipe in my own home and share my knowledge with others, rather than traveling as a lecturer.

In 1948 I met Phil Nash, who had come to Haiti to honeymoon in a local hotel and then been directed by an American friend to stay at the Ashtons' guest house. The Nashes moved into our top floor and stayed for at least a month that first time. Phil shared my interest in underwater photography, and among other things, he worked in the film industry. He began diving with Gustav and me, and the three of us became close friends. Later with their young daughter, the Nashes would stay with us for months at a time and eat their meals with our family.

I'll never forget the time when I was working on the underwater film *Shark Safari* with Gustav and Phil. The three of us often dove down twenty to thirty feet to make films. On this particular day Phil held the camera while Gustav and I hunted with spearguns. We suddenly jumped when a shark swam at Phil. As he frantically tried to focus the camera and capture the shot, the shark swam right between his legs!

Closer in age to my older son, Phil once made me laugh when he said in all seriousness that I was not in the least old-fashioned, and he was amazed at how active I was and how much a part of the scene. I think he enjoyed the permissive atmosphere in Haiti and in my home. One time, he found some fireworks—huge rockets that went for half a mile—and the three of us had great fun setting them off. No one bothered us, and we could do what we wanted.

Gustav Dalla Valle, Phil Nash, and I were pioneers in spearfishing and diving in Haiti. Scuba diving was uncommon, and diving equipment was very much in the experimental stages then. Gustav had arrived in Haiti in transit from Italy, hoping to work his way into the United States. I was retired by the time I met him, but I still had connections. Fortunately, he liked our tropical island so much that he ended up spending many years in Haiti. During that time I put in a few good words with the United States consul, and finally Gustav's visa came through.

He went to the United States and became very successful in the scuba industry. Eventually he sold his company, SCUBAPRO, which became a big name in scuba diving equipment, and retired to California. There, he started a vineyard, Dalla Valle Wines, which was another successful venture.

CHAPTER 38

Life in Haiti, 1950s

Horace

My eldest son, Burdette, went to the United States to attend school in Indianapolis in 1954. Butch was a teenager, and Todd was only seven years old. I think the large age differences between the brothers must have made it difficult for them to share much in common. They each had their own lives and very individual relationships with their parents. I often took Butch along on the diving trips with Gustav and Phil, as he was the right age at the time.

In 1953, Gordana received $50,000 from her wealthy aunt Militsa, partially a settlement for the equity of our house in McLean, which her aunt had loaned us the funds to purchase, and partially a gift.

I promised Gordana that I would build her the house of her dreams with the money. Knowing a grand home like the one she'd left behind in Yugoslavia was what she'd always wanted but never demanded, I felt at least something commensurate was nothing less than she deserved. She had sacrificed a great deal to marry me, and I adored her. This was my gift–wrapped opportunity to show her how much.

Butch had a playmate whose father was head of the Sugar Company in Haiti. We had become friends with the young man's parents, Mr. and Mrs. Brignac, the original owners of a spectacular house on the hilltop above Canapé Vert Hospital, which was built in 1930 by the well–known Haitian architect Villard. The Brignacs decided to leave

Haiti, and I bought their home for $30,000—a great deal of money to pay for a home in Haiti in 1953.

I consulted another architect about remodeling the villa, and he advised me to tear it down. As we'd had so much fun working together on other projects, Gordana and I decided to remodel the whole house ourselves. Butch helped me in my woodworking shop, and our father-and-son time there drew us closer together.

We removed walls to create a tiered terrace that let in the view below and built arches in front of the garage, which gave the parking area the look of an atrium. Not only did we renovate and decorate the inside of the villa splendidly, but I hung orchids in the trees, relandscaped the property, and added a swimming pool. We named our new home Villarosa.

My final touch was to fabricate a complex, entwined design of Vodou symbols on the wrought-iron front gate facing the view. In the end, we spent another $30,000 to rebuild the house and fix up the property, borrowing the additional $10,000 that we had no sure means to pay back at the time. I continued to think positively, for I truly believed that things would work out.

Gordana and I were very happy at Villarosa, where she continued her informal bed-and-breakfast for a number of years. We had a large table in the dining room that sat as many as fourteen. Many nights we held a big dinner for our guests, sometimes serving local dishes like spicy grilled chicken, fried sweet potatoes, and plantains. The meals always ended with fresh-roasted, locally grown coffee, served thick and strong and sweetened with molasses. Gordana always sat at the head of the long table, facing west, while I sat at the opposite end, facing east. I rarely had much of an appetite, and my wife shot me indulgently disapproving looks whenever she caught me feeding Bouki, my cocker spaniel, who sat at my feet under the table.

When Butch was ready to go to high school, I had been retired for several years and had no means to pay for his schooling in the United States. Gordana was the letter—writer who kept in touch with all our family members: mine in America and hers in Yugoslavia. During the five years we'd lived in Virginia, she had become good friends with my sister Eliza, and the two corresponded regularly.

Eliza was Butch's godmother and knew of our financial situation. As she and her husband had no children of their own, they offered to sponsor his education. When obstacles arose, I was proud of the way Butch took responsibility for his own education. He ultimately returned to Haiti and made a commitment to stay home and take care of his mother and me.

* * *

Throughout my years of travel, I did not always have the kind of opportunities to commune with nature as I'd had as a young man, although I never stopped being awed by nature. Now in my later years, I returned to my roots and explored the natural world of this tropical island, above and beneath the sea. My reputation as a scientist led to new scientific journeys.

I have always loved to observe all living things, and you may recall that one of my hobbies in my youth was herpetology. I've caught a number of snake specimens for the University of Florida, which is a harmless way to pass my time in the lush countryside, since there are no venomous snakes here. At one time our house was so full of snakes that my wife threatened to move out. That was only a temporary threat, however, because I shipped all the snakes out, and Gordana gladly remained.

Often groups from United States universities requested my help with their research. Once a group of ornithologists from Cornell University visited me and said they wanted to record the songs of our rare birds, such as the *l'oiseau musicien*. These creatures are seldom seen because they live in the mountains, sometimes at an altitude of 5,000 feet. Their song is clear and flute—like.

Another rare bird the group hoped to record was the Swayle's thrush. This bird had been seen only once by a Smithsonian expedition about forty years earlier when it appeared on the eastern slope of Morne La Selle at an altitude of 8,000 feet. The Cornell group asked me to accompany them as their guide, and I gladly accepted. I always did, for I loved any chance to go into the forests and find some rare orchids.

We drove a Jeep station wagon up to approximately 7,000 feet altitude, to Forêt des Pins and Morne Commissaire, where we spent the night and then started our long journey higher up the mountains at daybreak. The roads through the forest were clear for several miles until we started up Morne La Selle, and we encountered trees growing in the road, which prevented us from driving further.

We unloaded the equipment, including a recorder with a parabolic reflector to magnify sound, and continued on foot to an altitude of approximately 10,000 feet. I had no idea exactly where to find either bird, but when we reached an attractive glen in the rainforest, I suggested that we stop so I could make a brief orchid hunt. The ornithologists rigged up the recorder. Suddenly the forest came alive with song from a nearby musicien. Its call was being answered by two others not far off.

The group moved quickly to capture the sounds with their equipment while I searched for orchids. I found one or two small plants, sat down on a log, and lit my pipe. Just above my head, perched in the crotch of a tree not ten feet away, a bird burst into song. It was another musicien. I sat there studying the rare and seldom−seen bird for fifteen minutes. It was about the size of a robin, and its gray−brown color was beautifully camouflaged against the bark of the tree. Unlike other birds, it sat down low in the tree's crotch, not out on a limb. As long as I sat still and listened, the bird continued to weave its magical flute−like song around me. I could see my friends up the road taping this rare and wonderful music of nature.

When they had taped the musicien for over half an hour, we picked up our gear and continued our climb. Only thirty minutes later, as we passed along a fairly smooth trail cushioned with pine needles, I stopped the group again. I had spied a yellow blossom some distance below on top of a patch of wire bamboo. I left the rest of the group on the road and fought my way through the thick, sharp tangle of vines. Finally I reached a rare variety of yellow oncidium. These are small, dainty orchids commonly called "dancing dolls." I was thrilled to find it.

Starting back, I called out. One of the men signaled me to be silent by putting his finger over his lips. I returned quietly and saw they were watching a Swayle's thrush. The bird seemed calm, walking up and down a small bare branch on the ground less than fifteen feet from me. It sang to another thrush some distance away while my friends recorded its songs. You can imagine how happy we were.

When we returned to the city, my new friends gave an interview to the press and were generous in their praise of my guidance. I, too, felt fortunate to have heard the beautiful music and to have found some rare orchids.

About a year later two entomologists from the University of Florida came to Haiti and asked me to help them find a rare type of dragonfly called a damsel fly. There was only one specimen in any museum, and it had been collected about thirty-five years earlier on Morne La Visite. Now in the insect collection at Harvard, it was crumbling from age and handling.

Morne La Visite is not a peak but a plateau that covers an area of forty square miles on the western side of Morne La Selle. After consulting a group of monks who knew the area well, I was told that we couldn't go up to Morne La Visite at that time because the trails were slippery from recent rains, and we'd have to carry all our gear—sleeping bags, tents, and food—on our heads to keep them dry. We made a hundred-mile detour and approached from the south via Jacmel.

When we finally arrived in the plateau area, the morning was sunless and gray. The entomologists were sure no damsel flies would be moving about, since they only fly when the sun shines. I insisted that the scientists bring their nets just in case. They did, and we started off through the woods.

Not far along the trail we reached a steep ravine and heard the sound of water below. I stayed at the top but suggested that my colleagues go down into the ravine in search of the nymphs, which are the larva stage of damsel flies.

In less than a minute, the sun came out. I looked around and discovered a beautiful adult damsel fly, glistening blue in the sunlight, less than a yard from my nose. I backed away carefully. When I was far enough from the fly, I whistled and the men ran back. One of them deftly caught our prize in the net. A few minutes later, the clouds obscured the sun.

Several of the men returned to the ravine, where they found a number of nymphs clinging to the underside of rocks in the icy water. Normally one would expect them to breed in the still waters of the potholes on the mountain road, but this group of flies somehow attached their eggs to rocks under rushing water.

In half an hour, the sun came out again, and the scientists caught two more damsel flies not far from where I stood. "It's a miracle!" exclaimed one of the men. "To find a damsel fly, one of the rarest insects in the world, in an area of forty square miles is unbelievable. To find three is a miracle."

Afterward the Haitian government requested that I obtain a colored photograph of the damsel fly to use on a postage stamp to commemorate the event. I contacted my friends at the University of Florida in Gainesville, and they told me that the specimens were already mounted. In fact they had been folded in such a manner that no adequate photograph could be made.

Since these expeditions, I've never gone into the forest again without a camera. I have no pictures of the l'oiseau musicien, the Swayle's thrush, or the damsel fly. Perhaps if I had carried my camera, however, we would have found none of them.

CHAPTER 39

Confident

Butch
April 5, 2001
9:30 p.m.

Shortly after I promise my father I will tell his story if I escape with my life, the sixth safe house turns us away. The kidnapper that carried me up the steep steps and now back down again shoves me into the car. Slumped over in the passenger's seat, I pretend to drift in and out of consciousness.

After the sixth safe house, the killer apparently chooses to disappear or is left behind. I suspect this when I am shoved into the front seat, and I don't hear the back door slam. I no longer feel the Uzi against the back of my head. I breathe a little easier now, hoping that the Uzi-swinging, trigger-happy nutcase is no longer around. But that doesn't mean I am not still being held at gunpoint. I discover later that he has chosen graciously to leave the machine gun behind for the leader.

The driver speeds along the dark road to a seventh safe house. My eyes are still taped, but I can occasionally peer through the spot under the loosened duct tape. The car window is open just a crack for air, and I feel the spray of the light rain that continues to fall. I hope and wait for *facteur H* to kick in. Sooner or later my captors will make another childish blunder. I must remain mentally and physically prepared to seize even a split-second opportunity for escape.

Clearly, things are not going as planned for them. After holding me for almost eight hours they still have no ransom money, and they can't find anyone willing to take the risk and hide me. Their cohorts have fled the scene, and they are stuck with what they perceive to be a sick old man with little value. I become increasingly worried for my safety.

I force the negative thoughts aside and focus on my father's philosophy of positive thinking. It is my last resort. I have nothing to lose and everything to gain.

Suspending all my beliefs, I decide to become more like my father and watch for signs that will help me find my way out and back to my family safely. I think of how Dad used signs, such as the howl of a dog, to find his way out of the Sahara after his plane crashed. I may not have his experience, but I am Horace Ashton's son. With every ounce of inner strength I can muster, I pray for a sign.

Suddenly, in my mind I hear my father say, *"Mind over matter, son. You can do this. You can accomplish anything as long as you really want to."*

A rush of energy surges through my body. *Yes, Dad, I can. I can get myself out of this. I can save my life.*

* * *

As my father aged, I found myself running more and more errands for him. In his eighties Dad still had many interests. He cultivated his orchids and took up painting in addition to pursuing his spiritual quest. As he aged, he grew increasingly critical and demanding. Things had to be done a certain way. Every single day, he would make a new demand, especially when I was already rushed. He asked me to bring him stamps or to mail a letter. He wanted a certain color of paint for his art, one he didn't have, and he needed it now.

For years Myriam and I literally worked seven days a week from early morning until late at night. We tried to provide for our children and give them all the advantages we had not had growing up. We made sure my mother was properly taken care of and the house was properly maintained. We provided for all of my father's needs, and now every day it seemed he sent me out in the middle of my busy day to get something for him. The positive side of this was that my father was constantly occupied. He was always painting or tending his orchids or meditating or reading his *Daily Word*.

Sometimes I felt underappreciated by him and resented his lack of patience. To this day my father's demanding voice still lingers in my head. It pushes me to do more.

I have pondered his methods since and recognized our similarities. Back then, he was impossible to deal with and caused me aggravation. My feeling now is that in his way he was trying to educate me and better prepare me for life. If only I'd realized that this was his way of staying in the game, of being the active participant he had always been.

When his painting became successful, he approached life with renewed vigor. He was back in the game.

Excerpts Read at Horace Ashton's Painting Exhibit

Horace Ashton is an "old friend" of Haiti. His first visit to this country dates to 1906; since then, he has returned successively in 1912, in 1915, and 1919. Accompanied by his wife and family, he settled in Haiti in the position of first Cultural Attaché of the United States of America in 1940, and it was during this period that he contributed to the creation of the Haitian-American Institute, the Art Center, and the Union School.

The life of Mr. Ashton unfolds like a veritable historical romance. His eight decades of marvelous voyages could be summed up thus: a circuit of eight thousand miles in the Arctic, a travel of an entire week on the Trans-Siberian railroad, nine expeditions across South America and several explorations in Africa. His encounter with personalities in all parts of the globe go from a discussion on religion with the legendary Rasputin of Russia to the primitive hunt-

ers of the Amazon Basin, to American Chiefs of State and Sovereigns of Europe, to the Wright brothers in North Carolina on the historic day of the flight of the first American airplane. . . .

Almost as fantastic and as varied as his voyages have been his different occupations and his hobbies. He was among the first to make aerial photographs; was a war correspondent in the Russo-Japanese War of 1903; explorer and lecturer for thirty years and also a naturalist. One of his hobbies . . . is the culture of orchids. It has been two years since Mr. Ashton, at the age of eighty, started painting. He is an amateur who has never taken a lesson in the art of painting. . . . Horace Ashton . . . is in process of conveying his impressions of Haiti. . . .[66]

At the age of eighty-five, my dad had a minor car accident, and his driver's license was revoked. After that, I very tactfully hired him a driver. In fact, I gave him a car and a driver, but he simply would not accept the situation.

He put the driver in the passenger seat and drove down to the police headquarters, where he told the Port-au-Prince chief of police that he had been decorated by the president of Haiti. Therefore, his driver's license could not be taken away from him. Dad convinced the chief that he was in perfect control and able to drive safely. The chief returned his license. My father then traded four of his paintings for an MGB, and, to my horror, was back on the road in a sports car at the age of eighty-five!

Everything went along fine for a few years. Although he grew increasingly more demanding, always in need of painting or gardening supplies, he didn't crash the car again.

I was extremely proud of my father's accomplishments as an artist and to this day have many of his paintings. In his mid-eighties, he was invited to Mexico to display an exhibit of his paintings, and he went.

---

66   These paragraphs are excerpts from the "Biography of the Artist Horace Ashton," which was read in 1965 on the day Mr. Ashton's paintings were exhibited at the Haitian-American Institute in Port-au-Prince. The author is unknown.

He also is recognized as an important contributor to Haitian art. The *Town & Country* magazine article mentioned previously says that Horace Ashton and a few collaborators were instrumental in launching what has become known as the birth of Haiti's primitive art movement. "The creativity here has always been quite stunning and unexpected . . . Art is what put Haiti on the map."

Horace Ashton, at age eighty-three, painting in his studio

He was always impressed by the natural beauty of Haiti in his travels throughout the country over the years. He admired the innate aptitude and talent of the Haitians in their use and application of colors throughout. He was always impressed by the facility and grace with which Vodou symbols were drawn spontaneously, usually with cornmeal, on the ground, in preparation for a ceremony.

He gained strength from his surroundings. Will I have the strength to do what must be done to survive this ordeal? *Dad, please help me. I know you're here.*

CHAPTER 40

Vodou, 1940s–1950s

Horace

On my first visit to Haiti in 1906, I'd fallen in love with this island paradise that seduced me with her natural charms. I had never encountered so friendly a people, and even though the Haitians were among the poorest I'd ever seen, they showered me with hospitality.

When I finally settled there in 1940, my old friends welcomed me back with open arms, and because of my great affinity for the Vodou religion, I felt as if I had come home spiritually. As I continued to live in Haiti, I became an initiate and a practitioner of what I considered the world's first religion.

Unlike other established religions, Vodou has no official book, such as the Bible, the Talmud, or the Koran. Because of this, some individuals call it simply a superstition. A dictionary entry refers to it as "witchcraft," and I will admit there are two sides to Vodou. Houngans and mambos perpetuate the religious side, and a *bocor* is the black–magic witchdoctor who represents the evil side. During my learning process as a student of comparative religion, I encountered all aspects of Vodou, but I only worked with the priests and practiced the religious side.

In my research, I discovered that Vodou is the oldest recorded religion—at least 4,000 years older than Judaism and 8,000 years older than Christianity—although it has been handed down mostly through oral tradition. It is believed to have originated in Africa near what is now Ethiopia or Abyssinia, but no one knows exactly how long ago. We do know, however, that Moses, who was an Egyptian, had a remarkable black woman named Zipporah as his favorite wife. Zipporah was the daughter of Jethro, a priest of a cult known at that time as Iodu.[67] Its followers worshipped one God, known as Jove. Zipporah taught Moses the rituals and mysticism of Iodu. The practice of these rituals and the appeasement of the natural spirits enabled the Jews to live through that devastating forty years in the wilderness on their way to the Promised Land. During those years, Iodu was changed to Judah and Jove to Jehovah. Thus, Jewish history claims it was the first monotheistic religion. That statement is correct, but the origin of Judaism was in Iodu.

In Jamaica and the other British islands in the Caribbean, Vodou is called *Obeia*. In Brazil it has another name. Because there is no definitive text, the rituals vary, but basically this monotheistic religion has remained the same. In Haiti, where the slaves were compelled to become Catholics, nearly all Haitians today go to church on Sunday, but church attendance has nothing to do with their basic faith.

Vodou ceremonies can be held at many different times of the year. There are only two designated special days of worship: *La Cérémonie des Cimetières* on December 24, which has nothing to do with Christmas, and the Feast of the Three Kings on January 6, known in French as *La Fête des Trois Rois*. The Ceremony of the Cemeteries on December 24 is perhaps the most important date in the Vodou religion. Because of its coincidence with Christmas Eve and the tradition of tree trimming, the date often cost me some mild scolding from Gordana and my sons because of my absence from home.

My friend Duclos, who had built my first sailboat

---

67   The Bible, Exodus 2:21 and 4:18.

and also one for my son Butch, was a well–respected, powerful houngan, who conducted many of the ceremonies I attended. About fifteen years after Duclos's death, when I was getting on in age myself, a small boy approached my daughter–in–law at the grocery store.

"Are you Madame Butch?" he asked.

"Yes," she answered, knowing that many of the locals called my son by his nickname. She had never seen this boy before.

"Please tell your father–in–law that Duclos is going to appear tonight at the Ceremony of the Cemeteries and asked to see him."

Myriam returned home and gave me the message. I was not surprised to learn Duclos had called for me to be there when his spirit was going to "come down." I had been one of the key people in his life, and I looked forward to "seeing" my old friend again. I invited Myriam to accompany me, but she declined.

Every year on December 24, all the medicinal herbs, roots, and bark that have been gathered for healing to be used in the coming year are prepared. Late at night, when the devotees are assembled, a long, fascinating service is performed.

I'd witnessed it before, but I still watched in awe as a number of *hounsis*,[68] dressed in the white of angels, marched into the room, chanting, each carrying a large bundle of leaves in the apron of her skirt. With great ceremony the women encircled a large washtub on the floor, half–filled with water. As each approached, she emptied the leaves into the water and then joined the others already kneeling around the tub. With their hands in the water the hounsis kneaded and shredded the leaves, chanting all the while, until the liquid assumed a consistency of bright green pea soup. Occasionally, one of the women became possessed and had to be replaced, but the others continued to work.

I breathed the fragrant spicy odor that rose from the

---

68   Female Vodou initiates.

tub and permeated the room. As the evening progressed, the dry materials that had not been poured into the washtub, such as bark and roots, were pulverized in huge wooden mortars and beaten to powder by the rhythmic pounding of the pestles. Finally the powder was packaged into *Pacquets Congo*, small pear—shaped affairs used in healing, and they decorated them with bright ribbons. Separated by gender, the packets bore a cross at the top if they were to be placed by the head of a sick man, and colored feathers if they were intended for a woman.

Just after midnight, all the liquid containing the leaves that had been kneaded by the kneeling hounsis was poured into a large wooden washtub. This ceremonial tub was placed on two chairs in the middle of the room, and then rum and dabs of gunpowder were added as part of a dance by the devotees and ignited from time to time. Soon the whole room was infused with the heady odor of exploded gunpowder, herbs, and rum.

It was at this moment that Duclos chose to appear. I witnessed the glow of his spirit over the tub and watched it travel around the room, encompassing everyone in its warmth and love. The traditional chanting stopped momentarily, while the houngan called me forward to join him in a special chant that welcomed and honored the spirit of Duclos. I can't say that I heard a specific message from my friend, as some claim they receive from the spirits, but I felt very peaceful and happy.

That feeling stayed with me as the beautiful ceremony continued into the wee hours of the morning, and I watched the annual baptism of all the babies born that year. The infants, ranging from only weeks old to nearly one year of age, were stripped and tossed across the room to the houngan standing by the tub. He caught them dexterously and held them by a foot or an arm, waving them head—down through the flame of the burning rum in the tub two or three times. Then he would toss them back to their father or mother. In all the services I attended, including this one, I was astonished that I never once heard a baby cry. Generally, they would smile or laugh, depending on their age.

Later the older children were stripped to the waist, brought up to the tub, and smeared with the liquid by the houngan. Even some men and women leaned over and washed their faces in it. Because of Duclos, I stayed until just before daylight, when only a few worshippers were left. The houngan sat at the end of the room, as if in a receiving line. I came forward with the remaining people, and when he dipped the small coconut dipper into the tub and handed it to me, I took a big swallow of the blessed liquid used for baptism and smearing men, women, and children. It was a night I will never forget.

* * *

I sometimes took my friends Gustav and Phil and other guests who were interested to see the Vodou ceremonies. The houngans and mambos I had met were very approachable; generous, friendly people who welcomed spectators.

Besides containing rituals for the appeasement of nature's spirits, such as the sea, the forest, the brook, the mountains, the crossroads, and others too numerous to mention, Vodou is basically a religion for the people. It gets right down to the root of all their troubles—domestic, physical, and spiritual. A houngan or mambo, possessed by the spirit of a particular oracle and under that oracle's influence, can settle any domestic dispute or social difficulty clairvoyantly. Possessed by other specific spirits, they can cure almost any illness and meet all of the family's other spiritual needs. I have witnessed unbelievable demonstrations of clairvoyance and what could be only termed miraculous cures.

As a white man, I cannot even attempt to explain some of the phenomena, such as possession and self-immunization from heat and pain, which I have witnessed in the practice of Vodou. As a student of world religions,

I have seen many phenomena, like the skewers being stuck into bodies of the dervishes in Tunisia, attributed to faith. As a scientist, I admit and accept that these things simply cannot be explained from a scientific point of view.

Often I have seen a man possessed handling fiery-hot iron with his bare hands. In one instance I watched as a white-hot automobile spring that had been in a hot fire for forty-eight hours was placed on a piece of paper that burst into flames. This same spring was immediately held, unsupported, under a bare arm until it cooled. When I inspected the person's arm, I was amazed to see it had no burn or mark on it at all.

On another occasion a similar hot spring was placed on the shoulder of my thin white shirt for half a second. It left no mark and caused no pain. However, this same spring set a piece of paper afire immediately after it was placed on my shirt.

Although I have no memory of it, I am told my possession occurred in 1919 during the year I spent in Haiti as a scout for the United States Marines. Because of the United States occupation, all Vodou gatherings were prohibited at the time. I do recall participating in the secret Vodou service with a well-known mambo, held in the forest near Gros Morne, in the neighborhood of Port-de-Paix in the north. It reminded me of a nonstop carnival because nothing else seemed to exist for three days and nights, and there was much singing, dancing, and drumming.

Several hundred devotees attended the service. My memory lapse began at the end of the third day, when I'm told that I rode into town on horseback, screaming loudly and firing a Colt .45 into the air, accompanied by two women, also on horseback. Clad in khaki with red handkerchiefs flying from each elbow, I galloped along the main street of Port-de-Paix.

Naturally the marines stopped all three of us and took us to the gendarmerie. Being a friend of Captain

Howell, an American marine from Kentucky, I was put to bed on a blanket on the floor to await his return. The women were locked up, and I'm not sure what they did with our horses.

Apparently it started to rain while I was lying there. The downpour on the metal roof awakened me. When I opened my eyes, I saw a number of large horseflies on the ceiling. I grabbed my pistol and fired at the flies, making huge holes in the roof. The rain poured in, flooding the floor, and the marines on duty hauled me onto a chair. A sergeant took the pistol away from me.

When questioned the next day, the women who were arrested with me swore that during the night I had become possessed by Damballah, the snake spirit, who is one of the most revered in the Vodou hierarchy. They told the authorities that I had wriggled across the ground on my belly and up the trunk of a huge tree that could not be climbed in the ordinary manner. Poles had to be rigged, and they said it took four men over two hours to get me down with ropes. They said the mambo then brought me out of the trance.

I later confirmed this with the mambo and others present, and I've always wondered about this experience. The truth is that I never recalled anything that happened after sunset that day until shooting the flies in the gendarmerie.

While I cannot swear to my own possession, I witnessed an incidence of possession at a service one evening some time later. While I cannot explain these things, I can report what I observed and how I participated. I was seated at the side. A Haitian lady I'd seen earlier, dressed in a white eyelet embroidered dress, high-heeled white shoes, and a matching white linen hat, stood behind my chair. To my surprise she suddenly flew over my head and landed face down on the dirt floor among the dancing hounsis.

They quickly removed her shoes, hat, and earrings, so she would not injure herself and turned her over so that in some fashion only her heels and the back of her head touched the floor. She moved herself rapidly across the floor several times with her arms outstretched, her shoulders not touching the floor. The houngan stood on the woman's thighs, which were six inches above the floor, and beckoned me to straddle her forearms with my feet. The houngan and I faced each other, placing our hands on each other's shoulders while she moved twice around the room above the floor. Her heels and the back of her head were the only body parts that touched the floor. She moved effortlessly despite our total weight of more than three hundred pounds holding her down. When she came out of the possession about half an hour later, the hounsis brushed her off and helped her put on her shoes, hat, and earrings. The woman looked as fresh and clean as when she first arrived.

* * *

Because Haiti is an island nation, its people hold ceremonies to honor Agoue, the spirit of the sea. Ever since my birth in a sailboat, I'd had a profound connection with the spirit of the sea. In Haiti I often stood on the sand on the shore, listening to the music of the waves, and looking up at the sky filled with stars. It was these times that I felt completely one with nature, not just a mere human being, and it was no wonder that the ceremony to honor Agoue was one of my favorites.

This traditional Vodou service always took place in the early morning, usually on a Sunday or a holiday. I marched down to the water's edge, along with others, carrying a large tray laden with bottles of rum, perfume, cola, eggs, cakes, and bonbons, as offerings for Agoue. We waded into the water waist deep, chanting all the while, and launched the tray into the surf. The service was quite colorful and beautiful.

Another spectacular service I enjoyed watching was *brule zin* or *kanzo*, in which the new hounsis, women who were to serve with the houngan or mambo, were initiated. The initiates did most of the singing and dancing and were led by a *hounsi koun*, or queen of the hounsis, who kept things going at a lively pace during all the services.

These kanzo services took place only when there was a need for new hounsis, who were generally initiated in groups of three, five, or seven. The preparations for this sacred ritual began three days before the ceremony. At this time the candidates were "put down"; that is, they had to lie down in a row on the floor of the *hounfort*,[69] covered with a sheet. From the moment they were covered, they were not allowed to speak. Each could, however, whisper to her guide, a hounsi who kneeled at the initiate's head and took care of all her bodily needs. The guide also instructed the novice in the various rituals and taught her the accompanying chants and rhythms. Remember, nothing is written, and all must be learned by rote.

Over the years, I attended many different kanzo services, including one to initiate my son Burdette. I always enjoyed the kanzo, which took place at night in the hounfort with several Vodou priests and priestesses assisting. One chair for each candidate was placed around the *poteau mitan*, or central column, an ornate hardwood column that for all the world resembled a striped barber's pole. Each candidate's chair had three items in front of it: a small new ceramic dish about nine inches in diameter, three railroad spikes, and a bundle of kindling.

Guest houngans and mambos entered, seating themselves in the candidates' chairs around the poteau. They drove the three railroad spikes into the ground, placed the ceramic dish on them, and put a few splinters of kindling under each. Then they vacated the chairs as the ceremony commenced.

I could feel the energy rise as the drums began to beat, and a few hounsis entered the room carrying live chickens with which they *evantaille*, or fan, the audience.

---

69   Vodou temple.

The chickens were held up and offered to the north, south, east, and west. The room was dark except for long lighted tapers held by dancers who circled the room, moving to the rhythm of the drums. A signal was given, and the dancers paused before each dish, lit the kindling with the tapers, and started the fires.

At one initiation ceremony that I had brought my friends to see, I remember hearing Phil's gasp as the women who carried the chickens broke the birds' legs and wings, pulled out their tongues, and spilled a few drops of blood in small plates by each dish. All around the poteau there was a lot of activity. Other hounsis entered with small cruses of water and poured a little in each dish that sat over the fire. The women killed the chickens quickly, plucked them, and cut them up. While the chickens were being prepared, corn meal was added to the water in the dishes.

Suddenly the drum rhythms changed. The lights came on, and what appeared to be a huge white caterpillar came through the door of the hounfort. An already initiated hounsi led the odd-looking procession with her head poking out of the white covering. The candidates formed the body of the caterpillar and followed her in a human chain. Each leaned forward with her arms around the waist of the woman in front of her. The initiates were completely covered in fabric that resembled white bedspreads sewn together. No parts of their bodies were visible. The white chain entered the initiation area and slowly wove its way around the outside of the circle of chairs, where the visiting houngans and mambos tended the cooking dishes.

The great caterpillar stopped, and each initiate stood just to the right of each official. The houngans and mambos reached under the white covering, each taking an initiate's hand and making the sign of the cross on it, using a finger dipped in the plate containing the chicken blood mixed with oil. The officials then dipped their own hands into the boiling corn meal, removed some, and placed it in the palm of the initiate's hand. The initiates closed their fingers over the hot corn meal, making a sort of croquette, which then was removed and placed on a banana leaf on the floor. This ritual was repeated with the initiate's other hand. Nobody screamed in pain.

In a few minutes, the great caterpillar left the circle and moved back into the hounfort. At this point the chicken was added in small pieces to what remained of the corn meal in the dish. More water was added, and the chicken cooked for about ten minutes longer while the chanting and drumming continued. The contents of the cooking dishes were buried for the spirits.

The drumming ceased. A few hounsis came forward and picked up the hot dishes from which the cooked chicken and corn meal had been removed. Now blackened from the fire, the dishes were polished with oil until they shone like ebony. Then they were put back on the railroad spikes, more kindling was placed under them and ignited, and a bit of oil was poured into each dish.

The lights were extinguished once more, and the drumming and chanting resumed by candlelight. The covered initiates once again circled the poteau, each stopping beside the same official. I noticed that by now the oil in the dishes had ignited from the heat of the fire below and the old hounsis were screaming with delight, some becoming possessed.

Mesmerized, I watched as each official reached under the white cover and brought out a bare foot. The instep was crossed again with the chicken blood and oil, and then the foot was lightly placed on the edge of the hot dish. Each foot was then touched to the dish a little longer and then held directly above the flame for several seconds, being moved about slowly. After both feet of each candidate had been treated in this manner, the candidates left the hounfort.

The dancing and chanting built to a fever pitch, continuing faster and faster, as several more hounsis rolled on the ground, possessed. This final part of the initiation ceremony continued for several hours until everyone seemed exhausted.

Finally the newly initiated hounsis entered again, one at a time, each wearing a white dress and a white turban covered by a new Panama hat. As each was brought out and seated in a chair around the poteau, she received salutes from her new sisters.

These *hounsi–kanzo*, as they are called, comprised a sort of sorority, pledged to serve for life that particular houngan or mambo. During the day, they are working women. Some work in factories, others in the market, and many serve as domestics in the houses of the foreign residents. Actually, these hounsis are preferred as domestics because of their integrity.

The Vodou religion practiced in Haiti differs from Western religions, yet it is interesting to note that there are aspects of it quite similar to Catholic rituals. The initiates are wrapped in white sheets and must lie on the floor without speaking for three days. When Jesus died, he was wrapped in a shroud and buried in a cave. Three days later he was resurrected and emerged from the cave. After the three–day period when the candidates are shrouded in sheets, they enter the church as a giant white caterpillar. During the initiation ceremony, they emerge from their cocoon and become hounsis. Their metamorphosis is like that of the caterpillar who becomes a butterfly, a Christian symbol of immortality. In the Catholic Church on the night before Easter, there is the Rite of Initiation ceremony that welcomes new Catholics into the church. It is similar to the rite of initiation for new hounsis in that the church is completely dark, the candidates are dressed in white, and they enter the dark church carrying candles.

Kanzo initiation ceremonies also are held for practitioners, and I remember when Burdette was sixteen and took part in one. During all the prayers and chanting, they put hot cornmeal in his hands. As an initiate, he needed to have absolute faith that it was not going to burn him. The palms of his hands were not burned, but in the middle of the ceremony he lost faith. He was badly burned between his fingers because when he lost faith, he opened his hands and the cornmeal dribbled down between his fingers.

Butch, who as an adult refused to have anything to do with Vodou, had accompanied me that day to see his brother's initiation. Afterward, Butch said he'd always believed they put some kind of protective coating on the initiate's hands, but I explained that it wasn't the lack of protective coating that caused Burdette's fingers to be burned; it was the fact that he lost faith. None of my sons understood or accepted this religion as I did.

CHAPTER 41

Raising Orchids and Becoming an Artist, 1960s–1970s

Horace

In my youth, when I explored the Colombian jungle searching for the first white cattleya orchid, I knew nothing about these beautiful plants. The human toll this expedition took was sobering, and I never got over it. But I was a man on the move in those days, and growing plants did not fit into my adventurous lifestyle. It was not until I returned to Haiti in 1940 that I began to grow my own orchids.

I studied orchids the way I studied religion—immersing myself in the literature. Eventually, I became so knowledgeable that I served as president of the Orchid Society of Haiti in 1963, at the age of eighty. This group, which I was instrumental in establishing, is affiliated with the well–known American Orchid Society, which has thousands of members worldwide.

On my expeditions in the mountains and the rainforests, I collected many delicate, rare specimens and brought them home to the special orchid houses I'd designed and built, nestled in the lush gardens of Villarosa. I hung orchids in trees all over the property, and I walked around and tended them. It was as though they smiled at me every morning, which gave me great happiness. I would stop and talk to each orchid and caress the loveliness of her petals gently with my fingertips, at which point the flowers reached out to kiss me.

Eventually, I acquired some 5,000 orchids, including every species known to the Caribbean, and they thrived under my care. I took great joy in raising my orchids, and they became the children of my old age, or perhaps the mistresses, requiring daily nurturing to bring out their magnificent blooms. Having learned the meaning of love, not just for a person but for everything, I gave my heart to these perfect flowers and took great delight in painting them.

As I grew more and more orchids, I realized that I needed to share their beauty with the world. I rarely used my photography equipment anymore because it had become cumbersome. I had reached the advanced age of eighty-one, and the time had arrived in my life when I had to cut back on strenuous activity. I knew I would be miserable if I could not make myself busy in some useful manner, so I decided to pursue something I had wanted to do all my life—paint.

I had no formal training and never took an art lesson in my life, but I'd always had a good eye for composition and an ability to depict perspective, so I forged ahead. I leaned an old canvas against a chair and painted over the picture on it with white paint. Then, using only a palette knife, I created a picture of the entrance to Villarosa.

Luck was with me. The colors were just right, and everyone praised my picture. Their praises inspired me to continue to paint. It was a surprise to me—and I think my family, too—that at the age of eighty-one I would discover a new medium in which to express my creativity. Like everything else in my life that I took a notion to do, I simply became an artist. I painted with confidence and believed in myself. Immediately I sold four paintings.

My incredible memory also served me well. Some forty-seven years after I attended the bullfight in Spain with my friend Jimmy, the Duke de Alba, I dreamed about the event in full color. I could even smell the dust, hear the roar of the "*Olé, olé*" and actually relive the entire episode. When I awoke, I jumped out of bed, dashed into the studio, and made a quick charcoal sketch with color notes. A day or so later, I began work on it and in a couple of weeks had completed one of my best paintings.

Painting became my passion, and in three years I painted more than one hundred works. Fifty-one of my paintings were exhibited at the Mexican-American Cultural

Institute in Mexico City in 1968, immediately followed by an exhibit in Colombia. Eventually my paintings found their way to museums and residences in other major cities— Tehran, Persia (Iran); Caracas, Venezuela; Lima, Peru; the Virgin Islands; and many parts of the United States. Many remained at Villarosa for my family to enjoy.

Horace Ashton's painting graced the cover of the November 1968 *Foreign Service Journal.*

About the Cover . . .
Horace D. Ashton, the cover artist, was Cultural Attache at Port-au-Prince, 1941-46. He later retired to Haiti, where he took up painting at the age of 82. The cover painting is one recently exhibited in Mexico City and was loaned to the Journal by Robert S. Folsom.

My paintings depicted what I knew and loved. I painted more scenes of gingerbread houses, and one was featured on the magazine cover of the *Foreign Service Journal*.[70] I painted pictures of historic places in Haiti, ocean scenes, boats, flowers (mostly orchids), and birds.

I painted a special piece for my beloved Gordana—a large screen for our dining room of Dubrovnik, Yugoslavia—as a surprise. I spent three weeks on my hands and knees, painting the screen, laid out on the floor. When she returned to Haiti and I unveiled my work, Gordana looked at it for a moment, and all she said was "Too blue!" Nevertheless, it eventually became one of her favorites.

By now there were three houses on the property, as Butch and his family had built their own. They had an art studio built for me below the main house, surrounded by my orchid houses. It was a one–room affair that featured a huge bay window facing northeast with a view of the mountains and just the right light. Every day I sat in front of that window in a cane chair, propped the easel against the window, held the palette in my left hand, and using several brushes in my right, I painted from memory.

After a while, I moved out of the main house and into my art studio to spend most of my time painting. Gordana was so much younger than I, and she hadn't left the world of ambassadors and diplomats, while I was an old man happily studying religion, painting, and tending my orchids. I felt by this time that I had conquered the truth, and I was happy with the truth I had found.

The studio had a bed and everything I needed. A huge wall unit sat against one wall, cluttered with canvases, tubes of paint, brushes, mementos of my travels, and many books. My red Turkish rug warmed the floor and provided a bed for my dog Bouki.

I was rarely alone there. It seemed that someone always wanted to come and watch me paint or listen to my stories, which I never tired of telling.

---

70   Robert S. Folsom, in *Foreign Service Journal*, Port-au-Prince, Haiti, November 1968.

I always looked the same when I was painting; I wore a pale-colored, short-sleeved shirt that showed off my serpent tattoo to best advantage and a red, black, or burgundy bow tie (not the clip-on kind, of course).

I know that some people made fun of me as I got older—they thought I was a colorful, local character; a crazy old man who embellished his tales of adventure—except for Daska. I don't think my granddaughter, Daska, ever did. Even when she was no more than seven years old, every afternoon when she arrived home from school, she visited me in the studio. I'd lift her onto a tall bar stool, where she'd watch me paint and listen to my stories. Sometimes I would bribe her to stay, offering her some of the pastel-colored mints I always had on hand, because I loved having her there. One day, when I was painting the black and white birds I remembered from my trip on the Bosporus, she pointed to my canvas and said, "Deda, you already painted that one."

"No, I painted these birds flying east. This is a different painting because in this one they are flying west," I responded.

Dashkitsa, as I called her (meaning little Daska), was a somewhat mischievous, curious child. I remember the time she fell, cut her chin, and came to me crying.

"Does it hurt?" I asked.

She nodded through her tears.

"How do you know it hurts? Because you saw blood?" She stopped crying and forgot her pain as she watched me put a needle through my hand and saw the blood but realized I felt no pain. When her mother took her to the doctor, Daska told him it didn't hurt.

From an early age my granddaughter was spiritually curious. Like most young children in Haiti, Daska attended Catholic school. I taught her a few things that didn't sit well with the nuns. I told her that Jesus was a human being with extraordinary powers and that I could walk on water like he did. I told her that there was only one God, but God wasn't an old man with a white beard sitting in a chair, watching her. God was everything she breathed and walked on, everything that lived, everything she saw, touched, and felt. God was in every one of us.

CHAPTER 42

Farewell

Butch
April 5, 2001
9:35 p.m.

As I ponder my own death, I think of my father in his later years. He was always active, sometimes doing things a man his age should have avoided. Although he often asked for help, and I sometimes resented it, his independent spirit remained with him throughout his life. He had a strong will.

One day when Dad was eighty-nine, he climbed a ladder to hang one of his orchids, as he frequently did. Apparently he became distracted by our dogs that stood beneath the ladder, lost his balance, and fell. He had a stroke.

Fortunately, my younger brother, Todd, who had moved to the states for school and military service, was home for a short visit. Todd called the hospital but was told the ambulance driver had gone to lunch and taken the keys to the ambulance with him. Todd quickly drove to the hospital at the bottom of our hill, hot-wired the ambulance, and rushed Dad to the hospital.

A few days after Dad was hospitalized, the same young man who had approached Myriam in the grocery store—when the spirit of Duclos had supposedly requested my father's presence at a ceremony ten years earlier—arrived at our travel agency with an old woman completely dressed in white. The elderly woman of about eighty, who was a hounsi, or Vodou initiate, claimed that the spirit of Duclos had appeared at a recent ceremony. Duclos had instructed her to look for Mr. Ashton because Mr. Ashton was very ill and needed help urgently.

These people did not have access to phones or phone books. They operated by word of mouth. Since she had made such an effort, I reluctantly listened to her story and skeptically asked what she wanted me to do.

"Duclos told us you must bring your father to Arcachon, the place at the beach where they built his boat." I knew the place, where the two had also built the 150-foot pier. Our family had spent many Sundays there. I had learned to sail my first boat and to spearfish there at age eight.

Many years had gone by since then. Pollution and the erosion from deforestation had caused the sea to be very dirty now. This was no longer a place to go. "What do you want me to do with my father there?" I asked tolerantly. I was unsure whether I even wanted to continue this conversation but did not want to be disrespectful. It must have cost them money they didn't have, as well as time, to find me.

We were told to bathe my father in the dirty water and rub him down with the mud and sand. "If you don't do it, he will die," she insisted. "If you bathe him at Arcachon, he will recover and live much longer."

I didn't completely dismiss this as nonsense. I discussed it with the whole family that evening, and we decided that my father was just too ill and too fragile. We all agreed that bathing him in the dirty water wasn't the proper thing to do for him.

Dad had been in excellent health prior to this stroke. Although he seemed to recover physically and had no paralysis, he could no longer communicate by speaking. The man who had been such a great storyteller all his life now had to resort to writing down what he wanted to say. Even that came out garbled. He realized he was not getting his message across, and he grew increasingly frustrated and aggravated.

After about a year and a half of struggling to express himself, Dad invoked his strong will and basically shut his systems down. He began starving himself to death.

The last six months of his life were extremely distressing and sad. I tried to force him to eat, but he refused and fought my every effort. I actually resorted to force-feeding him. He would spit out the food and the beverage.

This was a very painful period of my life. Today I can't help but think this was just one last lesson from him of "mind over matter." He chose to end his life. As my father would say, he ventured into his next life on January 18, 1976.

* * *

I realize now that I am more like my father than I realized. I have the will to live, so I must find a way to escape and tell his amazing story. I will keep my promise to him.

CHAPTER 43

Freedom

Butch
April 5, 2001
9:48 p.m.

The car stops. My kidnapper gets out, leaves it running, and barks, "Don't do anything stupid, *blanc*." Then he slams his door.

I wait in the passenger's seat, silently praying for a miracle. I'm not sure if I hear the sound of voices over the rumble of the car engine, but it seems like a long time passes. I wonder what is happening. "Water. I need water, please," I beg, believing the other kidnapper is still behind me in the backseat with the Uzi at my head.

No one responds.

"Water, please give me some water," I say again.

Still no answer!

Oh, my God. Am I alone? Is this my facteur H that I've been praying for?

I reach into the backseat and feel around blindly, pleading, "I'm dying! I'm dying!" My hand touches cold metal, and I feel the shape of the machine gun lying on the seat—abandoned. I don't feel a person, and I rip the tape off my eyes, oblivious to the pain. I see the driver standing across the street, about twenty feet away from the driver's side of the car. Noticing my movement, he runs toward the car. This is it—my split-second opportunity, the answer to my prayers! The weapon lies within easy reach on the backseat. *Do I choose the gun or the car?*

Not knowing or wanting to risk whether the Uzi has ammunition or is jammed, I know that the car's engine is running, and I choose the car. I throw myself into the driver's seat, slam the car into gear, and floor it. Pistol in hand, the kidnapper dashes toward me. He attempts to open the door as I pull away. Three shots ring out.

I start to head home at breakneck speed but suddenly realize since this was where I was trapped. Some of their gang will probably be waiting for me. Almost airborne, the car flies through the rain-slicked streets. I instinctively decide to head for our Toyota dealership. Suddenly I remember that we recently placed guard dogs in the yard of the dealership at night, and we had armed guards inside the buildings. This makes me rethink my plan.

I pull into the nearest police station, which is only a couple of blocks from the dealership, and run inside. Only one policeman sits at a desk, listening to a radio and looking at a magazine. He casually looks up when I rush in, with no visible sign of concern.

"Help me!" My words tumble out in a rush of breath as I try to explain. "I'm Marc Ashton. I'm the person that was kidnapped this afternoon, and I just escaped. I need your help. I'm not sure if I'm still being chased. They're heavily armed. There are at least thirteen of them! You're going to need reinforcements."

The policeman looks up and shakes his head in disbelief, as if facing a deranged person.

"Look, can I use your phone? I need to call my wife."

He reluctantly hands me the phone and goes back to his magazine. I dial my number. It seems like our home phone just rings and rings. Finally, our daughter Militsa answers.

"Militsa, it's me. I'm okay! I'm at the Delmas Police Station near the Toyota dealership! Tell Mom not to pay any ransom! I need help! I want someone to come and get me out of here right away!"

"Dad!" I hear her scream with joy and then relay the news to Daska and Myriam.

The policeman finally reacts. He calls another officer, and they proceed to both put on bullet-proof jackets and take up arms, guarding the entrance to the station.

I wait for what seems like an eternity. No one comes.

I call home again. This time Myriam answers the phone. "*Cherie*! Where are you?"

"I'm still waiting at the police station. Myriam, I don't trust the surroundings! Don't you leave the house, but send someone now," I beg her. It's good to hear her voice.

"The girls left long ago with Gary to get you."

I know the Gary to whom she's referring is the Minister of Justice. The authorities had been working to find me after all.

* * *

Sometime around midnight, I arrive home in the Minister of Justice's bulletproof vehicle, driven by him personally, accompanied by our two daughters, the minister's bodyguard, and Thierry, another close mutual friend. A cheering crowd of approximately one hundred friends greets me at Villarosa. Overwhelmed, I fight off the urge to burst into tears.

Covered in mud, sweat, and my own blood, I feel years older than I had when I left the house that morning. After much hugging and kissing from my family, staff, and numerous friends, I ask, "Myriam, why are all these people here?"

"*Cherie*," she says, "this has been a crazy day. Sit down, and I'll explain."

"I really need to take a shower and clean up," I respond. "Come tell me while I'm patching myself up.

She starts at the beginning with her parents, our daughters, and grandchildren coming for lunch. They'd all just sat down to eat when our plumber, who lived down the road from us, called to say he'd seen four guys jump into my car and drive away with me.

She continues, "I told Daska to call everybody in your Rolodex. I immediately called the American Ambassador, your business partners, your brother Burdette in the United States, and the Prime Minister of Haiti. The United States Consul General advised me to negotiate with the kidnappers and string them along while the police tried to locate you. *Cherie*, we were worried sick, and we didn't know what else to do!"

As news of my kidnapping spread, people gathered at Villarosa to offer help and to follow the developments. Calls came from everywhere; everyone had a suggestion. Even my doctor, Michel, showed up because he was concerned about my health. He knew I needed medication and planned to get it to me somehow.

Myriam continues, "Someone told me that if I really believed in your father's guardian angel, I had to take the picture of him that we keep in our bedroom, go outside on the porch, look up at the sky, and ask for God's help." She smiles shyly, obviously unsure if I would want to hear this part of the story. "The girls and I went up to the terrace and did just that. I also took the wooden cross your father had carved, and we prayed for about fifteen to twenty minutes."

"Myriam, what time was that?"

She raised her brow. "About seven. Why?"

I smiled. "I was no doubt praying at the same time, and I think we might have had help from Dad. Our prayers were certainly answered!"

Myriam squeezed my hand. A look crossed her face, and I couldn't tell if it was one of amazement, relief, thankfulness, or a combination of it all.

* * *

April 6, 2001

Despite my escape, I know we will never again be safe at Villarosa. My kidnappers are still out there, and next time they will kill me. I realize there are more than a dozen people involved in my abduction—the kidnappers that held me hostage; the drivers of the cars that boxed me in; all those people in the seven different houses they took me to; plus, no doubt others assisted them. I had taken their machine gun and their car, and nobody made a penny. They have to be embarrassed, humiliated, and very frustrated. If they see me anywhere, they are going to blow me away.

"I want us all out of here immediately!" I tell Myriam.

A few minutes later, my good friend Bob calls from Key West, Florida. I had always suspected he might have worked "undercover" for the United States government before he became the chief pilot for the airline I started in the 1970s. He never confirmed it during all the years we've known each other. During those days, Bob spent many an evening on the terrace of Villarosa discussing religion and philosophy with my father. We had remained good friends over the years.

"Hey, Butch. I heard what happened yesterday. Listen, I'm coming down to help. You're not out of danger yet. Stay inside until I get there. How many Black Hawks do we need?"

His wife Pat interrupts the conversation. "Butch, please tell Bob you're okay. He's got about fifty of his crazy, old, retired buddies just dying for some action. They're itching to come with him."

Bob usually knows what he's talking about, so I take his advice very seriously.

That same afternoon, he arrives—alone—and immediately takes over our personal security, making his presence quite visible. He walks around Villarosa carrying my police-issue riot gun and his cell phone, occasionally making calls to give the appearance of frequent telephone updates.

It's not long before the word is out: "Washington has sent a special *blanc* to protect the Ashtons." In a country like Haiti, this makes a serious impact. It screams "Don't mess with me because I mean business!"

I stay out of sight. My mind is reeling, thinking over the events of yesterday. I marvel at how one single day, one single moment, can change our lives so drastically. One minute I'm on my way home to have lunch with my loved ones, and the next minute I'm not sure if I'll ever see them again.

The phone rings constantly all day. Myriam fields the calls, telling everyone that I left the country for the United States early that morning by private plane. She sets about the business of packing our important belongings. We will have to leave behind our long-time beloved home, her elderly parents, other family members, and many, many good friends.

Bob works on a plan to get me safely out of the country while he keeps his presence conspicuous. I make sure trustworthy security guards surround my family for the next few days. While Myriam and the girls pack, I keep a low profile. I wear a holstered pistol and never set foot outside the house. I am so unnerved that I only take the gun off to shower, and even wear it to bed, where I sleep fitfully.

On Saturday, April 7, 2001—two days after my kidnapping—I secretly leave Haiti forever. I swallow hard due to the lump in my throat and brush the wetness from my eyes as I watch the turquoise sea and green mountains of my faded island paradise— my home for over sixty years—disappear below the clouds. I leave our beloved Villarosa behind.

That day an article written by Yves Colon appeared in *The Herald*, a Miami newspaper, with a pull-quote that read, "Two Americans have been killed and another kidnapped in recent days." It told of my kidnapping and the murder of two other Americans after they were robbed. These crimes prompted the U.S. State

Department to issue a travel warning that U.S. citizens not go to Haiti.

> The murder . . . was followed by the kidnapping of American businessman Marc Ashton, who was abducted outside his home but managed to escape his kidnappers hours later. Ashton, known to his friends as Butch, is the son of a former U.S. diplomat who was stationed in Haiti, according to acquaintances, [who said] Ashton had left Haiti on a private airplane.[71]

Three days later, after my sad but safe departure, Bob accompanies Myriam, the girls, and our four dogs out of Haiti.

---

71   Yves Colon, "Haitian Police Increase Patrols After Attacks, *The Herald*, Miami, Florida, 7 April 2001.

AFTERWORD

The Spirit Endures

Butch
June 2003

For more than a decade before April 5, 2001—and the ten hours of terror that irrevocably changed our lives—our oasis in paradise was being strangled by the slums pushing against its walls. Living at Villarosa had become like living in a lifeboat, surrounded by drowning people in the middle of a churning sea. We loved Haiti desperately, but the changing situation and political unrest had given us reason to consider alternatives to how we were now living.

Myriam and I had talked it over extensively and decided to scale down, to sell our property, and buy a smaller place. Planning to spend six months of the year in the United States and six months in Haiti, we would still keep our business ventures going. I put our home on the market, and the Haitian government expressed interest in buying it. We began negotiations for the sale of this magnificent property to the Republic of Haiti.

Shortly after we left the country, the Haitian government purchased Villarosa, as agreed, and the prime minister moved into his new residence. Our houseboy Pressoir, who had lived and worked with us for more than twenty years, agreed to stay on to acclimate the new owners to the estate.

A few months later, Pressoir called to report that the prime minister had moved out. "Monsieur Butch, he says there is this old white man in a turban who roams the house at night, keeping his wife and sons awake. He believes the house is haunted!" Apparently the prime minister had told not only Pressoir but had even stated this publicly in a radio interview.

I laughed aloud when I heard the news and then turned around to salute the photo of my father that Myriam had used in prayer, which we still keep in our bedroom. Taken when Dad explored the Sahara, the picture shows him wearing the customary dress of the region, including a white turban.

Later I learned the prime minister had called in five of the most powerful houngans in the country. The houngans spent five days performing an exorcism at Villarosa to rid the house of the wandering spirit purported to be Horace Ashton. They scrubbed the walls of the house with a potion they prepared during a grand Vodou ceremony held in the front and back yards and used indigo to draw crosses above every door and window, trying to scare the spirit off. Finally, they left, claiming the spirit of Horace Ashton refused to leave Villarosa. Supposedly the houngans said his spirit was so strong, they believed that pursuing the exorcism might cause them to lose their own powers.

Today Villarosa stands empty. Or does it?

Reportedly, a man wearing a white turban is still seen roaming the halls. Superstition is embedded so deeply in the Haitian culture that naturally theories and stories abound about the spirit of Villarosa. Some say my father's presence was so powerful and dominant in Haiti for so long that the belief is if Ashtons cannot live in this home, then no one will.

When I learned there had been two attempts to kidnap our daughter Daska, who had since returned to Haiti and represented me at the dealership, it became obvious she had become as tempting a target as I had been. So that she would no longer have a reason or obligation to remain in Haiti, I decided to sell my shares in the dealership to my two partners and to sell the beach property as well.

* * *

In the early nineties, a young American lady who was helping at a local church-sponsored hospital rented my father's art studio for about a year. She claimed she frequently felt the presence of an elderly man. He smelled of Old Spice (my father's favorite cologne) and would sit on the cane chair and smoke a pipe. She had never known about Horace Ashton.

Shortly before my father died in 1976, a high Vodou priest contacted Myriam and insisted that *I* must accept and receive the powers and legacy I was meant to inherit from my father before he could be free to pass on. At the time, I felt I was being pushed into something I neither understood nor condoned. That feeling thrust me in the opposite direction and made me want to turn away completely. Some claim that this is the reason my father's spirit lingers. Others think that I actually did receive some of his powers anyway; the fact that I lived to tell my kidnapping story may be considered proof of it. I don't know if I will ever reconcile my feelings on this subject.

What I do know is that I have a strong desire to honor my promise and to honor my father. So with my deepest gratitude and highest respect, Dad, here is your book. Together, we share your stories with the world.

Horace D. Ashton as Cultural Attaché to the United States Embassy in Haiti

* * *

Tuesday, January 12, 2010
4:58 p.m.

A 7.0 magnitude earthquake struck Haiti. The epicenter was located fifteen miles outside of Port-au-Prince. There were fifty-nine aftershocks from the initial quake. A number of these were nearly as devastating as the initial impact, with some ranging from 4.2 to 5.9 magnitude in strength. Villarosa was completely destroyed.

Villarosa lies in ruins after the January 12, 2010, earthquake.

About the Authors

Horace Dade Ashton (1883–1976) was a pioneering news photographer, cinematographer, explorer, writer, lecturer, scientist, botanist, diplomat, and artist, who recorded stories from his life when he was eighty-six years old. These stories form the basis of this book.

Spanning the late nineteenth and three-quarters of the twentieth century, Horace's life was filled with adventure, much of it captured in magazines and newspapers. After Horace died, his son Marc received scrapbooks from his aunt that carefully preserved these publications and validated his father's amazing life story.

Horace Ashton's photographs appear in the Smithsonian Institution, the Nelson-Atkins Museum of Art, and other photography galleries and museums. They are featured in the book *An American Century of Photography: From Dry-Plate to Digital*, published by the Hallmark Photographic Collection.

 **Marc "Butch" Ashton** was born in Washington, D.C. and arrived in Haiti as an infant, when his father, Horace Dade Ashton, became cultural attaché to the United States Embassy. Marc remained in Haiti most of his life, marrying, raising a family, founding numerous businesses, employing thousands of people, and treating all he knew with respect. He remained on his beloved island until the day after he was kidnapped and held for ransom by four armed thugs. Marc retired to Boca Raton, Florida,

where he is involved in the community and serves as president of his homeowners' association. He remains active in Haitian-American relations.

 **Libby J. Atwater** has profiled individuals in entertainment, law, business, public service, medicine, education, and philanthropy while writing for nonprofits, educational institutions, magazines, and community newspapers for more than twenty-five years. She has assisted others with their life stories for the past eighteen years. Stories from her life appear in several anthologies, and she received first place in biography and memoir and tied for first place in other nonfiction for her riveting memoir *What Lies Within*, released in 2013.